Today, at one and the same time, scholarly publishing is drawn in two directions. On the one hand, this is a time of the most exciting theoretical, political and artistic projects that respond to and seek to move beyond global administered society. On the other hand, the publishing industries are vying for total control of the ever-lucrative arena of scholarly publication, creating a situation in which the means of distribution of books grounded in research and in radical interrogation of the present are increasingly restricted. In this context, MayFlyBooks has been established as an independent publishing house, publishing political, theoretical and aesthetic works on the question of organization. MayFlyBooks publications are published under Creative Commons license free online and in paperback. MayFlyBooks is a not-for-profit operation that publishes books that matter, not because they reinforce or reassure any existing market.

1. Herbert Marcuse, *Negations: Essays in Critical Theory*
2. Dag Aasland, *Ethics and Economy: After Levinas*
3. Gerald Raunig and Gene Ray (eds), *Art and Contemporary Critical Practice: Reinventing Institutional Critique*
4. Steffen Böhm and Siddhartha Dabhi (eds), *Upsetting the Offset: The Political Economy of Carbon Markets*
5. Peter Armstrong and Geoff Lightfoot (eds), *'The Leading Journal in the Field': Destabilizing Authority in the Social Sciences of Management*
6. Carl Cederström and Casper Hoedemaekers (eds), *Lacan and Organization*

LACAN AND ORGANIZATION

Lacan and Organization

Carl Cederström and Casper Hoedemaekers (eds)

may f l y

www.mayflybooks.org

First published by MayFlyBooks in paperback in London and free online at
www.mayflybooks.org in 2010.

Printed by the MPG Books Group in the UK

CC: The editors and authors 2010

ISBN (Print) 978-1-906948-10-8
ISBN (PDF) 978-1-906948-11-5

Contents

Contributors

Carl Cederström is a lecturer in Human Resource Management at Cardiff Business School, Cardiff University. His research focuses on Lacanian psychoanalysis, philosophy, politics, and work. He is the co-author of *How to Stop Living and Start Worrying* (Polity, 2010) and co-editor of *Impossible Objects* (Polity, 2011). His work on authenticity, happiness, health and love – among other subjects – has appeared in a range of journals and edited collections.

Peter Fleming is Professor of Work and Organization at Queen Mary College, University of London. He has previously held positions at Cambridge University and Melbourne University. One aspect of his research focuses on emergent forms of power in the workplace, especially as it pertains to bio-politics and 'biocracy'. Another interest is the social anthropology of corporate corruption. He is the author of the books *Contesting the Corporation* (2007, Cambridge University Press, with André Spicer), *Charting Corporate Corruption* (2009, Edward Elgar Press) and *Authenticity and the Cultural Politics of Work* (2009, Oxford University Press).

Jason Glynos is Senior Lecturer in Political Theory at the Department of Government, University of Essex, where he is director of the MA Programme in Ideology and Discourse Analysis. He has published widely in the areas of poststructuralist political theory and Lacanian psychoanalysis, focusing on theories of ideology, democracy, and freedom, and the philosophy and methodology of social science. He is co-author of *Logics of Critical Explanation in Social and Political Theory* (Routledge, 2007), and co-editor of *Traversing the Fantasy* (Ashgate, 2005) and *Lacan and Science* (Karnac, 2002). His current research explores the contributions of discourse analysis and psychoanalysis to the development of a critical political economy.

Rickard Grassman is a research and teaching associate in Organization Studies at Bristol Business School, University of the West of England. His research explores enjoyment, imaginings and images in the context of virtual networks and organizations, particularly by drawing on poststructuralist accounts. These interests are reflected in both journal articles and book chapters, including 'The Masochistic Reflexive Turn' (with Cederström, 2008), as well as 'Desire and Ideology in Virtual Social Networks' and 'The Will to Nothingness' (with Case, 2009). He is currently finishing his PhD, which focuses on dis-identification and dissociative identity symptoms ranging from cynicism and escapism to psychosis and pathologies.

Casper Hoedemaekers is a lecturer in Organization Studies at Cardiff Business School, Cardiff University. His research interests include Lacanian psychoanalytic theory, the study of subjectivity in the workplace, organizational control, transgressive practices in advertising and popular media, and the signification of creative labour. His work has appeared in a range of academic journals.

Campbell Jones, University of Leicester, UK, has published several studies of the reception of French theory in management and organization studies. To this end, he has also co-edited *Contemporary Organization Theory* (2005, Blackwell) and *Philosophy and Organization* (2007, Routledge), edited special issues of the journal *Business Ethics: A European Review* around the work of Emmanuel Levinas (2007), Jacques Derrida (2010) and Alain Badiou (forthcoming), and co-edited a special issue of the journal *Organization* on Jacques Lacan and organization studies. His most recent book is *Unmasking the Entrepreneur* (2009, Edward Elgar) and he is currently writing a book called *Can the Market Speak?*

Carol Owens is a practising and supervisory analyst in private practice in North County Dublin. She is a lecturer in the Department of Psychoanalysis at Independent College Dublin. She holds a PhD from the University of Reading, where she was formerly a member of the Beryl Curt research entity. She was editor of *The Letter – Lacanian*

Perspectives on Psychoanalysis for four years, and recently edited the *Annual Review of Critical Psychology* (http://www.discourseunit.com/arcp/7.htm) dedicated to the examination of Lacan and critical transdisciplinary research/theorising. She has published a number of articles and book chapters on the clinical practice of Lacanian psychoanalysis and on the application of Lacanian psychoanalysis to the fields of social psychology, queer theory and philosophy.

André Spicer is a Professor of Organization Studies at Warwick Business School, and a Visiting Research Fellow at Lund University, Sweden. He holds a PhD from the University of Melbourne, Australia. His research focuses on power and politics in and around organizations. His work has been extensively published in a wide range of journals and edited books. He has recently published books entitled *Contesting the Corporation* (Cambridge), *Unmasking the Entrepreneur* (Edward Elgar), *Understanding Corporate Life* (Sage), and *Understanding Leadership in the Real World* (Routledge).

Yannis Stavrakakis studied political science at Panteion University (Athens) and discourse analysis at Essex and has worked at the Universities of Essex and Nottingham. He is currently Associate Professor at the School of Political Sciences, Aristotle University of Thessaloniki. He is the author of *Lacan and the Political* (1999, Routledge) and *The Lacanian Left* (2007, Edinburgh University Press/SUNY Press) and co-editor of *Discourse Theory and Political Analysis* (2000, Manchester University Press) and *Lacan and Science* (2002, Karnac).

Preface

Carl Cederström and Casper Hoedemaekers

In 1975, the French psychoanalyst Jacques Lacan travelled to New York to give a series of talks. At that time he was already regarded as a celebrity within the Parisian context; indeed he was considered one of the charmed elite that helped define the intellectual spirit of the time. Upon arrival in New York City, and convinced of his own worldwide reputation, he requested a private screening at the Metropolitan Opera. His guide, in the interest of fulfilling Lacan's demand, told the well-cultured manager of the opera that she would be escorting the great French intellectual – whose name had become synonymous with French philosophy itself – Jean-Paul Sartre. That few had heard of him in the United States was apparently something that Lacan did not know, or perhaps, did not want to know.

Whether all details of this story are true or not, the reputation of this once obscure psychoanalyst, whose work was rarely discussed outside the circles of initiated psychoanalysts, and was generally neglected outside of his native France, has now travelled across the Atlantic. More than that, Lacanian psychoanalysis is today widely regarded as a distinct and influential school of clinical practice across the world: it is perhaps even the most widely practiced form of analytic treatment. In the last 40 years or so, Lacanian theory has found its way into all possible corners of the university – some expected, some less so. Among the many disciplines within the humanities and the social sciences (film theory, literary theory, French studies, feminist theory, sociology, political studies, and the like) this is perhaps not so surprising. That Lacan's influence is to be found in engineering, law, food studies, technology studies, and – the central object of this book – organization studies, is not something that could have been easily predicted.

There are at least two reasons why the reception of Lacan's work by organization scholars is somewhat odd. First, while organization studies include a broad register of phenomena, the main concern is with the study of organizations; and as far as we know, there's not a single statement in Lacan's work directly addressing organizations or the life within the walls of the corporation. Lacan had many interests – from wigs and cars, to art and antique books – but the study of organizations was simply not one of them. Second, organization studies have traditionally been occupied by questions of performance, control, and how corporations can be made more efficient, effective, and profitable. Such a starting point seems particularly incongruent with Lacanian theory. Throughout his career, Lacan violently combated all forms of psychology that aimed at the so-called 'improvement' of the human. With a sneer, he referred to such methods as forms of 'human engineering'.

The good news, however, is that organization studies are not exclusively obsessed with perfecting the corporation. Critical scholarship in organization studies goes back at least to the 1960s, although it was not until the early 1990s that a more organized movement began to take shape: what is today known as Critical Management Studies. Over the course of the last couple of decades, this conglomeration of critical management scholarship has found inspiration in the works of Weber, Durkheim, Marx, Foucault, Habermas and Bourdieu – to name only some of the more popular figures. Opposed to mainstream managerialism, they have critically addressed essential (but often unacknowledged) aspects of organizational life, including domination, identity regulation, gender, sexuality, control, power, resistance and emancipation.

Seen in this light, the reception of Lacanian studies is far from surprising. As is evident from a number of other disciplines, Lacan's work offers radically new insights into questions of subjectivity, power, and resistance. In addition, Lacan's path-breaking explorations in structural linguistics, together with his analyses of enjoyment, fantasy, and desire each offer distinguished contributions to popular themes in organization studies and beyond. More precisely, these theoretical examinations furnish an account that cuts to the heart of contemporary debates on language and emotions – debates which have become ever more relevant after the 'linguistic turn' and, more recently, the 'affective turn'.

Almost 30 years have now passed since Lacan's death, and much has happened over the years, not least in the universe of corporations and work politics. Yet, his contribution is arguably more topical than ever, especially for critical analyses of organization. For sure, Lacan's view that the autonomous ego is but a pure misrecognition firmly puts him at odds with the optimistic believes about self-potency and empowerment prevailing in contemporary management. In addition, Lacanian analysis offers a much-needed critique of the popular language of authenticity, happiness, and well-being that is today embraced and employed by management scholars, corporate leaders, and psychologists alike. In narcissistic times such as these, when the ego is erroneously deemed master in its own house, Lacan's lessons on subjectivity are surely more pertinent than ever. Famously, Lacan argued that psychoanalytic practice should never be geared towards the improvement of the analysand's well-being, let al.one the restoration of an authentic self, because such an endeavour would always be ideological. Ideological, insofar as it is aimed at an idealised self-image that is not only impossible to attain but based on a view of semi-stable personhood that is fundamentally a fiction. The pursuit of such an image, typically a romanticized view of the analyst, could only demonstrate to the analysand how painfully inadequate they are in relation to the ideal, thereby inadvertently opening up the gate for a flood of guilt, frustration, and narcissism.

Lacan's life-long battle against ego-psychology, as well as his rejection of psychologism, bears on the intimate relation between psychology and the organization. Today, increasing numbers of corporations turn their attention to the finer techniques of work psychology, psychotherapy and even the esoteric realm of 'New Age' self-improvement. Based on the assumption that they will become more efficient at work, employees at many corporations are routinely offered personality tests, as well as courses in meditation, yoga, inner-child therapy, and so forth. Perhaps this trend indicates that contemporary work life has become so alienating and soul-destroying that we need therapy to endure it? Another way of looking at it, however, is to see it as part of a more thoroughgoing transformation of workplace ideology. This latter view would imply that the control techniques exercised by corporations are now entirely all-encompassing, insofar as they seek to regulate not just the staged professional self, but also the private, authentic self. At work we are no longer allowed to be bored and alienated; it is no longer even enough to grudgingly ascribe to the 'core values' of the organizational culture. The application of our whole self, 'warts and all', seems to be what cutting edge management theory demands of us in the workplace. In some settings, organizational control appears to have evolved from merely governing behaviour (by governing beliefs), to influencing even our most intimate desires. And here, Lacanian theory proves particularly useful. It provides us with a sophisticated vocabulary through which we can begin to question the benevolence of the 'liberal workplace'. For instance, pointing to the complex relation between subjectivity and enjoyment (*jouissance*), Lacan reveals that the commandment to enjoy in fact leads to its opposite. When we are under the injunction to enjoy, we seem hopelessly incapable of administering our enjoyment.

These and many other themes will be developed in the course of this book. With contributions from organizational theorists, political theorists, and psychoanalysts, the following pages will provide the reader with a wide selection of Lacanian analyses of organization. To demonstrate the breadth and depth of the possible connections between Lacanian psychoanalysis and organization theory, the volume opens with a more comprehensive introduction by Casper Hoedemaekers, which focuses on Lacan's four discourses. Hoedemaekers diagnoses the need for a further interrogation of subjectivity within everyday work conditions and examines the business school as a site where the Master's discourse is produced, reproduced, and enacted. He suggests that a closer consideration of the hysteric's discourse would allow management scholars to account for the 'myriad of dysfunctionalities, travesties and fundamental contradictions' inherent in purportedly rational management practices.

The book then embarks on an examination of the necessary conditions for applying Lacan's work to management and organization. In his encyclopaedic account of the intersections of psychoanalysis and organization studies, Jason Glynos problematizes the application of psychoanalysis beyond the clinic. After noting two common fears linked to this form of interdisciplinary endeavour – whether 'psychoanalysis is true' or whether one is 'true to psychoanalysis' – he goes on to account for a variety of strategies by which psychoanalysis can be used for the study of organizations. This extensive review, leads Glynos to suggest Lacan's notion of fantasy has particular relevance for the study of organizations.

In chapter 3, Yannis Stavrakakis offers an in-depth analysis of the dialectic between subjectivity and the organized Other. He begins by arguing that Lacanian theory is particularly useful for understanding how attachment and obedience are established, and further, how this attachment is sustained on an affective level. What characterizes ideological domination here is the dual demand of obedience and transgression. In tracing the relation between these two demands, Stavrakakis shows how the transgression of particular ideals, like those promoted in organizations, often end up making the ideal more forceful. This argument is then developed in relation to the new spirit of capitalism and finally leads to an investigation of the hidden techniques corporations use for securing compliance and obedience among their employees.

In chapter 4, Carl Cederström and Rickard Grassman further take up this theme of affective attachment by investigating the relation between modern management ideologies and happiness. Proceeding from an interrogation of philosophical and popular-psychologistic notions of happiness, they demonstrate how a Lacanian take turns both the objective view and the subjective view of happiness on its head. They put forward the argument that happiness has taken on the status of a superegoic injunction that makes known its demands in the confines of the contemporary workplace as much as it does in the consumerist landscape. They conclude by analysing the ethical and political implications of the possible responses to this injunction.

In chapter 5, André Spicer and Carl Cederström ask why the question of love has been so underexplored in organization and management when it appears to be so central in underpinning contemporary discourses on work. How can work come to take up the place of a love object? And what sort of love might we direct at it? Drawing on contemporary philosophy, Lacanian psychoanalysis, and pop-management ephemera, they explore the strange cocktail of detachment, obsession, passion, and neurosis that work may inspire in each of us.

In the subsequent chapter, Peter Fleming explores the imaginary interstices of power and resistance by examining how contemporary ideology makes it possible for subjects to confirm, as well as transgress the commandments inherent in it. By closely reading Žižek's work on ideology with a sensitivity for how the Lacanian notion of transgression carries significant relevance for understanding state-of-the-art management techniques, Fleming shows how the subject relies on an implicit but ever-present Other to keep its consistency in the modern capitalist labour process.

In chapter 7, Lacanian psychoanalyst Carol Owens discusses how the recent developments in organizations manifest themselves in the clinic. Drawing on rich case histories from her analytic practice, she lays bare some of the fundamental dilemmas that arise when subjects attempt to assert themselves as productive, useful, and desirable employees within a fundamentally alienating symbolic order. Taking up some of the points concerning neo-normative control that are made by Cederström, Grassman, and Fleming, Owens sheds light on how individualised subjective trajectories intersect with the systematic level of capitalist ideologies.

Rounding off this collection, Campbell Jones raises the question of what it means to receive Lacan in organization studies. With attentiveness, Jones examines a variety of different ways in which Lacan has been prematurely received, or rather foreclosed, in recent years. Jones is keen to point out the potential dangers of carelessness and misappropriation in such scholarship, as he reflects on the difficulty of sustaining a productive engagement with a theory that demands that we check our ego at the door.

We would like to express our gratitude to a number of individuals who have encouraged us in this project and who have made it possible for us to edit this collection. We would firstly like to thank Alessia Contu, Michaela Driver, and Campbell Jones for planting the idea in us and for providing the inspiration for bringing it to fruition. Secondly, we would like to extend our gratitude to all our contributors, who have each provided spirited and profound contributions. Thirdly, we would like to thank Steffen Böhm and Armin Beverungen at MayflyBooks in helping us to prepare this volume for publication. And finally we would like to thank Todd Kesselman for his care and precision in helping us to prepare this manuscript.

1

Lacan and Organization: An Introduction

Casper Hoedemaekers

What should an introduction do? What should it do in a book such as this? Is it an inaugural statement? Perhaps it announces things to come. It might be like the programme that accompanies a classical concert or a theatre play, where we find a short description of what will follow: a cast of actors and a bit of background to help us interpret what we are about to witness in the 'proper' manner. At the same time, such a formal and pedantic format is usually dispensed with when we visit, let's say, a rock concert or a movie. Or perhaps the introduction is a frame, cast by the editor or curator to guide our interpretations in the right direction. That might be fair enough, in light of the mildly chaotic manner in which academic edited volumes tend to be composed. These books are compiled from the writings of a loose band of individuals, who might all have something more or less relevant to say on a scholarly topic. The editors then scramble frantically to find some sort of coherence between all these various scribblings. In such a way, the introduction may be seen as a text that frames with the aim of ordering.

In our own little corner of academia, we have been preoccupied over the past twenty years or so with the ordering effects of texts, and more specifically with such ordering effects in work organizations. Those of us with an interest in business, management and what passes for compliance and coercion in the workplace have long since taken up residence in the business school. Faced with decreasing union presence and membership, decreasing job security and labour intensification, many of those with a critical interest in management have taken a turn towards philosophy, or social and political theory in order to

1

understand the way in which control in organizations appears in ever more dispersed and insidious ways. Here, the influence of Foucault has been felt most strongly. Traditionally, critical scholars have seen management studies as a 'handmaiden to capitalism', and thus rejected them in favour of a variety of Marxist theoretical trajectories (among which labour process theory (Knights and Willmott, 1990) carried the most weight as a collective movement). The eventual turn to poststructuralism in critical studies of management and organization was due in large part to the need for an adequate theory of subjectivity. Such a theory would need to account for the growing individualism in society, coupled with decreasing levels of class struggle and class consciousness in the workplace – which had not been satisfactorily treated in more orthodox Marxist accounts (O'Doherty and Willmott, 2001).

However, this broad shift from labour process theory to poststructuralism within the critical arena of business schools should not distract us from the overwhelming dominance of the management studies 'mainstream'. This mainstream remains almost wholly functionalist and positivist in its make-up, and continues to unequivocally support the 'right to manage', or what can be better described as managerialism in the service of shareholder capitalism. On the basis of this dominance, one could say that critical management studies and other critical approaches have their own Big Other that engenders them, and to which they are indebted for their existence and their vocabulary. The critical is brought into being and sustained by the big managerialist Other. This dependency is further confirmed by what occurs in terms of education. It is only through the fantasy of countless students being trained to become successful managers that critical business academia can sustain itself within the business school. In this sense, we may wonder why Lacan is not read more widely in that context.

Faced as we are with a field of academic knowledge that relies upon the rampant fantasy of creating managers out of thousands of undergraduate students, and which, in the end, fails to inspire critical reflection or provide businesses with practicable insights – one would think this connection would be obvious. But here we stumble on what may be seen as a central repression at the heart of management studies. It cannot acknowledge its own dependency on the managerial fantasy, and it misrecognises the failure that lies at its heart. The managerial discipline is, much like the Lacanian subject, a split entity.

I will not try to give a Lacanian introduction here, or attempt to gauge what Lacan's oeuvre might mean for the study of organization. There is not an essence in Lacan that can be described readily that does not already carry its own defeat in it. Instead, what I will focus our discussion on is how Lacan views the role of the intellectual and what this might mean for the role of knowledge production in the field of management and organization studies. The question of subjectivity is a crucial one not just for those subjects that we might choose to study in organizations, but it is also a crucial question for the way in which we ourselves engage in the production of knowledge.

For this purpose, I would like to quote part of an exchange between a radical student activist and Lacan, whose weekly seminar at Vincennes was interrupted on December 3rd 1969 as follows:

> Student activist: "If we think that by listening to Lacan's discourse, or Foucault's, or someone else's we will obtain the means to criticise the ideology they are making us swallow, we're making a big mistake. I claim that we have to look outside to find the means to overthrow the university."

> Lacan: "But outside what? Because when you leave here you become aphasic [unable to speak]? When you leave here you continue to speak, consequently you continue to be inside." (Lacan, 2007: 205)

In this exchange Lacan expresses a fundamental point: the university and the knowledge it gives rise to do not exist independently of subjectivity. Rather, subjectivity is already enmeshed in and dependent upon the discourse of the university, just as it is enmeshed in and dependent upon discourses in the workplace, the family and elsewhere. This means that any reflection on the role of the university, scholarship and its relation to whatever social outcomes it seeks must include an account of the subject. Before a strategy for social critique can be formulated, we must make assumptions about the way in which subjectivity is impacted by language; why unconscious fantasies play such a rich part in human motivation; why the revolution has not taken place; and why we keep going to meetings that we know are pointless. To go one step further, we must learn to see the university as a seat in which the contradiction between the status quo and progressive forces is expressed at the level of subjectivity through scholarship and education.

In this respect, it is useful to look at the theory of the four discourses that Lacan offers (see also Sköld, 2010). Formulated against the backdrop of radical student protest in French society in the late 1960s, Lacan seeks a conversation with those who question the role of science and the university in society (but in classic Lacanian fashion, this is at once a misfired conversation in which mutual understanding is fraught and haphazard). The four discourses can be considered as different modalities of the subject in relation to signification, knowledge and desire. In formulating these four modes of Being-in-discourse, Lacan unearths some of the ways in which knowledge is itself inhabited by unconscious drives and desires. It forms a way of interrogating how the various knowledges on which we draw can be understood in relation to our selfhood, and to a shared sense of Being. As subjects, we move between types of knowledge in which notions of universal truth, use (or what Lacan calls mastery), need and want are variously the central criterion. What Lacan intends with his theory of the four discourses, is to probe these different knots of the subject to what it seeks to know. In this sense, we could also say that the four discourses represent different ideological constellations, various modes of being-in-the-world.

Lacan defines the four discourses by means of a mechanistic relation between two fractions, made up by four terms in total. Each separate discourse is articulated by a certain constellation of the terms in relation to each other. The first discourse that Lacan presents is what he calls the master's discourse. It is structured as follows:

$$\frac{agent}{truth} \longrightarrow \frac{work}{production}$$

$$\frac{S1}{\$} \longrightarrow \frac{S2}{a}$$

(Lacan, 2007: 169)

This quasi-mathematical style of representation is something Lacan often relies on, and it has led to some heated debates that I will not go into here (Sokal and Bricmont, 1998, and in response, Fink, 2004). In this case as in many others, Lacan uses various shorthand symbols to denote theoretical concepts and to explicate their relation to one another. Like all other signifiers, they should be taken as representative in a relational sense (namely in relation to Lacan's theoretical corpus) and like any other signifier, they can never 'say it all'.

Following Lacan's mathemes, we see here the imposition of supremacy of a master signifier upon the field of knowledge. This can be understood as a quilting point that is extraneously imposed upon a particular ideological field (see also Žižek, 1989). The master's discourse achieves a domination of a particular signifying assemblage by functioning as its central reference point. It 'hooks on, creates a discourse' (Lacan, 2007: 189).

If we follow Lacan's formula for the discourse of the master, we see that the lower left corner is occupied by $, the barred subject. This is the place of truth in the formula. This means that in the establishing of the master's discourse, the subject is produced as flawed and incomplete. The master signifier is at once foundational to its being, and lacking in positive content. The overriding importance of the master signifier is not questioned in the symbolic order, but at the same time it is a site of constant ideological investment. This can be seen in the formula where the lower left corner, the position of the by-product, is taken up by object *a*, the subject of desire.

What relevance does this type of discursive movement have for our understanding of scientific endeavours, let al.one the kind of scholarship that the business school produces? The question is whether we can see such a mode of subjectivising discourse, such a spectacular display of power, within academic debates. Perhaps the discourse of the master lets itself be felt in the capitalist imperative that is imposed on academia, and thus re-quilts the academic labour process. In such a way, we now find ourselves in search of 'academic excellence' and 'added value' for ever higher student numbers paying ever higher fees. In this way, academic relations of production in the business school and elsewhere become infused with the spectre of capital (see also Dunne et al., 2008).

What we can see in this figure is that the barred subject is in the position of truth here, in the lower left corner of the formula. Lacan states in this respect that the master's discourse masks the division of the subject (2007: 103). The subject is alienated by the imposition of a symbolic field of relations from which it is separated by the master signifier. If we take the example of subjectivity within the workplace, this master signifier is a quilting point that is at once alien to it ('if only they knew how much time I waste at work, how inefficient I am!') and intensely personal ('but no one gets the job done better than me!'). The vacillation between identification with the master signifier and its illicit transgression is what keeps it in place as the central reference point around which the libidinal economy is organized.

Besides the master's discourse, Lacan identifies the discourse of the university. This discursive modality broadly represents the production of knowledge and the role it plays in ordering social life. Lacan represents it in the following matheme:

$$\frac{S2}{S1} \longrightarrow \frac{a}{\$}$$

Here we see the quest for knowledge (S2) take the shape of the object of desire (object *a*). Knowledge (S2) seeks its completion, the missing bit of itself that would make it whole. Lacan formulates his discourse of the university as a way of describing the obsessive drive of modern science to chart, grasp, categorise and otherwise domesticate that which it studies (we might well look to Foucault's work to find ample evidence of this drive). Science colonises, and in doing so, it aims to fully and exhaustively document its object. It aims to have the final word on what it does. Knowledge (S2) must be imposed on the object; it must overlay and *cover* the object.

What is repressed here is S1, the master signifier. This is the quilting point, the central signifier at the heart of knowledge, which 'sutures the subject it implies' (Lacan, 2006: 744). This signifier that binds the field of knowledge together must represent everything to everyone for it to carry off that structural feat, and therefore by necessity it must be an empty signifier. The discourse of the university passes over this empty signifier. It can only but disavow the lack at its very heart, the lack that marks everything it stands for. Its only mode of being is that of *suture,* the covering over of the lack at the heart of discourse. In this spirit, we could say that conventional academic enterprise is characterised by a denial of its own fallibility. Lacan's theoretical and philosophical corpus allows us to see this function of the academic endeavour. In so doing, he helps us conceive of alternative ways of proceeding. But we are getting ahead of ourselves.

What is inadvertently produced in the discourse of the university is the barred subject. We find it in the lower right corner, which means for Lacan that it is something that results in the process of the production of knowledge, the search for scientific truth. How are we to understand this? In his formulation of the discourse of the university, Lacan stresses how the academy is built on a fantasy of completion, of exhaustive cataloguing, and ordering of the world that it seeks to study. Within this compulsion to document and to domesticate, the discourse of the university reproduces the symbolic relations in which human activity is embedded. Stronger still, as we know, the symbolic order is what gives the subject its consistency and its substance. The discourse produced under the banner of the university produces the subject in its alienated, objectified form.

It is safe to say that much of management studies produces knowledge in the form of the discourse of the university. This is clear in the epistemological fantasy of the positivist accumulation of knowledge that underlies the bulk of management theorising, as it is in the implicit utilitarian ambitions of serving the interests of business, consumers, workers and others all at once. The blatant and readily visible failure of mainstream management studies to fulfill either of these ambitions does not hamper its drive to stay its course. Following Lacan, this might be explained by saying that neither of these are the actual function of the discourse of the business school.

Lacan tells us that the discourse of the university still operates within the service of the master, which is invariably bound up with capitalism. Analogously, one could argue that the ultimate function of mainstream management studies is not to build social scientific knowledge or even to 'add value' for business. Rather, it fulfills the function of re-asserting the centrality of Capital as the master signifier, regardless of the myriad fantasies and intentions that underlie the knowledge production involved.

But if the discourse of the university is so well integrated into the master's discourse and what Lacan calls 'the service of goods', what scope is there for critique from within the business school? Or phrased otherwise, the question that has to preempt any notion of 'Lacan *and* organization' must be the following: what does Lacan have to say to organization? And if there is anything worth saying, how can we make it heard? This is where we must introduce the two further discourses that Lacan describes, namely that of the hysteric and that of the analyst.

The hysteric's discourse represents yet another constellation of subjectivity, language and desire. Here we see the terms make a clockwise turn from their positions in the formula for the master's discourse.

$$\frac{\$}{a} \longrightarrow \frac{S1}{S2}$$

What we see in this discourse is the questioning stance of the subject $ towards the master signifier S1. The barred subject is in place of the agent: it questions the master signifier in its place as the final word, the guarantor of truth. The clinical expression of this is the hysterical analysand who has taken it upon him or herself to expose the ignorance of the analyst by incessantly demanding interpretations, just to prove them wrong. The position of truth, the lower left corner in the figure, is here occupied by the object-cause of desire, object *a*. This is what describes the activity of the barred subject that seeks to catch the analyst off-guard: ultimately it is only chasing the impossible object of its desire, which continues to displace itself. Knowledge (S2) is not sought here, but produced as a remainder, an unwanted byproduct.

The hysteric's discourse reveals the relation of the master's discourse to *jouissance* (Lacan, 2007: 94), in the sense that in the hysteric's discourse, knowledge occupies the place of *jouissance*.

Lacan's final discourse is that of the analyst, which revolves around the analyst's ability to present him or herself as an enigma, thereby thwarting the attribution of the role of the 'subject supposed to know'. As our concern is with social critique as made possible by the university, we will forgo an in-depth discussion of the analyst's discourse here since it operates within the context of a number of parameters that are normally present within the clinical praxis of psychoanalysis, such as regularity of sessions, sacrifice (payment) and the ability of the analyst to punctuate a session by ending it at a certain moment. Although not unimaginable, these aspects cannot immediately be translated to the role of the scholar and their involvement in public debate.

Where does this short discussion on Lacan's four discourses leave us, and how does it address the question of how management studies might proceed from the work of Lacan? Here, I argue that the hysterical discourse is crucial to the role of the management scholar because it avoids either establishing a new discourse of mastery (or grand narrative, or metalanguage) or operating in the mortifying scheme of university discourse (which ends up in the service of the master in any case). How would a management studies that starts from the discourse of the hysteric look? Following Lacan, we might be tempted to cast this in terms of two fractions with four terms, like this:

$$\frac{\$\text{cholar}}{a} \rightarrow \frac{\text{Value}}{\text{Business education}}$$

This figure starts with the barred management scholar, the ~~management scholar~~. This subject is divided from itself, caught between not being and not thinking (Lacan, 2007: 103). The ~~management scholar~~ addresses hysterical questions to the central criterion of value that pins down management in all its guises: the management of work organizations, education, healthcare and elsewhere. Much like the hysterical subject who incessantly probes the knowledge of the analyst that they themselves have accorded the status of 'subject supposed to know', the ~~management scholar~~ questions the status of instrumental value. Wherein does this value reside? Who has it? What does it represent to us?

In lived reality, the seat of this value is empty. Business education, in its utopian form, could be the byproduct of this asking. As Harney (2010) has pointed out, today's business school does not produce value but does precisely the opposite: it warehouses unused labour, labour that must not work, study, or do anything else that might bring it to reflect on its status. By unsettling management studies's treatment of 'added value' as taken for granted, we might end up creating such a thing as business education that has a role to play of its own, rather than the current one that can neither create managers nor aid the practice of management.

What occupies the position of truth in such a scheme? What is repressed from the endless probing at the master signifier? According to Lacan, what is repressed in the hysteric's discourse is the object-cause of desire (*a*). Let us apply this to the notion that the role of academic work in contemporary business schools is invariably defined in terms of instrumental value: the business contribution of the knowledge we produce, or the revenue produced through teaching, and so on. The quilting operation that imposes the capitalist criterion of instrumental rationality on academia inadvertently gives rise to an object *a,* something that always escapes instrumental pursuits. At the heart of capitalist hegemony, we find flaws, slippage and transgression. It is only through a hysterical asking that we may venture upon this lack at the very heart of the ideological Other (see also Fleming, this volume).

This also raises another point. In the discourse of the university, there is an insistence on the representation and categorisation of the social life world. The master signifier here makes its presence felt in the form of the categorical imperative to 'keep on knowing' (Lacan, 2007: 105). In the discourse of the university, science must grasp, know, explain and deliver value for the master. Accordingly, the preoccupation in such work is to strive for breadth, for new phenomena that must be studied and understood. We can see this in the constant obsession of mainstream management studies to be 'cutting edge' and to be breaking into 'new' territory. Following Lacan's notion of the discourse of the university, we can understand this as a progressive imposition of codified knowledge on multiple sites of social life, with the aim of mastery.

In contrast, the discourse of the hysteric has no such pre-occupation with the new and undiscovered. Instead, it must seize upon the flaws, inconsistencies and contradictions that keep popping up as it probes the dominance of instrumental rationality in management, education, management education and elsewhere. Behind every smoothly presented management initiative there are a myriad of dysfunctionalities, travesties and fundamental contradictions.

Crucially, such critique in the hysteric's discourse must proceed not from an idealised position of a self-aware and resolved subject, but rather from that of a barred subject. Critical scholarship must come from a position of embodied lived experience, a position rife with emaciation and subjection. Critique can only proceed from a personalised locus in which the analyst him or herself is flawed. Engaged critique articulates itself in conjunction with its own symptom.

Management? Yes please!

Lacan's work directly and indirectly thwarts many of the assumptions on which management is based, such as the notion that employees act according to their intentions and their conscious motivations, or the idea that they act rationally in relation to things such as remuneration, institutionally defined criteria of efficiency and effectiveness, or even organizational politics. Theories that rely on these assumptions cannot be unproblematically maintained when we take seriously the notion of subjectivity as it is offered up by Lacan. More than a de-centered subject, what we find with Lacan is a subject that is intermittently included and excluded within a chain of signification. As such, Lacan allows us to address the subject in its radical dependency on discourse, but at the same time his work allows us to theoretically account for the inadequacy of discourse to inform fully, to provide meaning in a satisfying manner, or to give form to our desires.

Although the poststructuralist turn in organization and management has done much to undermine the notion of a transcendental worker-subject, we have seen that there have been serious difficulties in resolving the determining influences on subjectivity with personal socio-historical trajectories, without resorting to a backdoor essentialism in the form of identity politics. On the whole, the conceptualisation of resistant forms of identity that may be formulated in the face of power has relied on an implicit 'outside' of discourse and power, an untarnished location from whence such a response can be formulated. How can a subject formulate a resistant identity at work when its very being depends on the discursive context in which it resides? In this sense, it is important to recall that there is no 'outside' work. In the exchange that I quoted above, I raised Lacan's point that any outside is already inside, through the discursive constitution of subjectivity itself. The subject cannot place itself outside of the symbolic order, because its existence is always-already anchored within the symbolic. At the same time, the symbolic is not complete and the subject is not wholly encapsulated within it – not in the sense of retaining an authentic presence elsewhere, but in the sense of an ontological negativity that interrupts any and all 'stitched up' significations. In this negativity, the subject itself can be understood to find its most promising definition.

This 'extimate' conjunction of subject and symbolic does not just apply to disembodied academic papers that we might like to *'poubelle'*-ish in prestigious journals. It impacts on our everyday understanding of how we are subject to discourses in the workplace and elsewhere. While it is important to recognize that management discourses have been able to reframe social relations in which we exist (to the extent that instrumental forms of rationality hegemonically dominate over other considerations), we must simultaneously observe the slippage and failure that is displayed in the process. This failure is certainly present in the inability of management ideology to define the business school and other sites of business education fully, and to eradicate the activity of those who seek to interrogate the excesses of capitalism in terms of power, exploitation and inequality. It is in this space of im/possibility that we must engage with Lacan at work.

References

Dunne, S., S. Harney, M. Parker and T. Tinker (2008) 'Discussing the role of the business school', *ephemera*, 8(3): 271-293.

Fink, B. (2004) *Lacan To The Letter: Reading Écrits Closely*. Minneapolis: University of Minnesota Press.

Harney, S. (2010) 'In the business school', *Edu-Factory*, 0(January): 53-61.

Knights, D. and H. Willmott (eds) (1990) *Labour Process Theory*. London: MacMillan.

Lacan, J. (2007) *The Other Side of Psychoanalysis: The Seminar of Jacques Lacan, Book XVII, 1969-70*, trans. R. Grigg. New York: Norton.

Lacan, J. (2006) *Écrits*, trans. B. Fink, New York: Norton.

O'Doherty, D. and H. Willmott (2001) 'Debating labour process theory: the issue of subjectivity and the relevance of poststructuralism', *Sociology*, 35(2): 457-476.

Sköld, D. E. (2010) 'The other side of enjoyment: short-circuiting marketing and creativity in the experience economy', *Organization*, 17(3): 363-378.

Sokal, A. and J. Bricmont (1998) *Fashionable Nonsense: Postmodern Intellectuals' Abuse of Science*. New York: Picador.

2

Lacan at Work

Jason Glynos

As a site of wealth creation, work and the organization of work receive critical attention from many disciplines and from many traditions of thought. In this chapter I explore why one might want to supplement existing approaches to work and the organization of work – both psychoanalytic and non-psychoanalytic – with ideas drawn from the field of Lacanian psychoanalysis. I suggest that there are advantages to organizing this Lacanian intervention around the category of fantasy, but that there are also aspects of this approach that demand further development if we are to offer a convincing critical explanation of workplace phenomena.

Psychoanalysis Beyond the Clinic

The collection *Lacan and Organization* evokes a domain much larger than itself, a domain defined by the attempt to apply psychoanalytic theory to anything outside the clinic. It also evokes worries about the legitimacy and propriety of such applications. No doubt these basic worries are common to most domains in the social sciences, and are of a piece with Foucault's characterization of social science as essentially marked by the empirical-transcendental doublet. In this view, social science never ceases to doubt and revise its founding premises; never able, therefore, to 'move on' to the register of 'normal science'. And yet there also appears to be something provocative about psychoanalysis itself and the very idea of deploying *its* concepts and insights in a social science context.

Historically, of course, psychoanalytic theory has been applied to a wide range of social and political phenomena (the pathologies of various institutions, the behaviour of leaders and the masses, religion, art, architecture, theatre, film, literature, class, gender, crime, sexual perversion, and so on). Work initiated and inspired by the Frankfurt School is one of the most well known examples, involving the application of Freudian psychoanalysis to various social and cultural phenomena, such as political leadership, anti-Semitism, and consumption practices (Reich, 1970; Fromm, 1966; Marcuse, 1955; Adorno et al., 1950; Rieff, 1966; Brown, 1959; Lasch, 1980; Sloan, 1996; Sennett, 1998). And yet such applications have often been plagued by the twin fears of whether 'psychoanalysis is true' and whether one is 'true to psychoanalysis'.

Usually cast in the terms of positivist science, the first fear expresses a worry about whether clinical psychoanalysis, as a discipline, can generate predictions that can be verified or falsified in the same way as natural science. Not only does this entail the adoption of a highly restricted and restricting conceptualization of the relation between clinical psychoanalysis and science: unless it conforms to this sort of deductive-nomological model it also rules out, in an *a priori* fashion, the possibility that the conceptual grammar of psychoanalytic theory can be considered helpful to a field of inquiry beyond the clinic.

But if one is not particularly worried about whether psychoanalysis 'is true' in a 'scientific' or epistemological sense, there is still the fear that one is not being 'true to psychoanalysis'. What is at stake in this case is not the 'truth of psychoanalysis' as such. What is at stake is the *integrity* of psychoanalysis *beyond* the clinic: can one venture outside the clinic and still claim to exercise fidelity to the psychoanalytic enterprise? This question, of course, suggests that the extra-clinical articulation of psychoanalytic concepts is unorthodox in some sense. But as Ernesto Laclau points out in a different context, 'if by orthodox doxa one understands philological obsession and mechanical repetition of the same categories without 'developing' them as required by new contexts, it is clear that any intellectual intervention worth the name will be "heterodox"' (Laclau in Butler, Laclau, Žižek, 2000: 64-5).

Consider the emerging field of psycho-social studies (Clarke et al., 2008; Hoggett et al., 2010; Clarke, 2008; Layton, 2008a, 2008b; Hollway, 2004; Walkerdine, 2008; Frosh and Baraitser, 2008; Wetherell, 2008; Rustin, 2008: 407-11), a domain defined by the systematic use of psychoanalysis for social scientific research. Given that there are different schools of psychoanalysis it is obvious that there are also different heterodox forms of psycho-social studies. Frosh and Baraitser, for example, identify Kleinian and Lacanian psychoanalysis as the two main approaches in this kind of work in the UK (2008: 354). And what has been said of the application of psychoanalysis to social and political studies can also be said of the application of other traditions of thought to the analysis of social and political phenomena, such as hermeneutics, critical realism, and so on. Each of these domains is internally fragmented, generating a wide range of competing heterodox approaches to the study of social and political phenomena.

And yet the question remains how to evaluate the relative merits of competing 'heterodox' approaches, whether such approaches are inspired by psychoanalysis or not. It is difficult to conduct any sort of comparative evaluation at an abstract or purely theoretical level, so one way to proceed (that avoids the twin fallacies of positivism and 'orthodoxism') is to situate such approaches in relation to a problematized set of phenomena. We can, for example, consider a problem field linked to work and the organization of work.

The Problem with Work: Why Psychoanalysis?

When travel, preparation, and worry are added together, the time devoted to work-related activities in formal organizations can amount to a large chunk of one's life. And while the workplace continues to be regarded as a site of wealth production, social and technological change continually transform working practices, as a function of place, time, and control.[1]

In this context, it is not surprising that the concept of work itself becomes unstable. Is unpaid childcare work, for example? Should work be seen predominantly as a function of wage-labour? More broadly: how can or should people cope with changes in the workplace, including changing management practices? What role should resistance, struggle, and politics play in this context? How best to characterize and evaluate workplace practices, including the conditions under which these practices can or ought to be contested? What conditions might promote ethical and political responses to legitimate grievances, and/or avoid the building up of *ressentiment*?

Such questions force us to inquire further: what is a worker's relation to the wealth produced? Who should appropriate it? And how should it be distributed (see, for example, Resnick and Wolff, 1987; Gorz, 1999; Pettinger et al., 2005)? With the conceptual boundaries of work becoming increasingly permeable and fragile, answers to these sorts of questions will have implications whose effects will irradiate outward into many spheres of action, including the spheres of the family and the citizen.

With what resources can one tackle these sorts of questions, and why might one think that a psychoanalytic approach can supplement existing approaches? Labour process theory and the debates surrounding it, have been one important source of inspiration for those wishing to think critically about workplace practices; and so one way to understand the psychoanalytic intervention is to situate it in relation to such debates. For this reason it may be helpful to briefly sketch the basic parameters of this theoretical exchange, which range from more objectivist to more subjectivist understandings of workplace dynamics.[2] Firmly situated on the objectivist side of this debate, Harry Braverman's *Labour and Monopoly Capital* (1974), and other work it has inspired (e.g., Ackroyd and Thompson, 1999), deploy Marx's ideas in order to oppose the view that resistance in the workplace results from a conflict between the structure of the workplace and the personal goals of rational agents. Instead, resistance is conceived as a function of the 'objective' exploitation of labour by capital. In addition, Braverman expands upon Marx's remarks in *Capital* that managers function as 'special wage labourers'. He emphasizes how managers share 'in the subjugation and oppression that characterizes the lives of productive workers' (1974: 418), casting them as 'targets of capitalist control' and thus 'not simply or principally [as] its agents' (Willmott, 1997: 1334). In this view, managers are conceived as functional and subservient to capitalist imperatives just as much as traditional labourers.

Located somewhere in the middle of the macro-objectivist and micro-subjectivist poles of the debate is Michael Burawoy (1979, 1985), according to whom workers should not be reduced to their functional position in the process of capital accumulation. Influenced by critical theory and the work of Gramsci, Burawoy suggests that Braverman's account needs to be supplemented by an appreciation of the way capitalist structures are *reproduced* through the active participation of the workers, managers included. In this view, the political and ideological dimensions of workplace practices (conceived as the production of social relations, and the experience of those relations, respectively) are about as significant as the economic dimension (conceived in terms of the production of things). Showing that there is a place for the subjective judgement of workers in the capitalist process means that departures from dominant capitalist logics of accumulation are just as possible as their maintenance. Yet no sooner is the subjective dimension introduced by Burawoy than it is quickly reabsorbed into a higher level of objectivity, since the subjective dimensions identified are considered by him to be independent of the particular people who populate the workplace (Willmott, 1997: 1342).

Burawoy's failure to take the question of subjectivity sufficiently seriously has prompted many scholars working out of the labour process tradition to explore the potential of Foucauldian and poststructuralist approaches, in order to better exploit and develop Burawoy's original insights in a more satisfactory way (e.g., Knights and MacCabe, 2000, 2003; Thomas and Davies, 2005; O'Doherty and Willmott, 2001a, 2001b; Willmott, 2005; Fleming and Spicer, 2007; Spicer and Böhm, 2007). In the former case, the issue of subjectivity is cast in terms of identity. Here, the worker's identity is shaped and disciplined via technologies which impinge on his or her sense of self – technologies linked to performance and career anxieties, such as various audit and performance-related pay schemes. In the latter case, attention is paid to possible resistances to such micro-physics of power, and especially to the political dimension of workplace practices.

The tendency of many poststructuralist approaches to highlight the importance of the political dimension of workplace practices signals a desire to eschew the idea that the economy is an extra-discursive force outside of, and acting upon, politics, culture, and society. On the contrary, such a poststructuralist perspective seeks to make explicit the idea that the economy is discursively constructed and thus contestable. The political dimension of workplace practices is thus theorized in a way that diverges from the way politics and power are often understood. The concept of the political is theorized not as a function of the way that power is distributed in the organization, where power is understood in terms of identifiable sovereign authority, capacities, resources, interests, structures, or a dispersed micro-physics of power (Lukes, 1974; Knights and Willmott, 1989; Clegg, Courpasson, Phillips, 2006). From the point of view of poststructuralist theory, the political dimension of a practice is understood in relation to a negative ontology, where to subscribe to a negative ontology means simply to affirm the absence of any positive ontological foundations for the subject (or, to put it differently, to affirm the radical contingency of social relations). Far from leading to a kind of free fall into relativism, such a perspective expands the scope and relevance of critical analysis because it emphasizes the situated, precarious, and thus potentially political, character of interests and structures themselves.

The appeal of psychoanalysis can be understood in this context. The attraction of psychoanalysis – and I would argue the attraction of fantasy as a key psychoanalytic category in particular – can be understood in part by reflecting on the emergence and development of poststructuralist political theory and analysis. Central, in this regard, are what have been labelled the linguistic and affective turns. The linguistic turn (Rorty, 1967) signalled an appreciation of the symbolic dimension of political practices (Edelman, 1964), especially the importance of discourse and identity in thinking about political mobilization. Nationalist, feminist, environmental, and gay and lesbian movements emphasized the importance of the stories that people tell each other in shaping their political identity. More importantly, it highlighted the *constructed* character of political identity and discourse, calling for subjects to affirm this constructed and contingent character (e.g. Laclau and Mouffe, 1985; Connolly, 1995).

Many welcomed these developments because they marked a move beyond standard analyses that emphasized the 'givenness' of class, gender, and other interests. They pluralized perspectives on political mobilization and engagement beyond those grounded in interest-based rationalities. Nevertheless, there are many who feel that emphasizing the contingent and constructed character of discourse underestimates the inertia and force of social norms and practices. According to this view the roles of the emotions and passions have been neglected, and the analytical focus needs to shift to affects. The so-called 'affective turn' indicates a need or demand to acknowledge affects as central to political theory and analysis (e.g., Massumi, 1996; Ahmed, 2004; Stavrakakis, 2005; Stavrakakis and Chrysoloras, 2006).

Psychoanalytic theory possesses categories (such as fantasy, and associated concepts like transference, the unconscious, and so on), which are invoked specifically because they are able to capture the combined centrality of both the symbolic and affective dimensions of social and political life (see also Glynos and Stavrakakis, 2010). Against the background of the sorts of question I outlined earlier, a psychoanalytically-inflected poststructuralist approach can offer a decidedly critical – not simply constructivist – edge. Even so, a lot hangs on how the basic ontology underpinning psychoanalysis, including the idea that the subject is constitutively split between its symbolic and affective sides, is cashed out in theory as well as in practice. It is for this reason that it is helpful to explore the utility of psychoanalysis with reference to the specific domain of work and the organization of work. But which psychoanalysis?

The Problem with Work: Which Psychoanalysis?

Ever since its foundation in 1946, the Tavistock Institute of Human Relations has been a hub of activity where mainly Kleinian-inspired, object relations psychoanalytic theory was applied to areas outside the clinic, including, notably, the area of work and organizations (see Trist and Murray, 1990).[3] But there has also been a recent spate of anthologies exploring the connections between psychoanalysis and organizational studies (e.g., Contu et al., 2010; Essers et al., 2009; Carr, 2002; Walkerdine, 2008a; de Swarte, 1998; Carr and Gabriel, 2001; Hinshelwood and Skogstad, 2000; Hinshelwood and Chiesa, 2002; Neumann and Hirschhorn, 1999; Obholzer and Roberts, 1994). There are also those who have debated the utility of psychoanalysis for the understanding of organizations.[4] Nevertheless, many reviews of the current state of this interdisciplinary field call for a more critical and systematic uptake of psychoanalysis in the study of organizations and management (Carr, 2002: 344; Glynos, 2011; Glynos, 2008a; Glynos and Stavrakakis, 2008).

There are many ways one can classify the literature at the intersection of psychoanalysis and organization studies. Some have sought to do this by drawing a distinction between using psychoanalysis to *study* the nature and significance of particular organizations in relation to their wider social and cultural context on the one hand, and using psychoanalysis to draw out lessons about how to *intervene* into particular organizations with the purpose of achieving a specific aim or goal on the other (Carr and Gabriel, 2002).[5] In the former case, key psychoanalytic concepts are used to shed light on how people's personal histories are connected to their experiences in the organization (such as the unconscious or transference). In the latter case, analysts are concerned about how to reform management structures and how to overcome resistance to consultants' recommendations. Such a distinction, of course, should not be overdrawn. As Carr and Gabriel point out, many individual scholars have made important contributions to both sorts of literature (2002: 353). The work of Czander (1993) or Arnaud (1998), for instance, would be hard to classify as either a study or an intervention. It is, rather, a question of emphasis.

In addition, however, it is not possible, at this level of abstraction at least, to say anything concrete about the ontological, normative, and ethical assumptions of those whose work favours one of these two aspects.[6] In fact, the choice of such assumptions can itself become the source of alternative ways of slicing the literature in this interdisciplinary field. And this raises an interesting question. I have already mentioned that there is a basic, albeit healthy, debate about how to best deploy the insights of psychoanalysis in a non-clinical context. What is often not addressed in any systematic detail is why, beyond legitimate (and to a certain extent unavoidable) reasons concerning individual intellectual trajectories, one should choose to rely on one psychoanalytic tradition rather than another when addressing a non-clinical issue – concerning work relations or the management of an organization, for example.

It is well known how the history of clinical psychoanalysis is marked by multiple schisms. The field of clinical psychoanalysis bears the traces of this history, reflecting – to put it positively – a correspondingly rich pluralism. But what are less often examined when psychoanalytic theory is treated as a source of cross-disciplinary inspiration are the differential implications for a non-clinical problem as a function of a particular school of psychoanalysis. Scholars often elide this fundamental point, perhaps because there is an implicit awareness that such an admission would only reinforce the prejudice of psychoanalytic naysayers, or more likely, cause vacillators to misinterpret such an admission as an admission of weakness and invalidity. When there is disagreement over the sense and significance of basic psychoanalytic categories, such as transference and countertransference, ego ideal and anxiety, affect and meaning, interpretation and technique, fantasy and even the unconscious, it becomes difficult to sustain the idea that psychoanalysis is 'one'.[7]

The implication of this is two-fold. First, it encourages one to be more specific about the school presupposed in articulating a psychoanalytic perspective or category. (This helps rather than resolves the problem, because not only is there not 'one' psychoanalysis, there are also profound disagreements *within* each school.) Second, one can enhance the analytical potential of an adopted psychoanalytic perspective by comparing and contrasting it with other psychoanalytic approaches to similar sets of non-clinical issues. It is this set of issues that offers a vantage point from which to evaluate not only whether psychoanalysis is helpful in supplementing non-psychoanalytic approaches, but also in evaluating which sort of psychoanalytic approach is helpful and why.

This latter evaluative exercise has hardly been explored. Undertaking such an exercise would begin to answer some interesting questions not only about the substantive issues under investigation, but also about the nature and significance of the difference between psychoanalytic schools in a non-clinical context. It would shed light on how best to characterize the distinction between two sets of differences:

1. differences between approaches inspired by psychoanalysis and other approaches; and

2. differences between approaches inspired by different psychoanalytic schools.

Each of these sets of differences can be examined from the point of view of a concept, a problem, or both. Take the first set of differences, for example. One can pick out a key concept like fantasy and begin to examine how this concept (and related concepts such as utopia, metaphor, rhetoric, stereotype) has been deployed differently by psychoanalytically-inspired and non-psychoanalytic approaches. In what follows however I focus on the second set of differences (i.e., between approaches inspired by different psychoanalytic schools).

*

At the most abstract level, one could compare and contrast approaches in the plane of theory. That is to say, one can pick a category and examine how different psychoanalytic schools treat that category, say between Lacanian and Kleinian schools (see Burgoyne and Sullivan, 1997; Frosh and Baraitser, 2008). For example, Klein's more substantive conception of the unconscious could be compared and contrasted with Lacan's more dislocatory and substanceless conception. And the same can be done with respect to transference and countertransference, or the category of fantasy (see, for example, Steiner, 2003).

In the case of fantasy, what Klein and Lacan share is the rejection of the classical view that it should be linked in any simple way to the pleasure principle and to illusion. In the classical view, the aim is to make the subject's reliance on fantasy fade so as to better adjust to the demands of reality. Klein and Lacan, however, both question the epistemological premise upon which this stark separation between fantasy and reality is established and maintained. Rather than taking the demands of reality for granted, these are, on the contrary, put into question. But once reality is problematized in this fashion, so is its relation to fantasy. Instead of contrasting fantasy with reality, Klein and Lacan were keen to stress the role fantasy plays in structuring the subject's reality and were thus also keen to foster a stance toward the world which reflected this constitutively blurred boundary. Lacan's ethical injunction to 'traverse the fantasy' (as opposed to 'abandon the fantasy'), and Klein's privileging of the depressive position over the paranoid-schizoid position's overly strict dichotomization of the world into good/bad, fight/flight pairs, both seek to give expression to a subjective stance more tolerant of ambiguity and uncertainty.[8]

Nevertheless, there are also differences in their conceptualizations of fantasy – profound differences having to do with the role of the image, emotion, meaning, language, subjectivity, and libido (see Leader, 1997: 89-92). Yet the significance of these differences (and even the robustness of identified similarities) is hard to discern if we remain exclusively at the level of abstract theory. Clearly, there are clinical implications, which follow from these onto-theoretical differences (see, for example, Burgoyne and Sullivan, 1997). But I think it worth considering how such differences might also play themselves out in relation to problematized phenomena beyond the clinic too.

*

There have been attempts to separately apply Kleinian and Lacanian ideas to extra-clinical domains generally, and organization studies in particular. But it is striking that there has been virtually no work comparing Lacanian with other psychoanalytically-inspired approaches to work and the organization of work.[9] Comparative exercises generally are rare, but these are certainly more populous outside the Lacanian orbit (see, for example, Czander, 1993; and Czander et al., 2002). Czander (1993), for one, conducts a comparative exercise examining classical psychoanalysis, object relations, and self-psychology. A dialogue with Lacan may perhaps begin by critically engaging with Czander, and with others such as Hinshelwood et al. (Hinshelwood and Skogstad, 2000; Hinshelwood and Chiesa, 2002) or scholars linked to psychosocial studies (e.g., Clarke et al., 2008, Hoggett et al., 2006), by highlighting where convergences, divergences, and productive affinities lie.

An engagement with Czander from a Lacanian point of view might, for example, question the centrality attributed to the psychological health of the individual. This focus sets important limits upon the critical potential of this particular psychoanalytic approach – at least in the way it is being deployed here – because it marginalizes an ethics premised on split subjectivity. This underlying psychologistic tendency is evident in his self-psychological ideal of a mentally healthy person, who is 'a person with a firm or secure self system, motivated by a striving for power, a realization of basic idealized goals, and an ability to tap basic talents and skills that are consistent and capable of forming an arc between the person's ambitions and ideals' (Czander, 1993: 74).[10] It is also evident in Czander's invocation of a Kohutian self-psychological approach to issues of occupational choice. Using post-classical, Kleinian, and post-Kleinian ideas, Kohut (1971) and Kohut and Wolf (1978) develop a typology of characterological styles, and Czander seeks to relate these characterological styles to occupational choice (Czander, 1993: 79-80):

> These characterological styles are representative of fixed ways of interacting and negotiating relationships with objects in the world. Occupational choice is gratifying only when it is suitable to the individual's characterological style. Characterological style consists of traits and mannerisms adopted as a response to anxiety. If an occupation suits one's characterological style, it means that the occupation provides avenues for self-expression, anxiety will be reduced and a degree of comfort will be attained. These styles are self-protective in that they protect against anxiety but also protect the employee's

> fantasy life from real and imagined psychological injuries. (Czander, 1993: 80)

Czander thus presents a clear picture of the individual as necessarily possessing features drawn from a predefined set.

Apart from marginalizing an ethical perspective premised on split subjectivity, this psychologizing tendency also tends to marginalize wider critical perspectives, largely because Czander tends to take the aims and goals of organizations for granted (1993: 176-7, 200-1; see also Czander, 2001). In other words, the terms of the debate are defined by fairly narrow operational objectives, evident from the list of characteristics Czander regards as typical of an unhealthy organization: 'unprofitability; interpersonal conflict; high turnover; low morale; internal conflict; high absenteeism; no growth; poor labour-management relations; and work sabotage' (Czander, 1993: 198; see also 117-8, 122, 142-3).[11]

In general, however, we could say that the focus of a large swath of psychoanalytical approaches to work and the organization of work are concerned with problems which are defined in relation to a positivized conception of an individual's psychological health or a positivized conception of an organization's operational health. These health ideals frame a whole range of commonly analysed problems in this area: absenteeism, bullying, stress, workaholism, compulsiveness, occupational choice, motivations for continuing or abandoning work, reasons for particular style of management, trust, and sexual harassment.

These are, of course, important problems that deserve our attention. It is also true that such psychoanalytic perspectives, as commonly applied, contrast with and broaden the more conventional economic perspective on work and organizations. The latter assumes that the subject is motivated by material goods and must be managed on that basis. The former, on the other hand, suggests that the subject is moved by psychological motives such as the wish to control or be controlled by others, or to secure the approval of others, etc. However, psychoanalysis often gets deployed in a way that is too focused on the individual and how the individual copes psychically with the demands of the organization, and thus in a way that marginalizes the wider social and political significance of organizational norms and behaviour.

*

The task of comparing different psychoanalytic schools from the point of view of a specific problem area can be further refined by adding a particular psychoanalytic theme or category to the domain of work and organizations. Not many direct and systematic problem-driven, category-centred comparisons exist yet, even though the number of concept-oriented studies is increasing within approaches inspired by particular psychoanalytic schools. For example, key categories examined and explored from a Lacanian point of view in the context of organizational studies include transference (Stavrakakis, 2008; Arnaud, 1998); symptom (Cederström and Grassman, 2008); sinthome (Hoedemaekers, 2008); subjectivity (Cederström and Willmott, 2007; Hoedemaekers, 2007; Arnaud and Vanheule, 2007); jouissance (Kosmala and Herrbach, 2006); imaginary/symbolic/real (Hoedemaekers, 2009); the imaginary (Roberts, 2005; Vidaillet, 2007); demand/desire (Arnaud, 1998); interpassivity (Johnsen et al., 2009); fantasy (Chang and Glynos, 2011; Glynos, 2008a; Glynos and Stavrakakis, 2008; Willmott, 2007; Contu and Willmott, 2006; Bloom and Cederström, 2009; Fotaki, 2009; Hillier and Gunder, 2003, 2005, 2007); identification (Fleming and Spicer, 2003; Contu, 2008); master signifier /object *a* (Jones and Spicer, 2005). Outside the Lacanian orbit, these include: the oedipal complex (Lister, 2001, Baum, 1991), emotion (Carr, 2001; Antonacopoulou and Gabriel, 2001); and fantasy (Guinchard, 1998; Baum 1991, 1994; Gabriel 1995, 1997, 2008b; Walkerdine, 2005, 2006).

A concept promising considerable potential to yield insights in the field of organizations studies from a comparative point of view is the category of fantasy. As we saw earlier in relation to Lacan and Klein, the way fantasy is conceptualized within different psychoanalytic schools can diverge. Nevertheless, in most cases, fantasy raises common epistemological and ethical issues linked to the way the subject relates to the world in general and the world of work in particular. This suggests that a more systematic investigation of the way fantasy can be deployed in the analysis of workplace practices may be very productive, an investigation which could be enhanced further through a suitably constructed comparative exercise. As a general rule there have not been many studies that have focused their analytical interventions into workplace practices around the category of fantasy, and to my knowledge there has been no cross-psychoanalytic comparative work on fantasy in the workplace.

The works of Kernberg and Kets de Vries comprise two exceptions to this general rule (Kernberg, 1976, 1998; Kets de Vries, 1991; Kets de Vries and Miller, 1984) and they are not alone.[12] These particular 'theorists suggest that organizational structures are created to reflect the unconscious fantasies associated with the wishes and needs of executives' (Czander, 1993: 103). Taking a post-Kleinian, Bion-inspired approach, Kets de Vries has constructed a five-fold typology of organizations and corresponding dysfunctions, in terms of the motives and fantasies informing them: paranoid, compulsive, dramatic, depressive, and schizoid. Thus, fantasies of persecution, control, and dependency, for example, correspond to the paranoid, compulsive, and dramatic organizational structures respectively (Kersten, 2001: 458-10). Moreover, such a framework has been deployed to understand the shift from one to another structure (Kersten, 2007).

Nevertheless, there have been a number of drawbacks to this approach, as pointed out by sympathetic critics (Kersten, 2001; 2007). First is the tendency to treat as self-evident that a particular organization is dysfunctional (or not, as the case may be), there being little, if any, discussion of the criteria being deployed in order to make such a determination. Second, such an approach tends to view the relationship between executive management and employees in overly individualized and uni-directional terms, thus failing to grasp 'the dynamic and structural quality of power as well as its dialectical potential for generating its own resistance and denial' (Kersten, 2001: 462). As Kersten puts it:

> The key theme underlying most of the neurotic organization literature is that the neurotic style of top executives has a strong influence on the overall functioning of the organization, including its strategy, culture, structure, and the nature of group and interpersonal relations, such that individual pathology becomes organizational pathology. (Kersten, 2001: 458)

In this view, the employees' 'group fantasy both feeds and complements a management style that is insular, rigid, and fixed, based on the antagonistic impulses that characterize the various neurotic styles' (Kersten, 2007: 67). Remedies to the dysfunctional operation of organizations, then, involve targeting the top executives for therapeutic intervention, removing them, or hoping some major dislocation takes place (Kersten, 2001: 463). Employees tend to be treated as fairly passive subjects responding to the acts of their superiors.

Finally, the wider social, political, and ideological context tends to be ignored, implicitly regarding the latter as unimportant or marginal for the critical understanding of the organization. Kersten turns to Habermas' critical theory in developing this vantage point, in which the ideal of open and undistorted communication is held as a counterpoint to Kets de Vries' individualizing, personalizing, and psychologising tendencies. She appeals to critical theory in order to add a 'more specific consideration of the structural and ideological impact of the organizational and social context on psychodynamics' (Kersten, 2001: 453).

Using critical theory to articulate psychoanalytic insights to the organization (rather than, say, systems theory or indeed no socio-political theory whatsoever) is an important advance. Nevertheless, many problems remain. For example, there is no discussion of how best to conceive the relationship between psychodynamics and the wider social and political structures. There is also no systematic discussion of either the role of fantasy in thinking this relationship, or the content of fantasy, especially from the perspective of ontology, ethics, and methodology. This is especially crucial in light of a *prima facie* contradiction between the Habermasian ideal of undistorted communication and the Freudian ontology of split subjectivity in which miscommunication is considered – in important respects – ineliminable.

*

While both Kleinian and Lacanian traditions are considered influential in organization studies, and while the latter is still considered to be the 'new kid on the block', there are several reasons to be optimistic that a Lacanian-inflected political theory of discourse is better suited to help situate psychoanalytic insights in a way that can overcome some of the 'internalizing' and 'individualizing' tendencies already mentioned – tendencies which account either for the absence of critical engagement with company norms (Kets de Vries) or for the too abrupt imposition of other norms from the 'outside' (Kersten).

No doubt taking particular understandings of the health of an organization for granted is by no means a necessary outcome of adopting a Kleinian, object relations perspective. Yet it is an identifiable tendency, which may have its origins in Klein's widely-noted inclination to divide the world into an internal and external one, privileging the internal world in terms of explanatory efficacy (Leader, 2000: ch. 2). Leader, for example, argues that the object relations tradition

> tends to assume that the category of object is more or less a given (the mother, the breast, etc.) and that this given can be the subject of predicate qualification (for example, 'is good/bad'). A rich theory of judgement, if it had been formulated in this tradition, might well have encountered a number of counterexamples, and Lacan's work on this theme suggested that in fact the so-called 'object' was outside the field of predication. Rather than being the subject of meaningful predication, it could only be inferred from the points in a patient's speech where meaning seemed to collapse. (Leader, 2000: 209)

Of course the negativity of Lacanian thought, the absence of an explicit positive programme, has served for some as a counterpoint to Kleinian and object relations approaches to politics (cf. Rustin, 2001: ch. 7). Operating at a fairly high level of abstraction, this cannot be denied. However, there are advantages to abandoning the language of internality/externality from the point of view of political analysis. For a start, it allows one to avoid assuming 'that everything a patient might think of is… thought of as inside themselves' (Leader, 2000: 86) and so more likely to avoid taking it for granted as essential to them. Instead it shifts our attention to wider symbolic, cultural, and social factors (Leader, 2008: 107), suggesting that Lacan would be a more natural bridge to examining the political and ideological aspects of organizations, and organizational culture.

Lacan at Work

A turn to the category of fantasy offers one way to harness Lacan's psychoanalytic insights for the study of organizations.[13] As already mentioned, Kets de Vries and Kersten's work belong to a small but significant literature that explores workplace practices from the point of view of fantasies.[14] Such studies are significant because they represent initial attempts to document the content of workplace fantasies, trading on the powerful intuition that they have an important role to play in our understanding of how social practices – in this case workplace practices – are organized, sustained, or potentially transformed. They make interesting observations and generate some useful critical insights. In my view, it is possible to build on these insights by linking them more explicitly and systematically to the question of ideology, thereby making the political and normative significance of fantasy clearer. In order to see this I offer an initial sketch of the logic of fantasy (see also Lacan, 1966-7). I then use empirical material from existing literature to illustrate this logic. My strategy here is to narrow the focus of my inquiry to those scholars who explicitly appeal to a Lacanian understanding of psychoanalysis and fantasy – primarily to minimize conceptual overdetermination and ambiguities.

In a first approach we could say that the logic of fantasy names a narrative structure involving some reference to an idealized scenario promising an imaginary fullness or wholeness (the beatific side of fantasy) and, by implication, a disaster scenario (the horrific side of fantasy). This narrative structure will have a range of features, which will vary from context to context, of course, but one crucial element is the obstacle preventing the realization of one's fantasmatic desire. In Lacanian psychoanalysis, realizing one's fantasy is impossible because the subject (as a subject of desire) survives only insofar as its desire remains unsatisfied. But the obstacle, which often comes in the form of a prohibition or a threatening Other, transforms this impossibility into a 'mere difficulty', thus creating the impression that its realization is at least potentially possible. This gives rise to another important feature of fantasy, namely, its transgressive aspect: the subject secures a modicum of enjoyment by actively transgressing the ideals it officially affirms (see also Glynos, 2003a; 2008b), for example by trying to eliminate the identified obstacle through illicit means. In this view, there is a kind of complicity animating the relation between the official ideal and its transgressive enjoyment, since they rely on each other to sustain themselves. Fantasy, therefore, is not merely a narrative with its potentially infinite variations at the level of content, although it is of course this too. It also has a certain logic in which the subject's very being is implicated: the disruption or dissolution of the logic leads to what Lacan calls the *aphanisis*, or vanishing, of the subject (as a subject of desire). In sum, the logic of a fantasmatic narrative is such that it structures the subject's desire by presenting it with an ideal, an impediment to the realization of an ideal, as well as the enjoyment linked to the transgression of an ideal.[15]

This conception of fantasy can be readily linked to the literature in organizational studies. Several studies on employee cynicism, for example, suggest how transgressive acts can sometimes serve to stabilize an exploitative social practice, which they appear to subvert (Willmott, 1993; du Gay and Salaman, 1992; Fleming and Spicer, 2003; Contu, 2008). Taking their cue from Michael Burawoy's study of factory workers in *Manufacturing Consent* (1979), they draw the conclusion that informal games and cynical distance toward the control systems and company rules imposed by management often have the effect of sustaining the oppressive system which they ostensibly transgress.[16] In a related vein, and referring to Gideon Kunda's study of cynical workers in *Engineering Culture* (1992), Fleming and Spicer emphasise how 'employees performed their roles flawlessly and were highly productive' despite their recourse to 'humour, the mocking of pompous official rituals and sneering cynicism'. They suggest how cynicism could help sustain employees' belief that they are not mere cogs in a company machine, thereby allowing them to indulge in the fantasy that they are 'special' or 'unique' individuals (Fleming and Spicer, 2003: 164). That such cynical-transgressive acts sustain the social practice being transgressed appears to be corroborated by studies, which show how personnel officers of many companies actually advise workers not to identify with corporate culture ideals too strongly, and to retain a healthy distance from the company script (Ashforth and Humphrey, 1993; Leidner, 1993; Sturdy et al., 2001).

These studies point to the normative and political significance of workplace fantasies. In fact recent developments in political discourse theory bring into focus the critical potential of a Lacanian conception of fantasy by situating fantasmatic logics in relation to what have been called, following the work of Ernesto Laclau, social and political logics (Glynos and Howarth, 2007; see also Stavrakakis, 2007). My claim here is that appeal to these logics helps make clearer the normative and ethical implications of the category of fantasy (see also Glynos, 2008a). In general terms, the category of 'logics' seeks to capture the purposes, rules and self-understandings of a practice in a way that is sensitive to the radical contingency of social relations, or what in Lacanian parlance is called 'lack in the Other'. Logics thus furnish a language with which to characterize and critically explain the existence, maintenance, and transformation of practices, thus making the approach flexible enough to deal with the porous and shifting boundary of 'work' in a wide range of contemporary organizational practices. A practice is here understood in broad terms to comprise a network of activities and intersubjective relations, which is sufficiently individuated to allow us to talk about it meaningfully and which thus appears to cohere around a set of rules and/or other conditions of existence. In this view, a practice is always a *discursive* practice, which is meaningful and collectively sustained through the operation of three logics: social, political, and fantasmatic logics. If social logics assist in the task of directly characterizing a practice along a synchronic axis, then political logics can be said to focus more on the diachronic aspects of a practice, accounting for the way it has emerged or the way it is contested and/or transformed. And if political logics furnish us with the means to show how social practices come into being or are transformed, then fantasmatic logics disclose the way specific practices and regimes *grip* subjects ideologically (Glynos, 2001).

In the remainder of this section I continue to focus on the way the logic of fantasy *sustains* particular work relations and patterns. Fantasies supported by the prospect of big profits, generous pay packets, career advancement, consumption of prize commodities, and hobbies, are an obvious way to think about how patterns of work are affected and sustained by fantasies. But such fantasmatically-structured desires shape the nature and content of demands made by workers and by management, as well as the way they are responded to. But in what way, more specifically, does fantasy sustain the existing political economy of work? One way of thinking about this is in relation to the political dimension of social relations. Insofar as fantasies prevent or make difficult the politicization of existing social relations, relations of subordination inclusive, one can say that fantasy helps reinforce the *status quo*. The logic of fantasy, then, can be construed as a narrative affirmed by workers, often unconsciously, preventing the contestation of suspect social norms, and making less visible possible counter-logics.

Consider Willmott's reinterpretation of a study by Brown and Humphreys of a new further education college following the merger of two former colleges (Brown and Humphreys, 2006). In his reading of their study, Willmott finds both nostalgic fantasies of the past, as well as wishful fantasies projected onto the future (Willmott, 2007). According to Willmott, in the newly constituted college Alpha College, the *obstacle* preventing the realization of particular desires is key to understanding the function and significance of these fantasies.

Each member of the new staff belonged to one of three groups: ex-Beta employees (these are the new college staff that come from Beta college), ex-Gamma employees (these are the new college staff that came from Gamma college), and the new senior management team. Interviews with staff members revealed how each group became an element of narrative condensation for the others' fears and anxieties, serving as key talking points around which they could each consolidate their respective identities. Ex-Beta staff and ex-Gamma staff regarded the senior management team as incompetent; but they also regarded each other with suspicion and resentment. Precisely because these scapegoating fantasies enabled the construction of a common identity, which offered an informal and convenient receptacle for, or displacement of, their distinct grievances, it also suppressed an alternative articulation of grievances and the kind of cross-group collective mobilization that this may have made possible.

While Brown and Humphreys emphasize how employees' interactions tended to consolidate their differential and oppositional identities with respect to each other, Willmott points to alternative norms and possibilities present, but not emphasized, in the interview extracts presented. For example, both ex-Beta and ex-Gamma staff invariably evoked norms linked to educational and pedagogic ideals, which appeared to them to have been eclipsed by the dominant social logic of business efficiency and productivity. Alpha College was increasingly sedimented in the mould of a business. Contesting this norm in the name of an alternative educational norm may have served as a way to mobilize support *across* groups. The suggestion here is that such unofficial and collective grumblings were underpinned by scapegoating fantasies; and that *because* they offered individual groups a modicum of relief (or enjoyment in Lacanian terms), they were not easily jettisoned in favour of alternative pathways – more political pathways for example.

The above illustration suggests that fantasies play a role not just in sustaining workplace practices generally, but also in sustaining relations of domination or exploitation more specifically. In my view, there are both ethical *and* normative aspects at play here, and that these aspects are often conflated. My sense is that it is useful, from a critical point of view, to treat these aspects as analytically distinct where possible (see also Glynos, 2008a). While the ethical aspect of fantasy relates to the level of a subject's libidinal investment in its narrative, the normative aspect relates to the norms of the practice the fantasmatic narrative appears to sustain.

The claim here is that the more subjects are invested in fantasies, the more likely they are to read all aspects of their practice in terms of that fantasmatic narrative, and the less likely they are to 'read for difference'. Counter-logics are precisely those potential alternative discursive patterns that inhere in the interstices of workplace practices that would provide a counterpoint to a dominant social logic. The subject tends to use fantasy as a way to protect itself from ambiguities, uncertainties, and other features which evoke intimations of anxiety. But it is precisely those ambiguities that open up possibilities for critical distance and alternative 'becomings'. It thus becomes important to make explicit the normative framework that the researcher brings to the analysis and, through a process of *articulation*, to actively bring it into contact with those concrete alternatives residing in the practices themselves (Glynos and Howarth, 2007: 177-97).

The insights generated by such a Lacanian-inflected discursive approach to work and the organization may offer us a way to overcome some of the problems identified in approaches inspired by other psychoanalytic schools, and to generate a research programme intended to explore the links between ethics, fantasy, and normative critique in the study of organizations.[17] Such a research programme would address some fairly basic questions, which are important from the point of view of analysis and critique. For example: how should one characterize the workplace practice as a function of social logics and norms? In what sense is the researcher's implied conception of exploitation related to the idea that subjects ought to exercise meaningful control over their working conditions (or some other idea)? What aspects of a concrete workplace practice appear to reflect this implicit grievance or to embody alternative normative potentialities? Finally, how do the identified fantasies operate in such a way as to make less visible to the subjects themselves both the potential grievances and potential alternative ways of structuring workplace practice?

What Next?

To date there have been few systematic attempts to ascertain in a general way the political significance of fantasy and other key psychic processes, especially in relation to organizations. Moreover, most analyses that invoke the term 'fantasy' rarely elaborate the ontological, conceptual, and methodological parameters in detail or unproblematically, and so I believe we still need to determine the specificity and worth of fantasy for organizational studies in a much more rigorous and nuanced manner. There are at least three interrelated ways one can imagine the research programme of 'Lacan and Organization' advancing, each construed as addressing a particular deficit: a normative deficit, an ethico-empirical deficit, and a methodological deficit.

(1) The normative deficit

The critical impulse informing many studies that explore the role of fantasies and other psychic processes in organizations target norms, whose suspect nature is often taken for granted, branding them explicitly or implicitly as exploitative or oppressive, or as serving vested interests (often qualified as market capitalist interests). Consider the claim that transgressive 'indulgency patterns' (Gouldner, 1955; Mars, 1982; see also Roper, 1994) 'have long been recognized by researchers as an important part of maintaining workplace relations of power. In turning a blind eye to minor infringements such as petty pilfering and "fiddling"… more consequential disruptions [to, for example, profit maximizing activities] are avoided' (Fleming and Spicer, 2003: 167). This is clearly an important observation whose significance can be appreciated via Lacan's theory of subjectivity and fantasy. Indeed it points to the need to start engaging with the reasons why *particular* relations of power ought to be regarded as suspect, and how precisely such relations of power colour the content and modality of fantasmatic engagement. Here fantasies could be seen as key to understanding how such relations of power are maintained, but the norms embodied in these relations still need to be linked systematically and/or explicitly to broader normative theories informed by sociological and economic considerations. This would have the effect of transforming latent 'crypto-normative' tendencies into more explicit and convincing normative engagements.

In order to do this one could start by asking what contribution the appeal to fantasy and other psychic processes could make in critically engaging with the dominant norms of contemporary political economy, namely those norms for which markets and capitalist firms – and the neoclassical assumptions that usually underpin them – function as models or paradigms. From this point of view, advocates of the dominant conceptions of political economy are seen by many as apologists of the *status quo*, reinforcing existing power relations and ideals (Galbraith, 1975; Gorz, 1989, 1994, 1999). In challenging the hegemonic theories and practices of political economy, therefore, opposing approaches can be said to yield a fairly expansive definition of the field of *critical political economy*, which would include Marxist, post-Marxist, critical realist, feminist, environmentalist, and poststructuralist approaches within its ambit (e.g., Callinicos, 2001, 2006; Crouch, 2005; Jessop, 2002; Best and Connolly, 1982; Gibson-Graham, 1996, 2006; Resnick and Wolff, 1987, 2005; Ruccio and Amariglio, 2003).

A specifically Lacanian critical political economy, then, would begin with the assumption that economic life is embedded in social and political relations, highlighting the complex and overdetermined character of economic relations and identities. Here subjects are not only consumers, but 'also citizens, students, workers, lovers, and parents, and the lives they live in each of these roles affects their involvement in the others' (Best and Connolly, 1982: 39). Noting that subjects are multiply affiliated is not uncommon in the literature of course. The observation, however, raises a question about how best to understand the ways in which multiple subject positions combine, separate, or dissolve. From this point of view it is possible to draw on the hermeneutical, post-marxist, post-structuralist work of Best and Connolly (1982), Resnick and Wolff (1987, 2005), Gibson-Graham (2006), Laclau and Mouffe (1985), Laclau (1990) and others, to articulate a connection to Lacanian psychoanalytic theory (see also Glynos and Howarth, 2007; Ozselcuk, 2006; Madra, 2006; Ozselcuk and Madra, 2005). Such an exercise would help make a specifically Lacanian contribution to the critical political economy of work – a field which seeks to politicize dominant socio-economic arrangements, justifications of wealth and income inequality, as well as the various structures of accountability to stakeholders and the public at large (which secure and bolster the allegiance of those subject to such arrangements and structures).

Clearly this complicates our picture of the relation between psychological and economic interests, at least as traditionally understood. In emphasizing the symbolic and *undecidable* character of interests as such, a Lacanian-inflected political theory of discourse problematizes the traditional economic view in a profound way. It does not merely contest the view that the only interests that can act as key motivating factors are economic or material interests, and that these motivating interests need to be pluralized beyond material interests to include psychological or cultural interests. It also challenges the idea that such interests have a motivating force which is independent of the way they pass through the self-interpretations of subjects, thereby pointing to the fantasmatic and potentially political aspects of those interests. Such an approach, therefore, shares an important affinity with those cultural economists who argue that '[t]he economy does not exist, out there, but is enacted and constituted through the practices, decisions, and conversations of everyday life' (Deetz and Hegbloom, 2007: 325; see also du Gay, 1996; du Gay and Pryke, 2002; Pettinger et al., 2005). Noting the central role that work plays in social life, they suggest that its meaning and materiality demand careful and critical analysis that is rooted in context and history in order to evaluate the scope of its influence and possible trajectories of transformation. In this view, a focus on experimental, alternative, or minority community economies might serve as a way of throwing light on the historically contingent and normative character of dominant cultural economies (Gibson-Graham, 2006; Glynos, 2008a; Glynos and Speed, 2009). A Lacanian-inflected approach would clearly focus on aspects of those practices that exhibit the presence of split subjectivity, the unconscious, and fantasy, but it would seek to draw out the implications of such community economy analyses for normative and ethical critique.

One interesting and potentially rich case study with which to explore these themes would involve looking more closely at the organization of psychoanalytic practice itself. Some studies, for example, have already started to look at the tensions and paradoxes of ongoing attempts by the state to regulate the practice of psychoanalysis in the UK and Europe more generally. Such efforts reveal not only deep divisions between regulatory and psychoanalytic aims and objectives, they also point to divisions among different psychoanalytic organizations. This is because proposed new governance regimes entail the introduction of various guarantees and measurable quality standards that would, according to many scholars, spell the end of psychoanalysis (Parker and Revelli, 2008a; 2008b; Burgoyne, 2008; Litten, 2008; Leader, 2004, 2008). This implies that certain normative, sociological, and/or political economic conditions would have to be in place to make it possible for an 'ethics of psychoanalysis' to exist. Such a case study, moreover, would be further complicated by the fact that it would be considered relevant at multiple levels. For example, such a study may be expected to say something about the survival of psychoanalytic practice itself, defined in terms of concepts like split subjectivity and fantasy. But such a study would also involve invoking these categories to examine how political mobilization against such regulatory efforts succeeds, is pre-empted, or thwarted. It would explore the multiple roles that fantasy and ethics can play in policy making and in policy implementation, including the struggles engaged in by various agencies at and across each of these levels.

(2) Ethico-empirical deficit

Closely connected to the normative deficit is what I call the ethico-empirical deficit. There is a general consensus in the literature that the mode of engagement associated with an ethics of 'openness' is to be preferred, especially when thinking critically about the political economy and about the transformation of the organization of work more specifically. What receives much less attention in this literature, however, are questions about (1) what these alternative modes of engagement actually look like in practice; and (2) the conditions under which a transition is made from one to another mode of engagement.

There is of course considerable theoretical reflection on the concept of ethics in Lacan, which for many has become synonymous with the idea of 'traversing the fantasy'. But there is a need to add to these ontological discussions a more robust ontical base by, for example, building up a corpus of empirical examples, exemplars, or paradigms of different sorts of ethical engagement associated with the 'dissolution' of the logic of fantasy. This would entail supplementing existing studies that furnish negative critiques of modes of engagement characterized by 'closure' with rich phenomenological accounts of what appears on the 'other side' of posited fantasmatic traversals. This may offer us a way to deepen our theoretical understanding of the idea of a 'logic of fantasy', including how various ethical, normative, and sociological dimensions interconnect. In particular it would seek to show how various logics of fantasy can underpin either regressive or progressive programmes, and how the dissolution of such fantasmatic logics affects the normative trajectory of such programmes.

Such a shift of focus toward greater empirical detail and ethnographic nuance would also help avoid a temptation which Genevieve Morel finds even in a clinical context, namely, a temptation to subordinate 'the end of each analysis to a theory posited in advance' (Morel, 2004: 3). Noting how Lacan uses the expression 'traversing the fantasy' only once in his career (Morel, 2004: 1), she calls on analysts to heed Freud's and Lacan's reminders to affirm the analyst's non-knowledge as much as possible. Such a view is not without theoretical implications for socio-political analysis, since it would entail rearticulating the relation between ethics and fantasy in novel ways, mediating and amplifying them with the help of other concepts such as mourning.[18] One promising way to explore these themes may be to look more carefully at the ethical possibilities opened up by different configurations of workplace democracy. What conditions and devices, for example, might promote a specifically democratic ethos in organizations akin to a Lacanian 'ethics of the real'?[19]

(3) Methodological deficit

Finally, many scholars point to the dangers of abstract theory, of departing too much from the contextualized self-interpretations of the subjects under study, and of not reflecting sufficiently on the role of the analyst in the method and the manner in which the study is conducted (Ashcraft, 2008: 383-6; Deetz, 2008; Kenny, 2009). Of course the profound implications that unconscious processes have upon empirical data gathering techniques and analyses is widely recognized, discussed and debated in the context of the clinic. However, there is a striking gap in the literature dealing with the application of specifically Lacanian insights to extra-clinical domains generally, and the domain of work and organizations specifically. Though this is partly due to its relatively nascent status (Contu et al., 2010; Essers et al., 2009), it does nevertheless point to what I call a methodological deficit.

I construe the notion of a methodological deficit here in the widest possible sense, aiming to capture the full range of theoretical issues that arise when deploying psychoanalysis in the activity of describing, explaining, evaluating and criticizing in the social sciences, including those issues linked to the ontological and epistemological dimensions of any social inquiry. Many, for example, urge caution against the various dichotomizing, psychologizing, individualizing, and reductionist tendencies of some approaches (e.g., Wetherell, 2008; Branney, 2008; Layton, 2002, 2004, 2006, 2008a). Even so, the reference to a methodological deficit should also be understood to aim at more technical matters concerning, for example, the analysis of texts and other media, as well as the role that interviews, ethnographic observation and diary notes can play in drawing out the psychoanalytic dimension of analysis in forceful and convincing ways. Again, there is little systematic and sustained discussion of method in this narrower sense from a Lacanian point of view in organization studies or indeed in many other areas beyond the clinic.[20]

Interestingly, there is considerable debate and discussion outside Lacanian circles about these sorts of issues regarding the use of psychoanalysis beyond the clinic. And this suggests that cross-psychoanalytic comparative research with a methodological focus might provide another way forward for Lacanian-inspired organizational studies scholars.[21] Such an exploration would not only assist in the development of a robust and defensible stance on issues of methodology and technique, it would no doubt also carry important theoretical and empirical implications when these issues are reconsidered from the point of view of ontology and critique.

Conclusion

In this chapter I have suggested that a Lacanian conception of fantasy and associated psychic processes can provide a productive segue into the study of the organization of work. The focus on fantasy, in particular, is attractive for a number of reasons. Apart from its intuitive appeal and broad relevance for issues of normative and ideological critique, it neatly condenses many insights of psychoanalysis linked to the unconscious, transference, repression, and so on, thus serving as a way to focus and systematically tease out the psychoanalytic implications for the critical analysis of work, as well as the differential implications of different psychoanalytic schools in the domain of organization studies.

The privileging of culture, language, and ethics in Lacan's corpus suggests that the ideological, normative, and political aspects of work practices may be more readily discerned when examined through this particular psychoanalytic prism, thereby problematizing, rather than taking for granted, the nature and content of an individual's or organization's 'good psychological health'. A Lacanian-inflected political theory of discourse seeks to move beyond approaches that take the norms, ideals, and goals of organizations for granted, and could help throw light on the more collective and political aspects of such practices, highlighting the normative and ideological relevance of psychic processes. By situating the logics of fantasy alongside social and political logics, Lacanian insights can be brought to bear on the study of organizations by making this relevance explicit.

Notes

* I thank the editors Carl Cederström and Casper Hoedemaekers for their very helpful comments on earlier drafts of this chapter. Thanks also to Bob Hinshelwood, Mike Roper, Yannis Stavrakakis, and Hugh Willmott for their feedback.

1 Yiannis Gabriel uses the image of a 'glass cage' to capture the contemporary landscape of work and organization, in contrast to Weber's bureaucratic 'iron cage'. For Gabriel, the era of the 'glass cage' is characterized by the increasing role of the consumerist 'exit' strategy, the individual 'voice' at the expense of collective voice (unionism) and loyalty to the organization (Gabriel, 2008).

2 For useful overviews, see Jermier et al. (1994); Knights and Willmott (1990); Spicer and Böhm (2007: 1668-1672).

3 Cf. also the International Society for the Psychoanalytic Study of Organizations, founded in 1983: http://www.ispso.org/.

4 See, for example, the debate between Jaques (1995a; 1995b) and Amado (1995).

5 According to Carr and Gabriel (2002: 352-62), examples of the former include Sievers (1986; 1994; 1999) and Schwartz (1987; 1999); on transference: Baum (1987), Diamond (1988), Gabriel (1999), Oglensky (1995); on unconscious motivations to work: Baum (1987), Obholzer (1999), Smelser (1998), and Sievers (1986); on the way wider social and cultural norms and trends shape the organizational psychodynamics: Carr (1993), Maccoby (1976), Lasch (1980); on how organizations both provoke, and provide protection from, anxieties: Jaques (1952, 1955), Menzies (1960), Menzies-Lyth (1988), Trist (1950), Trist and Bamforth (1951), Miller (1976), Baum (1987), French and Vince (1999), Gould et al. (1999), Hirschhorn (1988), Stacey (1992), and Stein (2000); on how organizations can stimulate creativity and contentment and help realize collective visions: Baum (1989), Carr (1998), Gabriel (1993, 1999), Hirschhorn and Gilmore (1989), and

Schwartz (1987). To which can be added, on the role played by need, desire, and transference in the consultation process: Arnaud (1998); on the role of fantasy in absenteeism: Guinchard (1998); on the role of the mirror stage in workplace envy: Vidaillet (2007); on the role of the imaginary order in the context of workplace burnout: Vanheule and Verhaeghe (2004); on the relation of *jouissance* to cynicism in audit firms: Kosmala and Herrbach (2006). And examples of the latter include dealing with a wide range of themes, including consultancy and management themes. They come from people who have worked closely in or with the Tavistock clinic in the UK, such as Lewin (1947), Bion (1948/1962), Jaques (1952), Menzies-Lyth (1988), Trist and Bamforth (1951), Sofer (1961), Miller and Rice (1964), Miller (1976), Obholzer (1999), Obholzer and Roberts (1994), but they also include others, such as Mangham (1988), Kets de Vries (1991), Kets de Vries and Miller (1984), Levinson (1972, 1976, 1981), Zaleznick (1977, 1989a, 1989b), Gould et al. (1993, 1999), Krantz (1989, 1990), Hirschhorn (1988, 1999), Hirschhorn and Barnett (1993), Hirschhorn and Gilmore (1989), Diamond (1993, 1998), Stein (1998, 2001), Bain (1998), and Long (1999). Other examples include: on psychoanalytic coaching of managers: Brunner (1998); consultancy: Seel (2001); management of change: French (2001).

6   At some points, Carr and Gabriel appear to think this is possible; see, for example, Carr and Gabriel (2002: 353).

7   Consider the claim by Antonacopoulou and Gabriel, for example, that 'psychoanalytic approaches insist that there is a primitive, pre-linguistic, pre-cognitive and pre-social level of emotions, an inner world of passion, ambivalence and contradiction...' (2001: 438). This understanding of emotion, however, is not shared by all those who claim to adopt a psychoanalytic approach, foremost among these being Lacanians and discursive psychologists. Obviously, this throws into doubt the universalist aspiration attached to such a claim. Yet, this internal pluralism of psychoanalysis is recognised by many authors, even if sometimes only implicitly. In one article, for example, it is noted how a particular diagnosis of an organization's workings regarded as necessary a good understanding of Bion's psychoanalytic theory of groups (Paul, et al., 2002: 391). For examples of an explicit acknowledgement of this plurality, see Hoggett (2008: 379-80), Frosh (2008: 420), and Layton (2004; 2008a).

8   To this list we could add many other similar formulations, such as Bion's notion of 'negative capability' as a way of fostering a degree of ambiguity and paradox.

9   One example of a work which moves in this comparativist direction is Vidaillet (2007).

10 For a similar view, consider the following account of the possible uses of psychoanalysis in the study of organizations. 'As a technique which by strengthening the patient, aims at reconciling the pursuit of truth with the overcoming of resistances, psychoanalysis can make a contribution to organizational theorists and practitioners alike. As a theory of demystification, psychoanalysis can be a useful tool in dealing with the neurotic qualities of organizations' (Carr and Gabriel, 2002: 362).

11 For a critical assessment of Czander from a different vantage point, see Zaleznik (1995).

12 Other exceptions include Gabriel (1995, 1997, 2008a); Walkerdine (2005, 2006); Byrne and Healy (2006); Contu and Willmott (2006); and Willmott (2007).

13 There are, of course, scholars inspired by the Kleinian tradition who use fantasy as a central analytical device in the study of organizations, but it is by no means a common choice. Perhaps this is because, as Gabriel points out, if for Freud 'emotions derive from fantasies which, in turn, are compromise formations between desire and the forces of repression, for Klein, fantasies are derivatives, not causes of emotions' (Gabriel, 1999: 221; see also Isaacs, 1948). In addition, while Klein focuses much more on the meaning and content of language and fantasy, the accent falls much more on the structural or formal qualities in Lacan (Leader, 2000: 215-19; 2008: 130-1). For an illustration of how fantasy structures reality (including one's occupational choice, sexual relations, choice of partner, relations with family and friends) from a Lacanian point of view see Morel (2004: 15-19).

14 See also Walkerdine (2005; 2006); Gabriel (1995; 1997); Contu and Willmott (2006); Willmott (2007); and Byrne and Healy (2006).

15 Czander points out how '[f]antasies can generally be divided into categories, such as active or passive, dominating or submissive, aggressive or libidinal...' (Czande, 1993: 80-1). This presents an interesting attempt to clarify and refine the concept of fantasy into conceptions of fantasy. It may also warrant some close comparative analysis with a Lacanian concept of fantasy, especially given the following very resonant formulation by Czander: 'Unconsciously, success means that a wish may be gratified. If this wish is a merger with the gratifying object, the employee may unconsciously undermine or withdraw from the success out of the fear that the object will consume him/her, just as an overbearing mother may consume an infant. Thus the gratification of the unconscious fantasy may precipitate fears of engulfment' (Czander, 1993: 97).

16 On the role of games, play, and humour in work and organizations, see also Andersen, 2009 and Westwood and Rhodes, 2006.

17 For a similar set of ideas emerging outside the Lacanian orbit, consider Lynn Layton's notion of 'normative unconscious processes' (Layton, 2002; 2004; 2006; 2008a). For general issues concerning the ambiguous way the critical impulse manifests itself in Critical Management Studies research, see Brewis and Wray-Bliss (2008). Though operating with slightly different aims, assumptions, and emphases, there appears to be enough of a resonance to suggest that an exploratory comparative project may be productive in advancing our thinking about how best to relate an ethics of psychoanalysis to wider normative social and political concerns.

18 For a sample range of ways of thinking about mourning in this way, see Leader (2008), Butler (2004), Hoggett et al. (2006), and Gabriel (2008c).

19 For a call to explore the relation between a radical democratic ethos and an 'ethics of the real', see Mouffe (2000: conclusion); on this, see also Glynos (2003b). For a Kleinian approach to workplace democracy, see Diamond and Allcorn (2006).

20 This contrasts sharply with other (non-Lacanian) psychoanalytic approaches to social science research, which have considered these matters in considerable and systematic detail – e.g., Hollway and Jefferson (2000), Branney (2008), Hoggett et al. (2006), Clarke (2002; 2006; 2008), Hollway (2008), Gabriel (1999: ch. 11), Frosh and Young (2008), Hinshelwood and Skogstad (2000: ch. 2), Kvale (1999), Thomas (2007), Walkerdine (1997: ch. 4), and Walkerdine et al. (2001: ch. 4). The International Society for the Psychoanalytic Study of Organizations, founded in 1983, also focuses on exploring methods for identifying and accessing the unconscious dimensions of organizational life (see http://www.ispso.org/). However, examples of partial exceptions to this general rule exist: e.g., Parker (2010a; 2010b), Hoedemaekers (2007), Lapping (2007), Millar (2006), Branney (2006), Hollway (1989), and Walkerdine (1987).

21 How, for example, might techniques and methods from other psychoanalytic traditions be adopted and adapted from a Lacanian point of view? See, for example, Walkerdine (2008: 344), Branney (2008), Hoggett et al. (2006), Czander (1993: 123-143), Hollway and Jefferson (2000); Walkerdine et al. (2001), Frosh et al. (2002), Stopford (2004), Frosh and Baraitser (2008), Hinshelwood and Skogstad (2000).

References

Ackroyd, S. and P. Thompson (1999) *Organizational Misbehaviour*. London: Sage.

Adorno, T. W,, E. Frenkel-Brunswik, D. Levinson and N. Sanford (1950) *The Authoritarian Personality*. New York: Harper and Row.

Ahmed, S. (2004) *The Cultural Politics of Emotion*. Edinburgh: Edinburgh University Press.

Alvesson, M., K. L. Ashcraft and R. Thomas (2008) 'Identity matters: reflections on the construction of identity scholarship in organization studies', *Organization*, 15(1): 5-28.

Amado, G. (1995) 'Why the psychoanalytical knowledge helps us understand organizations', *Human Relations*, 48(4): 351-8.

Andersen, N. A. (2009) *Power at Play: The Relationships between Play, Work and Governance*. Basingstoke: Palgrave Macmillan.

Antonacopoulou, E. P. and Y. Gabriel (2001) 'Emotion, learning and organizational change: towards an integration of psychoanalytic and other perspectives', *Journal of Organizational Change Management*, 14(5): 435-451.

Arnaud, G. (1998) 'The obscure object of demand in consultancy: a psychoanalytic perspective', *Journal of Managerial Psychology*, 13(7): 469-84.

Ashcraft, K. L. (2008) 'Our stake in struggle (or is resistance something only others do?)', *Management Communication Quarterly*, 21(3): 380-386.

Ashforth, B. and R. Humphrey (1993) 'Emotional labour in service roles', *Academy of Management Review*, 18(1): 88-115.

Baum, H. S. (1991) 'Creating a family in the workplace', *Human Relations*, 44(11): 1137-59.

Baum, H. S. (1994) 'Community and consensus: reality and fantasy in planning', *Journal of Planning Education and Research*, 13(4): 251-62.

Best, M. H. and W. E. Connolly (1982) *The Politicized Economy*. Lexington, Massachusetts: D. C. Heath.

Bloom, P. and C. Cederström (2009) '"The sky's the limit": fantasy in the age of market rationality', *Journal of Organizational Change Management*, 22(2): 159-80.

Branney, P. (2008) 'Subjectivity, not personality: combining discourse analysis and psychoanalysis', *Social and Personality Psychology Compass*, 2(2): 574-590.

Braverman, H. (1974) *Labor and Monopoly Capital.* New York: Monthly Review Press.

Brewis, J. and E. Wray-Bliss (2008) 'Re-searching ethics: towards a more reflexive critical management studies', *Organization Studies*, 29(12): 1521-1540.

Brown, A. D. and M. Humphreys (2006) 'Organizational identity and place', *Journal of Management Studies*, 43(2): 231-57.

Brown, N. O. (1959) *Life Against Death.* New York: Random House.

Brunner, R. (1998) 'Psychoanalysis and coaching', *Journal of Managerial Psychology*, 13(7): 515-17.

Burawoy, M. (1979) *Manufacturing Consent.* Chicago: University of Chicago Press.

Burawoy, M. (1985) *The Politics of Production.* London: Verso.

Burgoyne, B. (2008) 'Psychoanalysis and state regulation' in I. Parker and S. Revelli (eds) *Psychoanalytic Practice and State Regulation.* London: Karnac.

Burgoyne, B. and M. Sullivan (eds) (1997) *The Klein-Lacan Dialogues.* London: Rebus Press.

Butler, J. (2004) *Precarious Life: The Powers of Mourning and Violence.* London: Verso.

Byrne, K., and S. Healy (2006) 'Cooperative subjects', *Rethinking Marxism*, 18(2): 241-258.

Callinicos, A. (2001) *Against the Third Way: An Anti-Capitalist Critique.* Cambridge: Polity.

Callinicos, A. (2006) *The Resources of Critique.* Cambridge: Polity.

Carr, A. (2001) 'Understanding emotion and emotionality in a process of change', *Journal of Organizational Change Management*, 14(5): 421-34.

Carr, A. (2002) 'Managing in a psychoanalytically-informed manner', *Journal of Management Psychology*, 17(5): 343-7.

Carr, A. and Gabriel, Y. (2002) 'Organizations, management and psychoanalysis: an overview', *Journal of Management Psychology*, 17(5): 348-65.

Carr, A. and Gabriel, Y. (eds) (2001) 'The psychodynamics of organizational change management: special issue', *Journal of Organizational Change Management*, 14(5).

Cederström, C. and R. Grassman (2008) 'The masochistic reflexive turn', *ephemera*, 8(1): 41-57.

Cederström, C. and H. Willmott (2007) 'Desiring agency', *Working Paper 3*, Lund Institute of Economic Research, Lund.

Chang, W.-Y. and J. Glynos (2011, forthcoming) 'Ideology and politics in the popular press', in L. Dahlberg and S. Phelan (eds) *Discourse Theory and Critical Media Politics*, London: Palgrave Macmillan.

Clarke, S. (2002) 'Learning from experience: psycho-social research methods in the social sciences', *Qualitative Research*, 2(2): 173-194.

Clarke, S. (2006) 'Theory and practice: psychoanalytic sociology as psycho-social studies', *Sociology*, 40(6): 1153-1169.

Clarke, S. (2008) 'Psycho-social research: relating self, identity, and Otherness' in S. Clarke, H. Hahn and P. Hoggett (eds) *Object Relations and Social Relations*. London: Karnac.

Clarke, S., H. Hahn and P. Hoggett (eds) (2008) *Object Relations and Social Relations*, London: Karnac.

Clegg, S. R., D. Courpasson and N. Phillips (2006) *Power and Organizations*. London: Sage.

Connolly, W. (1995) *The Ethos of Pluralization*. Minneapolis: University of Minnesota Press.

Connolly, W. (1999) *Why I am Not a Secularist*. Minneapolis: University of Minnesota Press.

Connolly, W. (2005) *Pluralism*. Durham: Duke University Press.

Contu, A. (2008) 'Decaf resistance: on misbehaviour, cynicism, and desire in liberal workplaces', *Management Communication Quarterly*, 21(3): 364-79.

Contu, A., M. Driver, and C. Jones (eds) (2010) 'Jacques Lacan with organization studies', *Organization*, 17, Special Issue.

Contu, A. and H. Willmott (2006) 'Studying practice', *Organization Studies*, 27(12): 1769-1782.

Copjec, J. (1994) *Read My Desire*. Cambridge, MA: MIT Press.

Crouch, C. (2005) *Capitalist Diversity and Change*. Oxford: OUP.

Czander, W. M. (1993) *The Psychodynamics of Work and Organizations: Theory and Application*. New York: Guilford Press.

Czander, W. M. (2001) 'The psycho-social analysis of employee commitment: how organizations induce and destroy commitment', Paper presented at ISPSO Symposium on Destructiveness and Creativity in Organizations, Paris.

Daly, G. (1999) 'Ideology and its paradoxes: dimensions of fantasy and enjoyment', *Journal of Political Ideologies*, 4(2): 219-38.

Daly, G. (2004) 'Radical(l)y political economy', *Review of International Political Economy*, 11(1): 1-32.

de Swarte, T. (ed.) (1998) 'Psychoanalysis and management: special issue', *Journal of Management Psychology*, 13(7).

Deetz, S. (2008) 'Resistance: would struggle by any other name be as sweet?', *Management Communication Quarterly*, 21(3): 387-92.

Deetz, S. and M. Hegbloom (2007) 'Situating the political economy and cultural studies conversation in the processes of living and working', *Communication and Critical/Cultural Studies*, 4(3): 323-26.

Diamond, M. A. and S. Allcorn (2006) 'Surfacing perversions of democracy in the workplace: a contemporary psychoanalytic project', *Psychoanalysis, Culture and Society*, 11(1): 54-73.

Du Gay, P. and G. Salaman (1992) 'The cult(ure) of the customer', *Journal of Management Studies*, 29(4): 616-33.

Du Gay, P. (1996) *Consumption and Identity at Work*. London: Sage.

Du Gay, P. and M. Pryke (eds) (2002) *Cultural Economy: Cultural Analysis and Commercial Life*. Thousand Oaks, CA: Sage.

Edelman, M. (1964) *The Symbolic Uses of Politics*. Urbana: University of Illinois Press.

Essers, J., S. Böhm and A. Contu (2009) 'Corporate Robespierres, ideologies of management and change', *Journal of Organizational Change Management*, 22(2): 129-40.

Essers, J., S. Böhm and A. Contu (eds) (2009) '"Corporate Robespierres": Ideologies of Management and Change', *Journal of Organizational Change Management*, 22(2), Special Issue.

Fleming, P. and A. Spicer (2003) 'Working at a cynical distance', *Organization*, 10(1): 157-79.

Fleming, P. and A. Spicer (2007) *Contesting the Corporation*. Cambridge: Cambridge University Press.

Fotaki, M. (2009) 'Maintaining the illusion of a free health care in post-socialism: a Lacanian analysis of transition from planned to market economy', *Journal of Organizational Change Management*, 22(2): 141-58.

French, R. (2001) '"Negative capability": managing the confusing uncertainties of change', *Journal of Organizational Change Management*, 14(5): 480-92.

Fromm, E. (1966) *Escape from Freedom*. New York: Avon Library.

Frosh, S. and L. Baraitser (2008) 'Psychoanalysis and psychosocial studies', *Psychoanalysis, Culture and Society*, 13(4): 346-65.

Frosh, S. and L. Young (2008) 'Psychoanalytic approaches to qualitative psychology', in C. Willig and W. Stainton-Rogers (eds) *The Sage Handbook of Qualitative Research in Psychology*. London: Sage.

Gabriel, Y. (1995) 'The unmanaged organization: stories, fantasies and subjectivity', *Organization Studies*, 16(3): 477-501.

Gabriel, Y. (1997) 'Meeting God: when organizational members come face to face with the supreme leader', *Human Relations*, 50(4): 315-342.

Gabriel, Y. (1999) *Organizations in Depth: The Psychoanalysis of Organizations*. London: Sage.

Gabriel, Y. (2008a) 'Spectacles of resistance and resistance of spectacles', *Management Communication Quarterly*, 21(3): 310-327.

Gabriel, Y. (2008b) 'Latte capitalism and late capitalism: reflections on fantasy and care as part of the service triangle', Keynote Presentation, Critical Management Studies Research Workshop, Academy of Management Conference, 7-8 August 2008, Anaheim.

Gabriel, Y. (2008c) 'Separation, abjection, loss and mourning: reflections on the phenomenon of organizational miasma', ESRC Seminar Series, University of Leicester, 28 May 2008.

Galbraith, K. (1975) *Economics and the Public Purpose*, Hammondworth: Penguin.

Gibson-Graham, J. K. (1996) *The End of Capitalism (As We Knew It): A Feminist Critique of Political Economy*. Oxford: Blackwell.

Gibson-Graham, J. K. (2006) *A Postcapitalist Politics*. Minneapolis: University of Minnesota Press.

Glynos, J. (2001) 'The grip of ideology: a Lacanian approach to the theory of ideology', *Journal of Political Ideologies*, 6(2): 191-214.

Glynos, J. (2003a) 'Self-transgression and freedom', *Critical Review of International Social and Political Philosophy*, 6(2): 1-20.

Glynos, J. (2003b) 'Radical democratic ethos, or, what is an authentic political act?', *Contemporary Political Theory*, 2(2): 187-208.

Glynos, J. (2008a) 'Ideological fantasy at work', *Journal of Political Ideologies*, 13(3): 275-296.

Glynos, J. (2008b) 'Self-transgressive enjoyment as a freedom fetter', *Political Studies*, 56(3): 679-704.

Glynos, J. (2011, forthcoming) 'On the ideological and political significance of fantasy in the organization of work', *Psychoanalysis, Culture and Society*.

Glynos, J. and D. Howarth (2007) *Logics of Critical Explanation in Social and Political Theory*. Abingdon: Routledge.

Glynos, J, and E. Speed (2009) 'Timebanking as a community economy? A political discourse theory approach to health-related social economy policy initiatives', ESRC Networks of Methodological Innovation, Discourse Analysis Network Conference, University of Essex.

Glynos, J. and Y. Stavrakakis (2008) 'Lacan and political subjectivity', *Subjectivity. International Journal of Critical Psychology*, 24(1): 256-274.

Glynos, J. and Y. Stavrakakis (eds) (2010) 'Politics and the unconscious', *Subjectivity*, 3(3), Special Issue.

Gorz, A. (1989) *Critique of Economic Reason*. London: Verso.

Gorz, A. (1994) *Capitalism, Socialism, Ecology*. London: Verso.

Gorz, A. (1999) *Reclaiming Work: Beyond the Wage-Based Society*. Cambridge: Polity.

Gouldner, A. (1955) *Wildcat Strike*. London: Routledge and Kegan Paul.

Guinchard, R. (1998) 'Absenteeism and phantasy', *Journal of Managerial Psychology*, 13(7): 485-97.

Hillier, J. and M. Gunder (2007) 'Planning as urban therapeutic', *Environment and Planning A*, 39(2): 467-86.

Hillier, J. and M. Gunder (2005) 'Not over your dead bodies! A Lacanian interpretation of planning discourse and practice', *Environment and Planning A*, 37(6): 1049-1066.

Hillier, J. and M. Gunder (2003) 'Planning fantasies? An exploration of a potential Lacanian framework for understanding development assessment planning', *Planning Theory*, 2(3): 225-248.

Hinshelwood, R, and W. Skogstad (2000) *Observing Organizations*. London: Routledge.

Hinshelwood, R. D. and M. Chiesa (eds) (2002) *Organizations, Anxieties, and Defences: Toward a Psychoanalytic Social Psychology*. London: Whurr Publishers.

Hoedemaekers, C. (2007) *Performance, Pinned Down: A Lacanian Analysis of Subjectivity at Work*. Rotterdam: ERIM.

Hoedemaekers, C. (2008) 'Toward a sinthomatology of organization?', *ephemera*, 8(1): 58-78.

Hoedemaekers, C. (2009) 'Traversing the empty promise: management, subjectivity and the Other's desire', *Journal of Organizational Change Management*, 22(2): 181-201.

Hoggett, P. (2008) 'What's in a hyphen? reconstructing psychosocial studies', *Psychoanalysis, Culture and Society*, 13(4): 379-84.

Hoggett, P., P. Beedell, L. Jimenez, M. Mayo, and C. Miller (2006) 'Identity, life history and commitment to welfare', *Journal of Social Policy*, 35(4): 689-704.

Hoggett, P., P. Beedell, L. Jimenez, M. Mayo, and C. Miller (2010) 'Working psycho-socially and dialogically in research', *Psychoanalysis, Culture and Society*, 15(2): 173-188.

Hollway, W. (1989) *Subjectivity and Method in Psychology: Gender, Meaning, and Science*. London: Sage.

Hollway, W. (2008) 'Doing intellectual disagreement differently?', *Psychoanalysis, Culture and Society*, 13(4): 385-96.

Hollway, W. (2008) 'The importance of relational thinking in the practice of psycho-social Research: ontology, epistemology, methodology, and ethics' in S. Clarke, H. Hahn, and P. Hoggett (eds) *Object Relations and Social Relations*, London: Karnac.

Hollway, W. (ed.) (2004) 'Special volume on psycho-social research', *Critical Psychology: The International Journal of Critical Psychology*, 10, Special Issue.

Hollway, W. and T. Jefferson (2000) *Doing Qualitative Research Differently: Free Association, Narrative, and the Interview Method.* London: Sage.

Isaacs, S. (1948) 'The nature and function of phantasy', in R. Steiner (ed.) (2003) *Unconscious Phantasy*, London: Karnac.

Jaques, E. (1952) *The Changing Culture of the Factory.* London: Tavistock

Jaques, E. (1955) 'Social systems as a defence against persecutory and depressive anxiety' in M. Klein, P. Heimann and R. Money-Kyrle (eds) *New Directions in Psychoanalysis.* London: Tavistock.

Jaques, E. (1995a) 'Why the psychoanalytical approach to understanding organizations?', *Human Relations*, 48(4): 343-50.

Jaques, E. (1995b) 'Reply to Dr Gilles Amado', *Human Relations*, 48(4): 359-69.

Jermier, J. M., D. Knights and W. R. Nord (eds) (1994) *Resistance and Power in Organizations.* London: Routledge.

Jessop, B. (2002) *The Future of the Capitalist State.* Cambridge: Polity.

Johnsen, R., S. L. Muhr, and M. Pedersen (2009) 'The frantic gesture of interpassivity: maintaining the separation between the corporate and authentic self', *Journal of Organizational Change Management*, 22(2): 202-13.

Jones, C. and A. Spicer (2005) 'The sublime object of entrepreneurship', *Organization*, 12(2): 223-46.

Kenny, K. (2009) 'Heeding the stains: Lacan and organizational change', *Journal of Organizational Change Management*, 22(2): 214-28.

Kernberg, O. (1976) *Object Relations Theory and Clinical Psychoanalysis.* New York: Jason Aronson.

Kernberg, O. (1998) *Ideology, Conflict, and Leadership in Groups and Organizations.* New Haven, CT: Yale University Press.

Kersten, A. (2001) 'Organizing for powerlessness: a critical perspective on psychodynamics and dysfunctionality', *Journal of Organizational Change Management*, 14(5): 452-67.

Kersten, A. (2007) 'Fantastic performance and neurotic fantasy: a case-based exploration of psychodynamic development', *Tamara: Journal of Critical Postmodern Organization Science*, 6(1/2): 65-82.

Kets de Vries, M. (ed.) (1991) *Organizations on the Couch*. San Francisco, CA: Jossey-Bass.

Kets de Vries, M., and D. Miller (1984) *The Neurotic Organization*. San Francisco, CA: Jossey-Bass.

Knights, D. and D. McCabe (2000) "Ain't misbehavin'? Opportunities for resistance under new forms of 'quality' management', *Sociology*, 34(3): 421-436.

Knights, D. and D. McCabe (2003) 'Governing through teamwork: reconstituting subjectivity in a call centre', *Journal of Management Studies*, 40(7): 1587-1619.

Knights, D. and H. Willmott (1989) 'Power and subjectivity at work: from degradation to subjugation in social relations', *Sociology* 23(4): 535-558.

Knights, D. and H. Willmott (eds) (1990) *Labour Process Theory*, London: MacMillan.

Kosmala, K. and O. Herrbach (2006) 'The ambivalence of professional identity: on cynicism and jouissance in audit firms', *Human Relations*, 59(10): 1393-428.

Kunda, G. (1992) *Engineering Culture*. Philadelphia: Temple University Press.

Kvale, S. (1999) 'The psychoanalytic interview as qualitative research', *Qualitative Inquiry*, 5(1): 87-113.

Lacan, J. (1966-7) *The Logic of Fantasy, The Seminar of Jacques Lacan, Book XIV*, trans. C. Gallagher. Unpublished.

Laclau, E. (1991) 'The impossibility of society', *Canadian Journal of Political and Social Science*, 15(1/3): 24-27.

Laclau, E. (2000) 'Identity and hegemony' in J. Butler, E. Laclau, and S. Žižek *Contingency, Hegemony, Universality*. London: Verso.

Laclau, E. (2005) *On Populist Reason*. London: Verso.

Laclau, E. and C. Mouffe (1985) *Hegemony and Socialist Strategy*. London: Verso.

Laplanche, J. and J.-B. Pontalis (1988) *The Language of Psycho-Analysis*, London: Norton.

Lapping, C. (2007) 'Interpreting "resistance" sociologically: a reflection on the recontextualization of psychoanalytic concepts into sociological analysis', *Sociology*, 41(4): 627-44.

Lasch, C. (1980) *The Culture of Narcissism*. London: Abacus.

Layton, L. (2002) 'Psychoanalysis and the "free" individual', *Journal of Psycho-social Studies*, 1(1): 1-13.

Layton, L. (2004) 'A fork in the royal road: on "defining" the unconscious and its stakes for social theory', *Psychoanalysis, Culture and Society*, 9(1): 33-51.

Layton, L. (2006) 'Racial identities, racial enactments, and normative unconscious processes', *Psychoanalytic Quarterly*, 75(1): 237-69.

Layton, L. (2008a) 'What divides the subject? Psychoanalytic reflections on subjectivity, subjection, and resistance', *Subjectivity*, 22(1): 60-72.

Layton, L. (2008b) 'Relational thinking: from culture to couch and couch to culture', in S. Clarke, H. Hahn and P. Hoggett (eds) *Object Relations and Social Relations*, London: Karnac.

Leader, D. (1997) 'Phantasy in Klein and Lacan', in B. Burgoyne and M. Sullivan (eds) *The Klein-Lacan Dialogues*, London: Rebus Press.

Leader, D. (2000) *Freud's Footnotes*. London: Faber and Faber.

Leader, D. (2004) 'The Future of Psychotherapy?', *Papers for the College of Psychoanalysts UK*, available at http://www.psychoanalysis-cpuk.org/HTML/DarianFuturePaper.htm.

Leader, D. (2008a) *The New Black*. London: Penguin.

Leader, D. (2008b) 'Psychoanalysis and regulation' in I. Parker and S. Revelli (eds) *Psychoanalytic Practice and State Regulation*. London: Karnac.

Leidner, R. (1993) *Fast Food, Fast Talk*. London: UCLA Press.

Lister, E. A. (2001) 'Organizational change: tales of intergenerational and sibling rivalry', *Journal of Organizational Change Management*, 14(5): 468-79.

Litten, R. (2008) 'Responsibility and accountability in psychoanalysis' in I. Parker and S. Revelli (eds) *Psychoanalytic Practice and State Regulation*. London: Karnac.

Lukes, S. (1974) *Power: A Radical View*. London: Macmillan.

Madra, Y. M. (2006) 'Questions of communism', *Rethinking Marxism*, 18(2): 205-224.

Marcuse, H. (1955) *Eros and Civilization: A Philosophical Inquiry into Freud*. Boston: Beacon.

Mars, G. (1982) *Cheats at Work*. London: Allen and Unwin.

Massumi, B. (1996) 'The autonomy of affect', in P. Patton (ed.) *Deleuze: A Critical Reader*, Oxford: Blackwell.

Menzies-Lyth, I. (1988) *Containing Anxiety in Institutions: Selected Essays*. London: Free Association Books.

Menzies, I. (1960) 'A case study in functioning of social systems as a defence against anxiety', *Human Relations*, 13: 95-121.

Millar, A. (2006) *Socio-Ideological Fantasy and the Northern Ireland Conflict: The Other Side*. Manchester: Manchester University Press.

Morel, G. (2004) 'Fundamental phantasy and the symptom as a pathology of the Law', *The Centre for Freudian Analysis Research Web Journal*, available at http://www.cfar.org.uk/pdf/Morel.pdf.

Mouffe, C. (2000) *The Democratic Paradox*, London: Verso.

Neumann, J. and L. Hirschhorn (eds) (1999) 'The challenge of integrating psychodynamic and organizational theory: special issue', *Human Relations*, 52(6).

O'Doherty, D. and H. Willmott (2001a) 'The question of subjectivity and the labor process', *International Studies of Management and Organization*, 30(4): 112-132.

O'Doherty, D. and H. Willmott (2001b) 'Debating labour process theory: the issue of subjectivity and the relevance of poststructuralism', *Sociology*, 35(2): 457-476.

Obholzer, A. (1999) 'Managing the unconscious at work', in R. French and R. Vince (eds) *Group Relations, Management, and Organization*. Oxford: Oxford University Press.

Obholzer, A. and V. Roberts (eds) (1994) *The Unconscious at Work: Individual and Organizational Stress in the Human Services*. London: Routledge.

Ozselcuk, C. (2006) 'Mourning, melancholy, and the politics of class transformation', *Rethinking Marxism*, 18(2): 225-240.

Ozselcuk, C. and Y. M. Madra (2005) 'Psychoanalysis and Marxism', *Psychoanalysis, Culture and Society*, 10(1): 79-97.

Parker, I. (2010a) 'Psychosocial studies: Lacanian discourse analysis negotiating interview text', *Psychoanalysis, Culture and Society*, 15(2): 156-72.

Parker, I. (2010b) 'The place of transference in psychosocial research', *Journal of Theoretical and Philosophical Psychology*, 30(1): 17-31.

Parker, I. and S. Revelli (2008a) 'Introduction' in I. Parker and S. Revelli (eds) *Psychoanalytic Practice and State Regulation*, London: Karnac.

Parker, I. and S. Revelli (eds) (2008b) *Psychoanalytic Practice and State Regulation*. London: Karnac.

Paul, J., C. Strbiak, and N. Landrum (2002) 'Psychoanalytic diagnosis of top management team dysfunction', *Journal of Managerial Psychology*, 8(17): 381-93.

Pettinger, L., J. Parry, R. Taylor and A. Glucksmann (eds) (2005) *A New Sociology of Work?* Oxford: Blackwell.

Reich, W. (1970) *The Mass Psychology of Fascism*. New York: Farrar, Strauss and Giroux.

Resnick, S. A., and R. D. Wolff (1987) *Knowledge and Class: A Marxian Critique of Political Economy*. Chicago: University of Chicago Press.

Resnick, S. A., and R. D.Wolff (2005) 'The point and purpose of Marx's notion of class', *Rethinking Marxism*, 17(1): 33-7.

Rieff, P. (1966) *The Triumph of the Therapeutic*. New York: Harper and Row.

Roberts, J. (2005) 'The power of the Imaginary in disciplinary processes', *Organization*, 12(5): 619-42.

Roper, M. (1994) *Masculinity and the British Organization Man since 1945*. Oxford: Oxford University Press.

Rorty, R. (ed.) (1967) *The Linguistic Turn*. Chicago: University of Chicago Press.

Ruccio, D. F. and J. Amariglio (2003) *Postmodern Moments in Modern Economics*. Princeton: Princeton University Press.

Rustin, M. (2001) *Reason and Unreason: Psychoanalysis, Science, and Politics*. London: Continuum.

Rustin, M. (2008) 'For dialogue between psychoanalysis and constructionism', *Psychoanalysis, Culture and Society*, 13(4): 406-15.

Seel, R. (2001) 'Anxiety and incompetence in the large group: a psychodynamic perspective', *Journal of Organizational Change Management*, 14(5): 493-503.

Sennett, R. (1998) *The Corrosion of Character: The Personal Consequences of Work in the New Capitalism*. New York: Norton.

Sennett, R. and J. Cobb (1977) *The Hidden Injuries of Class*. Cambridge: Cambridge University Press.

Shapiro, T. (1990) 'Unconscious fantasy', *Journal of American Psychoanalytic Association*, 38(1): 39-46.

Sloan, T. (1996) *Damaged Life: The Crisis of the Modern Psyche*. London: Routledge.

Spicer, A. and P. Fleming (2007) *Contesting the Corporation*. Cambridge: Cambridge University Press.

Spicer, A. and S. Böhm (2007) 'Moving management: theorizing struggles against the hegemony of management', *Organization Studies*, 28(11): 1667-1698.

Stavrakakis, Y. (1999) *Lacan and the Political*. London: Routledge.

Stavrakakis, Y. (2005) 'Passions of identification: discourse, enjoyment, and European identity', in D. Howarth and J. Torfing (eds) *Discourse Theory in European Politics*. London: Palgrave.

Stavrakakis, Y. (2008) 'Subjectivity and the organized Other: between Symbolic authority and fantasmatic enjoyment', *Organization Studies*, 29(7): 1037-59.

Stavrakakis, Y. and N. Chrysoloras (2006) '(I can't get no) enjoyment: Lacanian theory and the analysis of nationalism', *Psychoanalysis, Culture and Society* 11(2): 144-63.

Steiner, R. (ed.) (2003). *Unconscious Phantasy*. London: Karnac.

Stopford, A. (2004) 'Researching postcolonial subjectivities', *International Journal of Critical Psychology*, 10: 13-35.

Sturdy, A., I. Grugulis and H. Willmott (2001) *Customer Service: Empowerment and Entrapment*. London: Palgrave.

Sturdy, A., D. Knights and H. Willmott (eds) (1992) *Skill and Consent*. London: Routledge.

Swanson, J. (2007) 'The economy and its relation to politics', *Polity*, 39(2): 208-233.

Thomas, M. (2007) 'The implications of psychoanalysis for qualitative methodology: the case of interviews and narrative data analysis', *The Professional Geographer*, 59(4): 537-46.

Thomas, R. and A. Davies (2005) 'Theorizing the micro-politics of resistance: new public management and managerial identities in the UK public services', *Organization Studies*, 26(5): 683-706.

Trist, E. and H. Murray (eds) (1990) *The Social Engagement of Social Science, Volume 1: The Socio-Psychological Perspective*. London: Free Association Books.

Trist, E., and K. Bamforth (1951), 'Some social and psychological consequences of the Longwall method of coal getting', *Human Relations*, 4(1): 3-38.

Vanheule, S. and P. Verhaeghe (2004) 'Powerlessness and impossibility in special education: a qualitative study from a Lacanian perspective', *Human Relations*, 56(3): 321-38.

Vidaillet, B. (2007) 'Lacanian theory's contribution to the study of workplace envy', *Human Relations*, 60(11): 1669-701.

Walkerdine, V. (1987) 'No laughing matter: girls' comics and the preparation for adolescent sexuality', in Broughton, J. M. (ed.) *Critical Theories of Psychological Development*, New York: Plenum Press.

Walkerdine, V. (1997) *Daddy's Girl: Young Girls and Popular Culture*. London: MacMillan.

Walkerdine, V. (2005) 'Freedom, psychology and the neoliberal worker', *Soundings*, 29: 47-61.

Walkerdine, V. (2006) 'Workers in the new economy: transformation as border crossing', *Ethos*, 34(1): 10-41.

Walkerdine, V. (2008) 'Contextualizing debates about psychosocial studies', *Psychoanalysis, Culture and Society*, 13(4): 341-5.

Walkerdine, V., H. Lucey, and J. Melody (2001) *Growing Up Girl: Psychosocial Explorations of Gender and Class*. London: Palgrave.

Wetherell, M. (2008) 'Subjectivity or psycho-discursive Practices? Investigating complex intersectional identities', *Subjectivity*, 22: 73-81.

Westwood, R. and C. Rhodes (eds) (2006) *Humour, Work and Organization*. London: Routledge.

Willmott, H. (1993) 'Strength is ignorance; slavery is freedom', *Journal of Management Studies*, 50(4): 515-52.

Willmott, H. (1997) 'Rethinking management and managerial work: capitalism, control, and subjectivity', *Human Relations*, 50(11): 1329-1359.

Willmott, H. (2005) 'Theorizing contemporary control: some post-structuralist responses to some critical realist questions', *Organization*, 12(5): 747-780.

Willmott, H. (2007) 'Identities in organizations', unpublished.

Zaleznik, A. (1995) 'Review of Czander, W. M., *The Psychodynamics of Work Organizations*', *Psychoanalytic Quarterly*, 64: 815-819.

Žižek, S. (1989) *The Sublime Object of Ideology*. London: Verso.

Žižek, S. (1994) *The Metastases of Enjoyment*. London: Verso.

Žižek, S. (2002) *For They Know Not What They Do*. London: Verso.

3

Symbolic Authority, Fantasmatic Enjoyment and the Spirits of Capitalism: Genealogies of Mutual Engagement

Yannis Stavrakakis

Psychoanalysis – especially Lacanian theory – is gradually being acknowledged as an important resource in illuminating the institutional and organizational aspects of social life, as an important tool in cultural analysis and critical socio-political theory. Indeed, Lacan articulates a novel approach by illuminating the desire behind identity construction (agency), the reliance of this process on the Other (structure), as well as the limits marking both the subject and the socio-symbolic order conditioning her options.

In effect, what a Lacanian perspective highlights is the non-teleological dialectic between subject and Other which operates, unfolds, in a variety of distinct but, as we shall see, deeply inter-implicated levels: on the one hand, at the level of the *symbolic*, of socio-semiotic construction; on the other hand, at the level of affective investment, of the mobilization of the passions, of what Lacan calls *jouissance* (enjoyment). Within this context, it can account for obedience and attachment to particular identifications, for the depth and salience they can acquire, in at least two ways. First, by focusing on the symbolic presuppositions of authority and power, on the irresistibility of the Other's command and the symbolic dependence of subjectivity; and, second, by exploring the role of fantasy and enjoyment, of the affective domain, in sustaining them and in neutralizing resistance.

In this context, I will be initially highlighting the role of the symbolic in sustaining subjection and obedience to authority through the performative function of the symbolic command. However, given the alienating limitations that affect the consistency of organized frameworks of social life – limitations that Lacanian theory relates to the impossibility of symbolizing/capturing the real of enjoyment – the symbolic command of the Law can only be credible if supported by a fantasy dealing with our lack of enjoyment and perpetuating desire (as desire of the Other). Only thus can obedience and social reproduction be secured. And only through a shift in the ob/scene aspects of subjective attachment – in the particular modes of such ideological overinvestment – can new symbolic identifications emerge and new ethical orientations be envisaged.

After providing a brief sketch of this argument, in the broadest lines possible, I will then focus my attention on the *relation* between these different levels, the predominantly symbolic on the one hand, fantasy and enjoyment on the other. How are these distinct dimensions related in producing a salient identification? Apart from instances of straightforward and visible synergy, psychoanalytic research points to dialectics of mutual engagement that very often take the form of antithesis and dis-identification. The problematics of self-transgression and cultural intimacy signify, in this perspective, two parallel ways – emanating from psychoanalysis and social anthropology respectively – that aim to capture such a paradoxical *modality of mutual engagement* between official ideal and ob/scene practice, explicit normativity and the terrain of habits, the symbolic and the real; to capture, in other words, a dialectic that is often crucial in understanding the ability of hegemonic identifications to co-opt what initially emerges as a transgressive act of resistance.

A further hypothesis explored in this essay is that, by highlighting the mutual engagement between these dimensions, such a focus can also prove helpful in understanding the ethical/cultural preconditions of consumption and production within capitalist societies. Hence, if the first aim of this essay is to argue that every successful identification involves an overdetermined blend or articulation of *form* and *force*[1] (symbolic weight and affective investment) – crystallized and redoubled into contingent and often paradoxical distributions along axes such as visible/invisible, scene/obscene, conscious/unconscious, dry/sticky, etc. – the second aim is to examine under this light the 'spiritual' genealogy of capitalism. In fact, within the milieu of capitalist societies, we can observe a whole (synchronic and diachronic) dialectic between distinct distributions of this type, through the social matrices of prohibition and commanded enjoyment and their association with different – but, as we shall see, deeply inter-connected – 'spirits' of capitalism.

1. Subject and Other: Between Symbolic Authority and Fantasmatic Enjoyment

The relation between individual/subject and social order/Other has often been described in terms that reduce the one pole to the other. I do agree with Jones and Spicer that 'a particularly powerful approach to these questions might be found in the work of Jacques Lacan' (Jones and Spicer, 2005: 224-5). In fact, it could be argued that Lacan can offer an extremely nuanced and productive escape from the two dominant paradigms in subject-power relations and their associated limitations, namely from the paradigm of (transcendent) externality – where a pre-constituted individual encounters the Other as a force limiting its subjective autonomy from the outside – and that of (immanent) internality – where the subject becomes a mere effect of the Other's ideological/discursive construction.

For a start, Lacanian theory radically questions the credibility of individualism and subjectivism by advancing a novel conception of subjectivity: the subject of lack.[2] The benefits of such a conceptualization are obvious. First, it avoids positing a positively defined essence of subjectivity and thus moves beyond psychological reductionism and individualism. Second, it permits a thorough grasping of the socio-symbolic dependence of subjectivity: due to the centrality of lack in the Lacanian conception of the subject, subjectivity becomes the space where a whole 'politics' of *identification* takes place. Lack stimulates desire and thus necessitates the constitution of every identity through processes of identification with socially available objects, such as family roles, political ideologies, patterns of consumption and professional ideals. This is bound to create a truly symbiotic relation between subjectivity and power.

But, for Lacan, this is not the end of the story. Not only does Lacanian psychoanalysis explode the whole individualist/subjectivist tradition but it also puts in radical doubt its objectivist or immanentist inversions. If, on the one hand, subjective lack stimulates the desire for identifications that rely on the organized Other, the inability of all acts of identification to produce a full identity – subsuming subjective division – (re)produces the radical ex-centricity of the subject and, along with it, a whole negative dialectic of partial fixation (in the dual form of partial determination and partial resistance).

True, ideological/discursive determination is unavoidable, even *necessary*. No social reality and subjective identity can emerge without it; and no management of subjective lack. At the same time it is ultimately *impossible*. No ideological determination is ever complete. Social construction is always an imperfect exercise, and the social subject cannot transcend the ontological horizon of lack. Something always escapes from both orders – Lacan reserves a special name for that: the *real*, an excessive quantum of enjoyment (*jouissance*) resisting representation and control. Something that the subject has been forced to sacrifice upon entering organized society, and which, although lost and inaccessible/unrepresentable forever, does not stop causing all our attempts to encounter it through our identification acts.

Clearly, the administration of this constitutive lack of enjoyment takes place in a field transcending simplistic dichotomies (individual vs. collective, for instance). But how exactly can we access this field? And what can Lacanian theory contribute to our understanding of its formation and functioning? Of how subjects are constituted, human lives are lived and social orders and institutions are organized and sustained? Where is power and authority exactly located in this play? And how are their symbolic and fantasmatic dimensions, language and enjoyment, inter-implicated?

In Lacanian terms, the *symbolic* is always central as far as the constitution of the subject is concerned. If the imaginary representation of ourselves, the mirror image – and imaginary relations in general, such as the early one between mother and child – is ultimately incapable of providing us with a stable and functional identity, if it reproduces instead of resolving alienation, the only option left for acquiring one seems to be the field of linguistic representation, the symbolic register. Humans are predominantly linguistic creatures. By submitting to the laws of language every child becomes a subject in language; it inhabits and is inhabited by language, and hopes to gain an adequate representation through the world of words. In the early structuralist phase of his work, Lacan will highlight this symbolic dependence, the priority of the symbolic over the subject: 'The subject in question has nothing to do with what we call the subjective in the vague sense, in a sense that muddles everything up, and nor does it have anything to do with the individual. The subject is what I define in the strict sense as an effect of the signifier' (Lacan, 2008: 79).

This, however, should not lead to the conclusion that entering the symbolic overcomes alienation by producing a solid identity. Lacan was never an orthodox structuralist. On the contrary, the subject constituted on the acceptance of the laws of language, of symbolic Law – a function embodied, within the Oedipal setting, in what Lacan calls 'the Name-of-the-Father', the agent of symbolic castration – is the subject of lack *par excellence*.[3] Alienation is not resolved but displaced into another (symbolic) level, to the register of the signifier. On the one hand, due to the 'universality' of language, to the linguistic constitution of human reality, the signifier offers to the subject an almost 'immortal', 'neutral' representation; only this representation is incapable of capturing and communicating the *real* 'singularity' of the subject. In that sense, it is clear that something is always missing from the symbolic; the Other is a lacking, an incomplete Other. The structure is always an open, a failed structure, even – or, perhaps, especially – when closure is sought: everything originates in 'breaks, in a succession of trials and openings that have at every stage deluded us into thinking that we could launch into a totality' (Lacan, 2008: 95). This critique of semiotic closure is what has permitted the poststructuralist appropriation of Lacan. The emergence of the subject in the socio-symbolic terrain presupposes a division between reality and the real, language and *jouissance* (a pre-symbolic, real enjoyment), a division that consolidates the alienation of the subject in the signifier and reveals the lack in the Other. The Other, initially presented as a solution to subjective lack, is now also revealed as what retroactively produces/consolidates this lack. It promises to offer the subject some symbolic consistency, but the price to be paid is the sacrifice – imposed by the symbolic command – of all access to pre-symbolic real enjoyment – which now becomes the object of fantasy.[4]

However, experiencing such alienation is not enough to effect a lessening of the bonds attaching us to the socio-symbolic Other. Simply put, subjects are willing to do whatever may be necessary in order to repress or disavow the lack in the Other. This insight is crucial in understanding power relations. Moving beyond the banal level of raw coercion, which – although not unimportant – cannot form the basis of sustainable hegemony, everyone seeking to understand how certain power structures institute themselves as objects of long-term identification and how people get attached to them is sooner or later led to a variety of phenomena associated with what, since de la Boétie, is debated under the rubric of 'voluntary servitude'. The central question here is simple: Why are people so willing and often enthusiastic – or at least relieved – to submit themselves to conditions of subordination, to the forces of hierarchical order? Why are they so keen to comply with the commands of authority often irrespective of their content? Obviously, the Oedipal structure implicit in the social ordering of our societies (the role of what Lacan calls 'the Name-of-the-Father' in structuring reality through the (castrating) imposition of the Law), predisposes social subjects to accept and obey what seems to be emanating from the big Other. That is, socially sedimented points of reference invested with the imaginary gloss of authority and presented as embodying and sustaining the symbolic order, organize (subjective and objective) reality: 'Whilst there is no such thing as a collective consciousness, we might perhaps note that the function of the desire of the Other really does have to be taken into consideration when it comes to the organization of societies, especially these days' (Lacan, 2008: 48). Suspension of the command is thus often experienced or imagined as threatening the consistency of (symbolic) reality itself to the extent that the Law is what stands at the foundation of this reality. This central Freudian-Lacanian insight can indeed explain a lot. And there are numerous examples demonstrating this central role of the command of the Law, the role of authority.[5]

If this structural and structuring role of the command provides the ontological nexus within which the subject learns to interact with its social environment – the symbolic preconditions of subjection and obedience – it cannot explain, however, why some commands produce obedient behaviour and others are ignored. It cannot account for the occurrence of disobedience and for instances of resistance. In fact, if we were to stay at this level, it would be impossible to account both for the failure of certain commands and for the complex 'extra-symbolic' means through which the organized Other supports and/or attempts to reinstitute its authority. Here, the Lacanian answer is simple. On the one hand, the real exceeds the subject and the lack this inscribes within subjective identity is what stimulates desire (for subjection to the Other). On the other hand, the real also exceeds the Other and the lack this inscribes in the Other explains the ultimate failure of fully determining subjectivity. It is this second failure that makes resistance possible, at least in principle. It is in the traumatic fact that the Other cannot fully determine the subject that a space for freedom starts to emerge. But this is a freedom that the subject has learned to fear. As Judith Butler has formulated it, this predicament of the subject is usually resolved with the adoption of the following stance: 'I would rather exist in subordination than not exist' (1997: 7). Both the Other and the subject prefer to repress or disavow, to defer this realization of the lack in the Other.[6] But in order to attempt that in a persuasive manner, the symbolic command is not enough. Something more positive is needed, given the fact that the lack marking subject and Other is a lack of *jouissance*. This is what *fantasy* attempts to offer. Focusing on the symbolic aspects of identity – although a necessary step, a step that, as already shown, Lacan has also taken – is not sufficient in order to reach a rigorous understanding of the drive behind identification acts, to explain why certain identifications prove to be more forceful and alluring than others, and to realize why none can be totally successful.

Let me recapitulate my argument so far. Our dependence on the organized Other is not reproduced merely at the level of knowledge and conscious consent. What is much more important is the formal (symbolic) structure of power relations that social ordering presupposes. The subject very often prefers not to realize the performative function of the symbolic command – the fact that what promises to deal with subjective lack is what reproduces this lack, perpetuating the subject's desire for subjection. Most crucially, the reproduction of this formal structure relies on a libidinal, affective support that binds subjects to the conditions of their symbolic subordination. What makes the lack in the Other 'invisible' – and thus sustains the credibility of the organized Other and the integrity of its desire – is a fantasmatic dialectic manipulating our relation to a lost/impossible enjoyment. It is impossible to un-block and displace identifications and passionate attachments without paying attention to this important dimension.

Our discussion is now entering a delicate phase, because we have started sketching the different levels at which identification matters. And we have already seen that any analysis that purports to capture the complex relation between subject and structure cannot remain at the level of signification, although the role of the symbolic command remains extremely important. Here, contrary to what is widely believed, Lacan does not limit his insights within the level of representation and signification. Indeed, one needs to stress the productivity of the

Lacanian distinction between the 'subject of the signifier' and the 'subject of enjoyment/*jouissance*' in addressing this question. For example, psychoanalysis alerts us to the fact that attachment to the nation cannot be reduced to rational self-interested motivations, economic conditions, and institutional dynamics. As important as the aforementioned factors may be, the play of identifications should be at the heart of any effort to study group actions and human agency in nationalist movements. However, highlighting the discursive/semiotic aspect of identification processes is also not enough. No matter how much a national identification is deconstructed there is still something that resists and this is why shifting such attachments is so difficult. Above all else, the ecumenical appeal of discourses like nationalism rests on their ability to mobilize human desire for identity and to promise an encounter with (national) enjoyment. The study of nationalism should therefore emphasize the workings of the processes of identification and the way dialectics of enjoyment are played out in different national contexts. Undoubtedly, the nation is a symbolic construction internalized through socialization, but what gives (imaginary) consistency to this discursive construction of the nation is a fantasy promising our encounter with the fullness of enjoyment supposedly located at the roots of national history, an enjoyment denied to us by the evil action of the enemy figure. This fantasy often permeates official channels and narratives: education, national myths, ritualized practices like army parades, etc. However, such imaginarized promises acquire the gloss of the real – enhancing their depth and salience – through the partial enjoyment obtained from mostly unofficial, and often secretive, ob/scene practices: an enjoyment reproduced through characteristic everyday rituals, customs, culinary preferences and traditions, etc. (especially in cases where what is consumed is considered inedible or even disgusting in other cultures and what is practiced is not usually shared with non-members of the community).[7]

2. Self-transgressive Enjoyment and Cultural Intimacy

As we have seen, a plurality of distinct but inter-implicated levels is always involved in a successful identification. The *symbolic* call emanating from the site of the Law that institutes social reality, the first level, relies on a second level consisting of a fantasmatic narrative that deals with the lack of enjoyment the symbolic command entails (*imaginary*); and this, in its turn, presupposes practices of partial enjoyment (*real*). Now, let us go one step further. What are the precise forms this synergy between the various levels involved in this process can take? In particular, how can we account for the far-from-uncommon fact that symbiosis can appear as antithesis and can even metamorphose into transgression and/or resistance?

My main hypothesis in this text is that, apart from the simple case of straightforward synergy between the different dimensions on which identifications operate, this system can often take the extremely sophisticated form of complex form/force articulations which then undergo a certain process of distribution or *splitting* – to use a Kleinian category – along a set of different axes (public/private, scene/obscene, visible/invisible, explicit/implicit etc.). This (unevenly structured and invested) distribution very often conceals the symbiotic relation between the two – or more – poles involved or produced in the process. The emergence of an oppositional polarity camouflages, disavows, a synergy reproducing the hegemonic structure/order.[8] The reproduction of workplace identifications offers a revealing example in this respect. Here, one can again notice the play between symbolic obligation, fantasy and enjoyment, which often appear as seemingly unconnected or even antithetical dimensions, while in effect they symbiotically sustain relations of power and attachment to authority. Thus, the established distinction between *formal* and *informal* organization can be seen under a new light.

A very good illustration is offered by Alessia Contu and Hugh Willmott in 'Studying Practice: Situating Talking About Machines', in which they offer a challenging interpretation of the complexity of the work practices of Xerox technicians described by Julian Orr. What one observes here is the apparent antagonism between the symbolic command emanating from Xerox management, a call for strict compliance with instructions included in repair manuals and the actual (unrecognized and undervalued) practice of technicians, which often favors improvisation and creative experimentation not sanctioned by bureaucratic procedure (Contu and Willmott, 2006: 1771, 1773). What we seem to have here is a form of transgression of the (Xerox) Law (*symbolic*) by technicians who enjoy (*real*) – and take pride (*imaginary*) – in enacting a different course of doing their job. Sometimes such ironic and/or cynical transgressive acts are presented as effective forms of resistance.

Now, what is the catch here? It may, at first, sound insanely counterintuitive, but what if the transgression of an ideal serves to reinforce the ideal's capacity to secure compliance and obedience (Glynos, 2003)? This is because this transgression – and the concomitant failure to meet a publicly affirmed ideal – can serve as a source of enjoyment. For example, military communities have practices and codes of conduct that often transgress the public ideals of the institution (ideals like fair and equal treatment) but which are kept secret – the practice of 'hazing' or initiation ceremonies, for instance. The established private or officer is well aware that forcing a new recruit to undergo a series of painful and humiliating experiences transgresses the military institution's ideals, which he officially avows. However, the claim here would be that not only are these ideals not subverted by such practices, but rather, they make possible the enjoyment of their transgression which, in turn, sustains those very same ideals: 'Such an *institutional unconscious* designates the obscene disavowed underside, that, precisely as disavowed, sustains the public institution. In the army, this underside consists of the obscene sexualised rituals of fragging which sustain group solidarity' (Žižek, 2008a: 142). Fantasmatically structured enjoyment thus alerts us to the politically salient idea that oftentimes it may be more productive to consider the possibility that concrete ideals may be sustained rather than subverted by their transgression. And this is exactly what happens in Xerox. Although apparently transgressive, the 'misbehaviour' of Xerox technicians ultimately functions in a 'conservative' way that ultimately benefits the corporation: 'By improvising and applying fixes and short cuts, the technicians minimize the expense of machine repairs and replacements and reduce costumer frustration associated with delays in restoring machine use' (Contu and Willmott, 2006: 1775). Thus partial deviance from the publicly sanctioned Law – a deviance limited within the confines of the closed community of technicians – 'is indeed functional for, the goal of cost-effectiveness, customer satisfaction and, ultimately, corporate profitability' (Contu and Willmott, 2006: 1776).[9]

This should not cause surprise, especially given that the idea that 'some forms of transgression can be a preserving force' is not entirely new within management studies (Fleming and Spicer, 2003: 162). At any rate, it makes absolute sense from the point of view of a problematic of self-transgression, which – with its focus on fantasy and enjoyment – can illuminate this paradox: 'The ideal and the enjoyment procured through transgression are *co-constitutive*: one sustains the other' (Glynos, 2008b: 687). On the one hand, the symbolic ideal forms the background for the transgressive practice; on the other, this practice, through the enjoyment it procures, may serve 'to bolster the ideal and the objectives it structures' (Glynos, 2008b: 694; also see Glynos and Stavrakakis, 2008: 267-9). Every effective hegemony has to operate on all these levels, co-opting opposition and neutralizing its radical potential – and undergoing, in the process, gradual shifts that, however, do not threaten the reproduction of hierarchical order (the basic parameters of domination).

In his *The Practice of Everyday Life*, Michel de Certeau designates such tactics of everyday practice as the 'art of the weak' (de Certeau, 1988: 37). For de Certeau, these practices still possess a transformative potential within the limits of an established hegemony. In his schema, consent and submission to rules (rituals, representations and/or laws) imposed by one group (for example, the Spanish colonizers) on another group of people (the indigenous Indians) do not preclude the possibility of a form of inverted syncretism: subversion 'not by rejecting or altering them, but by using them with respect to ends and references foreign to the system they had no choice but to accept' (de Certeau, 1988: xiii). De Certeau's somewhat anti-Foucauldian approach aims at bringing to light the procedures of everyday creativity through which groups or individuals transform disciplinary techniques into an 'antidiscipline' (de Certeau, 1988: xv), procedures that connect '*manipulating* and *enjoying*, the fleeting and massive reality of a social activity at play with the order that contains it' (de Certeau, 1988: xxiv). In this view, the (playful, joyful) enactment of particular uses of imposed systems can transform them, constituting 'subtle, stubborn, resistant' forms of activity (de Certeau, 1988: 18). Interestingly, one of the examples he offers comes from workplace practices. It involves what the French call '*le perruque*'. What we encounter here is

> the worker's own work disguised as work for his employer. It differs from pilfering in that nothing of material value is stolen. It differs from absenteeism in that the worker is officially on the job... In the very place where the machine he must serve reigns supreme, he cunningly takes pleasure in finding a way to create gratuitous products whose sole purpose is to signify his own capabilities through his work and to confirm his solidarity with other workers or his family through *spending* his time in this way. (de Certeau, 1988: 25-6)

Thus 'order is *tricked* by an art' (de Certeau, 1988: 26), albeit this art is only allowed a parasitic status with respect to this order that, more or less, retains its dominance.

Already in the 1960s and 1970s – if not earlier – Cornelius Castoriadis had observed that whenever the rules are strictly observed in an organization – this is the case of *working to rule* and *grève du zèle* – what ensues is not better order but total chaos (Castoriadis, 2000: 75). Indeed, such practices of *over-identification* 'can have a devastating impact on the smooth functioning of the work process' (Fleming and Spicer, 2003: 172). Paradoxically then, 'production can only take place to the extent that workers transgress the rules and develop the initiative, creativity, and inventiveness production requires' (Castoriadis, 2000: 75). Hence a whole informal, unofficial quasi-organization is formed (2000: 77). On the one hand, Castoriadis discerns here the possibility of future transformation in the direction of autonomy. Such parallel organization, formed on the basis of a certain cultivation of creativity, can enhance struggles for autonomy and self-direction (ibid.). On the other hand, activities of this sort are crucial in sustaining the system – the system could not be reproduced without such innovation and creativity, which also introduces gradual alterations: 'Thus, the life and the activities of innumerable human beings continually introduce infinitesimal alterations in the ways of doing things as well as in the manner of effectively living, or "interpreting" (re-creating for themselves), the instituted social imaginary significations. As a result, a slow – and, of course, nonconscious – self-alteration is always in process in actual social life' (Castoriadis, 2005: 179). Likewise, to retain its grip, every hegemonic ideology needs to take into account in advance its own failure, its own limits, and to condition its own (partial) transgression. Here, we see the lacking Other, an incomplete power structure, indirectly acknowledging this lack, allowing a certain degree of dis-identification, providing a breathing space for its subjects, on the condition, of course, that this remains under control: 'Ideology is effective precisely by constructing a space of *false disidentification*' (Žižek in Fleming and Spicer, 2003: 167).

In his recent work Slavoj Žižek has also stressed this intimate relation between the rules, the visible symbolic/legal order, and its obscene, unconscious other side. He designates this institutional unconscious as the terrain of habits:

> The particular ethnic substance, our 'lifeworld', which resists universality, is made up of habits. But what are habits? Every legal order or every order of explicit normativeness has to rely on a complex network of informal rules which tell us how we are to relate to explicit norms: how we are to apply them; to what extent we are to take them literally; and how and when we are allowed, even solicited, to disregard them. These informal rules make up the domain of habits. To know the habits of a society is to know the meta-rules of how to apply its explicit norms. (Žižek, 2008a: 134)

Habits, in this perspective, incarnate our effective social being, 'often in contrast with our perception of what we are' (Žižek, 2008a: 140). They also provide ideology with its most important mechanism; the public ideological message is sustained by a series of obscene supplements that make resistance really tricky: the official order may change; what is really difficult to change is 'this obscene underground, the unconscious terrain of habits' (Žižek, 2008a: 143). In that sense, the most essential dimension in ideology critique involves 'not directly changing the explicit text of the law but, rather, intervening in its obscene virtual supplement' (Žižek, 2008a: 145).

This ultimately symbiotic engagement between publicly affirmed ideal and secret transgression, between what happens *off stage* and what is *on display* (Shryock, 2004) in their mutual co-constitution – observable in a variety of socio-political settings from national identifications to workplace practices – has been extremely well documented by social anthropologists,[10] especially through the problematic of *cultural intimacy* (Herzfeld, 2005). According to this extremely challenging body of work, the production of public identities seems to create, of necessity, 'a special terrain of things, relations and activities that cannot themselves be public but are essential aspects of whatever reality and value public things might possess' (Shryock, 2004: 3); it is this terrain that has been described by Michael Herzfeld as a terrain of 'cultural intimacy' (Herzfeld, 2005). If we go back to our example of the nation, Herzfeld's analysis also points to the operation of distinct logics in the constitution and reproduction of national identity. On the one hand, we have a dimension of self-construction of often elaborate ideologies of self-glorification, and, on the other, the popular support these are able to enjoy 'precisely because they can carry a far greater load of dirty secrets – grounded in everyday experience'; cultural intimacy 'is always th[is] space of the dirty linen' (Herzfeld, 2004: 320, 329).

Herzfeld captures cogently this dialectic between the formal narrative of national identity and its *envers*, a dimension of spirited, personal (social) poetics that involve fantasies of transgression and practices procuring partial enjoyment. This crucial other side is most often dismissed, obscured, repressed; but remains absolutely crucial:

> the formal operations of the national states depend on coexistence – usually inconvenient, always uneasy – with various realizations of cultural intimacy… That is hardly the stuff of which the rhetoric of national unity is officially made, yet it informs the mutual recognition that one finds among a country's citizens everywhere – even among its state functionaries. (Herzfeld, 2005: 4)

What we have here, in other words, is 'a direct mutual engagement between the official state and the sometimes disruptive popular practices whose existence it often denies, but whose vitality is the ironic condition of its own continuation' (Herzfeld, 2005: 5). This mutual dependence of the formal and the intimate aspect of national identity is missed in top-down accounts of the nation-state that dismiss as mere anecdote the intimate social spaces constituting our ways of life and moving people to action (Herzfeld, 2005: 6, 24).

Like this anthropological tradition, Lacan-inspired socio-political analysis moves beyond the limits of such top-down mainstream academic approaches, by orienting its research toward the disavowed dimension implicated in identification and social reproduction; that of cultural intimacy as the *other scene* where administrations of enjoyment are formulated, fantasized and (partially) enacted. Likewise, both intellectual traditions (psychoanalysis and social anthropology) register the importance of the aforementioned problematic of self-transgression. As Herzfeld points out, the adherence to static cultural ideals has a surprising consequence: 'it permits and perhaps even encourages the day-to-day subversion of norms' (Herzfeld, 2005: 22). In other words, 'norms are both perpetuated and reworked through the deformation of social conventions in everyday interaction' (Herzfeld, 2005: 37). Wasn't this also the lesson from the Xerox example? Indeed the public Law, the space of the officially sanctioned ideals, is revealed as incomplete, and – paradoxically – it receives support from a clandestine supplement of self-transgression (Contu, 2008: 369); the lack in the Other demands a fantasy support, ultimately an indirect anchoring in the (partial) *jouissance* of the body.[11]

3. Prohibition, Enjoyment and the Spirits of Capitalism

We have seen how Lacanian theory illuminates the dialectic between subject and organized Other by focusing on both the symbolic level, the formal presuppositions of authority (the irresistibility of the Other's command), and the level of affect and *jouissance*, the fantasmatic administration of real enjoyment and its lack, which – through a series of complex articulations and oppositional distributions – sustains the credibility of the lacking Other through the dynamics of self-transgression and cultural intimacy. This orientation needs, however, to encounter more consistently the field of historical experience. There are good reasons for that, both theoretical and strategic. On the one hand, it is important to move beyond the obsolete stereotype of psychoanalytic interpretation as an a-historical one, as one trapping us within a suffocating, all-encompassing and eternal structure. In fact, it is precisely Lacan's incomplete structure, the lacking Other, that demands a consistent engagement with history:

> You know the nonsense they've come up with now. There is structure and there is history. The people they've put in the 'structure' category, which includes me – it wasn't me who put me there, they put me there, just like that – supposedly spit on history. That's absurd. There can obviously be no structure without reference to history. (Lacan 2008: 68)[12]

On the other, it is obviously impossible to analyze and effectively critique capitalist hegemony without closely following its often revolutionary and unexpected mutations, without locating the shifting distributions of form and force securing its reproduction within the broader anthropological, historical and moral picture.

Indeed every age, every historical conjuncture, every socio-political order, will institute its own blend of coercion, symbolic authority as well as fantasmatic and self-transgressive *jouissance*. Here historical contextualization is able to provide fruitful intuitions and thus I will be devoting the third section of this text to this enterprise. Todd McGowan's recent study *The End of Dissatisfaction? Jacques Lacan and the Emerging Society of Enjoyment* (2004) provides a convenient starting point for such an exploration. McGowan begins by registering the enjoyment explosion surrounding us in consumer society and develops the hypothesis that it marks a significant shift in the structure of the social bond, in social organization (2004: 1). In particular, he speaks of a passage from a *society of prohibition* into a *society of commanded enjoyment* (2004: 2). While more traditional forms of social organization 'required subjects to renounce their private enjoyment in the name of social duty, today the only duty seems to consist in enjoying oneself as much as possible' (ibid.). This is the call that is addressed to us from all sides: the media, advertisements, even our own friends. Societies of prohibition were founded on an idealisation of sacrifice, of sacrificing enjoyment for the sake of social duty; in our societies of commanded enjoyment, 'the private enjoyment that threatened the stability of the society of prohibition becomes a stabilizing force and even acquires the status of a duty' (2004: 3).

In McGowan's schema, this emerging society of commanded enjoyment is not concomitant with capitalism in general; it characterises, in particular, late capitalism. In its initial phases, with its reliance on 'work ethic' and delayed gratification, 'capitalism sustained and necessitated its own form of prohibition' (McGowan, 2004: 31). Simply put, early capitalism 'thwarted enjoyment to the same extent that [many] traditional societies did' (ibid.). According to this perspective, the classical bourgeois attitude – and bourgeois political economy – was initially based on 'postponment, the deferral of jouissances, patient retention with a view to the supplementary jouissance that is calculated. Accumulate in order to accumulate, produce in order to produce' (Goux, 1990: 203-4). This is the first spirit of capitalism – in the Weberian sense, where 'spirit' implies a particular form of obligation, a distinct ethical mode, a type of categorical imperative (Weber, 2006: 45, 267) – associated with a sense of professional duty based on 'rational asceticism' – a gradually secularized version of protestant asceticism – and the concomitant tabooing of enjoyment, conspicuous consumption (in Thorstein Veblen's sense) and luxury (Weber, 2006: 149). One of the nodal points of this framework of sacrifice is 'saving':

> In the form of the first spirit of capitalism that dominated the nineteenth century and the first third of the twentieth, saving constituted the main means of access to the world of capital and the instrument of social advancement. It was, in large part, by means of inculcating an ethic of saving that the values of self-control, moderation, restraint, hard work, regularity, perseverance, and stability prized by firms was transmitted. (Boltanski and Chiapello, 2005: 152)

In *The System of Objects*, Baudrillard had also described this shift from an ascetic model of ethics organized around sacrifice to a new morality of enjoyment:

> the status of a whole civilization changes along with the way in which its everyday objects make themselves present and the way in which they are enjoyed… The ascetic mode of accumulation, rooted in forethought, in sacrifice… was the foundation of a whole civilization of thrift which enjoyed its own heroic period. (Baudrillard, 1996: 172)

This simple model, incorporating the insights of sociology classics like Max Weber, postmodernists like Baudrillard and even Lacanians like McGowan, can be extremely helpful; but it may also be in need of some revision that would be able to produce a more nuanced account, alert to the paradoxes of mutual engagement. In fact, the whole problematic elaborated in this essay justifies a problematization of this model of clear-cut differentiation and periodization between prohibition/asceticism and enjoyment/luxury. Such a problematization can and should proceed on both the synchronic and the diachronic axes. On the one hand, at the synchronic level, the consumerist call to enjoy may be less liberating than it seems; McGowan himself points to its irreducible link to power and duty. In that sense, what we are dealing with, instead of a strict antithesis or opposition between restraining asceticism and liberating enjoyment are articulations of ethics/morality and enjoyment distributed along two seemingly antithetical but, in effect, mutually reinforcing axes, in effect comprising one single, paradoxical but, more or less, functional structure. On the other, at the diachronic level, the idea – present in the original model – of a straightforward linear movement from prohibition to enjoyment, from the first to the second spirit, also needs to be re-examined; and here recent historical research of consumption patterns can be extremely revealing.

But let's take one step at a time. As far as synchronic differentiation is concerned, what a careful comparison between the two spirits reveals is that, with all their differences, they do not signify a radical break of cosmological proportions. As we have seen, from a psychoanalytic point of view, the administration of enjoyment and the structuration of desire are always implicated in the institution of the social bond. Every society has to come to terms with the impossibility of attaining *jouissance* as fullness; it is only the fantasies produced and circulated to mask or at least domesticate this trauma that can vary, and in fact do vary immensely. Prohibition and commanded enjoyment are two distinct such strategies designed to institute the social bond and legitimize authority, social hierarchy and power in different ways. Nevertheless, in both cases, certain things remain unchanged. What remains the same is, first of all, the impossibility of realising the fantasy: 'The fundamental thing to recognize about the society of enjoyment is that in it the pursuit of enjoyment has misfired: the society of enjoyment has not provided the enjoyment that it promises' (McGowan, 2004: 7). But if this is the case, then the command to enjoy is only revealed as 'a more nuanced form of prohibition; it continues – with other means – the traditional function of symbolic Law and power' (McGowan, 2004: 39). Greater autonomy associated with the new spirit of capitalism 'conceals more constraints' (Boltanski and Chiapello, 2005: 254).[13]

In societies of commanded enjoyment, enjoyment makes sense predominantly as a duty: 'duty is transformed into a duty to enjoy, which is precisely the commandment of the superego' (McGowan, 2004: 34). The seemingly innocent and benevolent call to 'enjoy!' – as in 'Enjoy Coca-Cola!' – embodies the violent dimension of an irresistible commandment. Echoing the astute reference to *forced enjoyment* by Paul Lafargue, Marx's son in law, in his extremely perceptive and provocative *Le Droit à la Paresse* [The Right to be Lazy], first published as a series of articles in 1880 (Lafargue, 1999), Lacan was perhaps the first to elaborate on the importance of this paradoxical hybrid when he linked the command 'enjoy!' with the superego: 'The superego is the imperative of *jouissance* – Enjoy!' (Lacan, 1999: 3). He was, indeed, one of the first to detect in this innocent call the unmistakable mark of power and authority. Thus Lacan is offering a revealing insight on what has been described as the 'consuming paradox': while consumerism seems to broaden our opportunities, choices and experiences as individuals, it also directs us towards predetermined channels of behaviour and thus it 'is ultimately as constraining as it is enabling' (Miles, 1998: 147). The desire stimulated – and *imposed* – by advertising discourse is, in this sense, the desire of the Other *par excellence*. Already in 1968, Baudrillard had captured this moral dynamics of an 'obligation to buy', and recent consumption research is becoming increasingly more alert to this *forced choice* of consumerism: 'It is now something of a duty to explore personal identity through consumption' (Daunton and Hilton, 2001: 31). In late capitalist consumer society this is how a symbolic command and a fantasy regulating/manipulating the pursuit of our lacking enjoyment attempt to construct us as social subjects, a process revealing – once more – the inextricable dialectic between symbolic authority and fantasmatic enjoyment. Thus, apart from products and advertising fantasies, what are also manufactured are consumers (Fine, 2002: 168). It is here that 'the triumph of advertising' is located, as Adorno and Horkheimer already knew: 'consumers feel compelled to buy and use its products even though they see through them' (Adorno and Horkheimer, 1997: 167).

To be fair, it seems that, once more, Lafargue – with his caustic irony and incisive observations, 'at once funny and serious, witty and profound, elegant and forceful', 'an ironist as much as a Marxist' (Hope, 1999: v, vi) – was here first, and deserves to be quoted at some length:

> The abstinence with which the productive class condemns itself to inordinate output obligates the bourgeoisie to consecrate itself to over-consumption. At the debut of capitalist production (a century or two ago) the bourgeoisie was orderly, morally reasonable and peaceful. The bourgeois man was more or less happy with his wife, he didn't drink except to slake his thirst, nor eat to excess. He relegated the noble virtues of a debauched life to courtesans and court jesters. Today, every son of new money takes it upon himself to develop prostitution and 'mercurialize' himself to provide a goal for the work that workers in mercury mines impose on themselves. Now every bourgeois gorges himself with truffle-stuffed capons and fine wine to encourage the farmers of La Flèche and the growers of Bordelais. This occupation rapidly destroys the body – hair falls out, gums recede, spines curve, bellies distend, breathing becomes difficult, movement slows, joints stiffen, and fingers twist into knots. And others, too weak to handle the strains of debauchery, but nonetheless endowed with the hunch of the honest man, dry up their minds like the Garniers of political economy and the Acollas of legal philosophy, elaborating thick, soporific books to occupy the leisure time of typesetters and printers.

> The women of the world live the lives of martyrs when they display themselves in the fairy-like dresses seamstresses kill themselves to make: like a weaver's shuttle, women shift into one dress after another; for hours they hand over their empty heads to hairdressers who, for the right price, want to assuage ladies' passion for the creation of false chignons. Bound in corsets, stuffed in boots and packed into dresses cut low enough to make a coal miner blush, they twirl entire nights

away at charity balls to collect a few cents for the poor. Holy souls!
(Lafargue, 1999: 18-9)

In our consumer societies, societies of enforced or commanded
enjoyment, authority and symbolic power are as operative as in
'societies of prohibition': the 'enforced happiness and enjoyment' is the
equivalent of the traditional imperatives to work and produce
(Baudrillard, 1998: 80). In that sense, the structure of obedience and
subjection discussed in the first section of this essay is still relevant here.
Indeed, McGowan uses the word 'obedience' to refer to our attachment
to the enjoyment commandment. The command to enjoy is nothing but
an advanced, much more nuanced – and much more difficult to resist –
form of power. It is more effective than the traditional model not
because it is less constraining or less binding but because its violent
exclusionary aspect is masked by its fantasmatic vow to enhance
enjoyment, by its productive, enabling *facade*: it does not oppose and
prohibit but openly attempts to embrace and appropriate *the subject of
enjoyment*. Not only is this novel articulation of power and enjoyment
hard to recognize and to thematize; it is even harder to de-legitimize in
practice, to dis-invest consumption acts and dis-identify with
consumerism. However, without such a dis-investment and the
cultivation of alternative (ethical) administrations of *jouissance*, no real
change can be effected.

4. A Genealogy of Spirit(s)

There are two general wants that mankind is born with; the wants of
the body and the wants of the mind...

Wares, that have their value from supplying the wants of the mind, are
all such things that can satisfy desire; desire implies want: it is the
appetite of the soul, and is as natural to the soul, as hunger is to the
body.

The wants of the mind are infinite, man naturally aspires, and as his
mind is elevated, his senses grow more refined, and more capable of
delight; his desires are inlarged, and his wants increase with his wishes,
which is for every thing that is rare, can gratifie his senses, adorn his
body, and promote the ease, pleasure and pomp of life.

Nicholas Barbon (1690)

Le superflu, chose très nécessaire.

Voltaire (1736)

Once convinced that instead of wishing them harm, we want to free
them from the work of over-consumption and waste that they've been
overburdened since birth, the capitalists and stock-holders will be first
to rally to the popular party.

Paul Lafargue (1880)

Clearly, a psychoanalytic perspective is bound to introduce a more
nuanced picture on the differentiation between the different spirits of
capitalism. A similar conclusion follows from a more careful
examination of periodization. As we have seen, most analysts locate the
shift from the first to the second spirit of capitalism around the middle
of twentieth century. According to most accounts, it is in the second
half of the twentieth century – after 1950 – that puritanism gives place
to enjoyment (Lipovetsky, 1983: 73). Recent research, however, has
revealed that 'whatever forces were working to challenge the Protestant
ethic they were hardly recent, but could be found to have a pedigree
which extended back to a time well before the twentieth century'
(Campbell 2005: 5). Indeed, signs of erosion of the first spirit of
capitalism started to become visible and/or conscious well before that.
Writing in 1880, Lafargue describes vividly how mass production
prepared the ground for the development of a consumer culture unified
around 'the command to enjoy': 'In the face of this double folly of
workers killing themselves with overproduction and vegetating in
abstinence, the big problem of capitalist production isn't finding
producers and increasing their force, but finding consumers, exciting
their appetites and creating artificial needs' (Lafargue, 1999: 21-2). It
could even be argued that a first wave of hedonism/consumerism
affected the middle ranks of English society by the second half of the
eighteenth century (Campbell, 2005). Drawing on and renewing a
neglected tradition going back to Sombart's work,[14] recent historical
research has documented an unparalleled product and consumer
revolution that took place in eighteenth century Britain; this revolution
involved the fascination with new consumer goods now embraced by a
'bourgeoning middling class extending to professionals, merchants, and
industrialists to ordinary trades people and artisans' (Berg, 2005: 15).
Far from being the invention of the post-Cold War era, a 'global

consumer society' is thus revealed as 'the very foundation of the industrial world' (Berg, 2005: 329).

Indeed, it would be a mistake to associate the emergence of enforced enjoyment with modernity itself. This is clearly not the first time in history that such an order of commanded enjoyment was instituted. It is, in fact, possible to trace the genealogy of this administration of enjoyment, of such an authority/fantasmatic structure, back to what is often called 'Court Society'. A few centuries before the sedimentation of the bourgeois ascetic ideal, European aristocracy, the feudal ruling class, asserted itself through its exemption from 'industrial occupations' and a rejection of any purposive-rational orientation in consumption, that is to say through its devotion to leisure and the unproductive and conspicuous consumption of goods and luxuries (Veblen, 2005: 1, 43; Elias, 1983: 38). However, one should not mistake the wealth of members of this class with a state of perfect happiness free from all social restraint. On the contrary, as Norbert Elias has masterfully shown, a powerful ethics of obligation is operating here: 'What appears as extravagance from the standpoint of the bourgeois economic ethic... is in reality the expression of the seigniorial ethos of rank... It is not freely chosen' (Elias, 1983: 53). Indeed, 'expenditure on prestige and display is for the upper classes a necessity which they cannot avoid' (Elias, 1983: 63). In the words of a contemporary, 'luxury is to them as much an affliction as poverty is to the poor' (Mercier in Sombart, 1967: 59).

To complicate things a bit more, it is also important to keep in mind that a similar logic of enforced expenditure and consumption is something observable in many pre-modern societies. This explains why Georges Bataille recognises in it the most important factor in life, the nodal point of what he calls 'general economy' – as opposed to 'restrictive economy', the economy of rational regulation of production and development: 'The history of life on earth is mainly the effect of wild exuberance; the dominant event is the development of luxury, the production of increasingly burdensome forms of life' (Bataille, 1989: 9, 33). A central example here is offered by the institution of potlatch, a means of circulating wealth found in many traditional societies. Potlatch denotes

> the solemn giving of considerable riches offered by one chief to his rival for the purpose of humiliating, challenging and obligating him. The

recipient has to erase the humiliation and take up the challenge; he must satisfy the obligation that was contracted by accepting... by means of a new potlatch, more generous than the first. (Bataille, 1989: 67-8)

What we observe here is a particular use of the surplus produced by a community – the non-productive consumption of excess wealth – in the service of acquiring differential status for this community. In certain cases, 'consumption and destruction of goods really go beyond all bounds... one must expend all that one has, keeping nothing back' (Mauss, 1990: 37). It is the same principle that will guide the ethos of prestige consumption regulating the Court Society: 'hundreds and often thousands of people were bound together in one place by peculiar restraints which they and outsiders applied to each other and to themselves... a more or less fixed hierarchy, a precise etiquette bound them together' (Elias, 1983: 35).

In both cases, obligation plays a crucial role. The rival chief is obliged to compete in this antagonism of generosity the potlatch kicks off. This element of obligation is particularly stressed in Marcel Mauss's seminal analysis of the relevant anthropological observations by Boas, Malinowski and others. In the potlatch, what initially appears as voluntary, free and disinterested is eventually revealed as 'constrained and self-interested', as guided by social obligation (Mauss, 1990: 3): 'Material and moral life, and exchange, function... in a form that is both disinterested and obligatory' (Mauss, 1990: 33). Obligation is thus absolutely central, under pain of losing authority and prestige (Mauss, 1990: 8): 'The obligation to reciprocate worthily is imperative. One loses face for ever if one does not reciprocate, or if one does not carry out destruction of equivalent value' (Mauss, 1990: 42). Likewise, the aristocrat is obliged to consume in order to retain and increase his prestige within the Court:

> The obligation to spend on a scale befitting one's rank demands an education in the use of money that differs from bourgeois conceptions. We find a paradigmatic expression of this social ethos in an action of the Duc de Richelieu related by Taine. He gives his son a purse full of money so that he can learn to spend it like a grand seigneur, and when the young man brings the money back his father throws the purse out of the window before his eyes. This is socialization in keeping with a social tradition that imprints on the individual the duty imposed on him by his rank to be prodigal. (Elias, 1983: 67)[15]

81

Isn't a similar type of superegoic obligation discernible behind the call to enjoy, the nodal point of consumer society?[16]

It is even more important to note that, although such behaviour was anathema to dominant bourgeois ethics, the pursuit of luxury never receded from the horizon; it remained a disavowed/postponed fantasy that influenced considerably the development of capitalism, if not in theory then certainly in practice. Certainly, the capitalist ascetic ethic channels surplus into accumulation and industrial growth through a critique of luxury (Bataille, 1989: 107): 'What differentiates the medieval economy from the capitalist economy is that to a very large extent the former, static economy made a non-productive consumption of the excess wealth, while the latter accumulates and determines a dynamic growth of the production apparatus' (Bataille, 1989: 116). But is this the full story? What if the relation between commanded enjoyment and bourgeois asceticism was not one of substitution or succession but one of co-constitution? Gilles Lipovetsky has described this as a central contradiction of modernity – the simultaneous idealisation of duty and sacrifice (observable in economic behaviour as well as in national identification) and their transgression – that found expression in the works of Mandeville, Smith, Sade and others (Lipovetsky, 1992) – an indirect justification of the need to consider together *Kant avec Sade*, as Lacan did (Lacan, 2006). Indeed, for Mandeville, writing in 1714, *private vices* produce *public benefits* (Mandeville, 1989); clearly a relation of mutual engagement if not of self-transgressive co-constitution. And an argument that – in its essence, although not in its radical formulation – will be ultimately endorsed by Adam Smith in his *Theory of Moral Sentiments* (Smith, 2006: 307-12). Similarly, Vico sublimates vices like ferocity, avarice and ambition into conditions of civil happiness (Hirschman, 1997: 17). In the words of Abbe Coyer: 'Luxury is akin to fire: it may be beneficial as well as destructive. In ruining the houses of the rich, it sustains our factories. In devouring the inheritance of the spendthrift, it feeds our workers. In diminishing the property of the few, it increases the prosperity of the many' (Sombart, 1967: 115).

In his *Luxury and Capitalism*, Werner Sombart goes so far as to argue that luxury 'gave birth to capitalism' and that 'increase in the consumption of luxury goods' has been the deciding factor in capitalist development (Sombart, 1967: 169, 171). Sombart's schema thus reveals the disavowed genealogy of the late capitalist ethos of commanded enjoyment. It emerges with Court Society and passes gradually to parts of the bourgeoisie through the 'amalgamation of noble ancestry and bourgeois money' (Sombart, 1967: 9-10):

> The luxury prevailing at the courts spread gradually to all the circles that were in any way connected with the court or saw fulfilment of their ambitions identified with court life. This description, we may safely state, applies to the entire moneyed class, which was gripped with the same fondness for luxury as the court circles. (Sombart, 1967: 80)

This stress on the importance of luxury is corroborated by more recent accounts: 'contrary to popular impression, the manufacturing industries most closely associated with the early Industrial Revolution were those producing consumer rather than capital goods and among these, those which produced objects for "luxury" consumption predominated' (Campbell, 2005: 25). Of course, the new classes were quick to distinguish their own luxury from its corrupt ancestors. While the 'old' or 'ancient' luxury was negatively associated with foreign imports and 'elite ostentatious display', with the decaying Court Society, a 'new', 'modern' luxury now emerged, one associated with middling class 'domestic interiors and dress' (Berg, 2005: 5, 21, 32). In fact, the way bourgeois luxury presented itself was always as a radical shift 'from the conspicuous display of opulence to a more refined demonstration of elegance, refinement and fastidious discrimination' (Thomas, 2009: 15).

However, if this is the case, then we may have to rethink the relation between the ethics of asceticism/prohibition and the ethics of enjoyment. This is the task that Colin Campbell sets to himself in *The Romantic Ethic and the Spirit of Modern Consumerism*. How did the new propensity to consume occur? (Campbell, 2005: 32). This is his central research question. He starts with an evaluation of the aforementioned Sombart-Veblen line of argumentation, that is to say with the hypothesis that it is the emulation of aristocratic behaviour which accounts for the shift from one spirit of capitalism to the other. There is 'no doubt [that] there were ways in which the emerging bourgeoisie of the period 'imitated' the aristocracy' (Campbell, 2005: 33) – such as the adoption of the aesthetic sensibility, which was 'imported from the nobility' (Campbell, 2005: 204). For Campbell, though, this argument is not entirely satisfactory. His own answer also involves an attempt to remedy what he perceives as the incompleteness of Weber's account (Campbell, 2005: 103). In his view, the emergence of modern consumerist hedonism was not the effect of factors exogenous to the religious ethic of the emerging middle classes. What permits this conclusion is the hypothesis that there were, indeed, two distinct cultural and ethical traditions 'which developed out of English Puritanism in the eighteenth century'. Apart from the well-known ascetic tradition, immortalized by Max Weber, there was a second one (linked to Arminianism and the Cambridge Platonists), which led to the development of a whole Romantic ethic that legitimized early consumerism (Campbell, 2005: 136-7).

Given the prevalence of logics of enforced enjoyment in traditional societies, Campbell's analysis is justified in tracing the foundations of consumer culture and the development of its cultural and ethical preconditions that early. What remains puzzling is his insistence to dissociate modern hedonism from its traditional (aristocratic) cousin. His main argument here is that the hedonism characteristic of the Court Society was permeated by a restraining code of conduct and civility, by a sense of obligation (Campbell, 2005: 163) unlike modern 'autonomous' hedonism, which 'presents all individuals with the possibility of being their own despot, exercising total control over the stimuli they experience, and hence the pleasure they receive' (Campbell, 2005: 76-7). My fear is that what we encounter here is a grossly exaggerated and idealized account of modern consumerism that ignores its heteronomous, restraining character. We have already examined in detail the way consumption is elevated to a duty within (late) modern capitalist societies. Whether this is effected within a more reflexive attitude in comparison to that of the Court Society does not really make that much difference; an 'enlightened false consciousness' – to use Žižek's phrase – remains a false consciousness. Besides, as Norbert Elias has shown, modern society has indeed embraced with great fervor not only the hedonism but also the rules of civility formulated within Court Society. Indeed the social conventions defining membership to the nobility have gradually spread throughout European societies – more easily in France, less easily in Germany – constituting a whole civilizing process slowly encompassing segments of the lower classes as well as neighbouring countries and peoples (Elias, 1997: 108, 194). Court Society seems to have formulated the models of status, distinction and consumption that became gradually desirable to lower social strata, as well as the types of socialization necessary to internalize the mechanisms of self-control, of voluntary servitude, necessary to achieve such model behaviour (Elias, 1997: 199, 253).

Yet – and no matter whether what he calls 'the Romantic ethic' and modern hedonism/consumerism developed out of the emulation of Court behaviour or out of a novel play of intellectual and moral forces and/or group cohesion mechanisms[17] – what remains truly fascinating in Campbell's account is that, even though Weberian rational asceticism may have hegemonized for a certain period moral debates – the field of the official ideal – this has always proceeded in coexistence if not in a paradoxical symbiosis with its supposed opposite; with what is assumed to transgress it. Even in Weber, the protestant ethic is presented as an ideal type, and it is

> a fundamental mistake to confuse such a cultural ideal type with that total pattern of behaviour which might be identified as characterizing the conduct of individuals or social groups, and hence to confuse an ethic with a type of personality or the behaviour typical of a given social position. In theory, individuals cannot conform to two ethics; in practice, it may not be so difficult. (Campbell, 2005: 220)

In fact, Campbell's reference to the *symbiotic* relationship between the two opposed ethical orientations (Campbell, 2005: 217) introduces a similar problematic to that of mutual engagement and self-transgression discussed in previous parts of this chapter, a problematic of simultaneous contrast, even contradiction, but also – and most crucially – of interdependence: 'these twin cultures ensured the continued performance of those contrasted but interdependent forms of behaviour essential to the perpetuation of industrial societies, matching consumption with production, play with work' (Campbell, 2005: 227), official ideal with self-transgression/habit, a distribution of form/force in which symbolic authority is dominant under the form of ascetic prohibition with another distribution in which fantasmatic enjoyment is dominant under the form of a call to enjoy. As we learn from Lafargue, almost from the beginning of bourgeois society, next to the ascetic bourgeois is the bourgeois who has delivered himself to 'frenetic luxury, exotic indigestion and syphilitic debauch' (Lafargue, 1999: 19). Very soon after acquiring its dominant status, 'the capitalist class found itself condemned to laziness and forced hapiness, to unproductiveness and over-consumption' (Lafargue, 1999: 18). Such mutual engagement, such 'cultural tango', has characterized modern societies 'from their birth, and appears essential to their continued existence' (Campbell 2005: 227).[18]

This cultural tango also affected the lower classes. Gradually, the new goods had also become, at least in principle, accessible even to labourers; especially after the lifting of sumptuary laws (Berg, 2005: 29):

> Lower down the social scale, among the working poor, the new goods had little initial impact... though, by the later 18th century, cotton and linen, peuter, pottery, tea sets, and decorative household items would reach even labourers' cottages... Even when undernourished and poorly housed, the lower classes were prepared to devote some of their limited resources to goods which boosted their self-esteem and helped them to create social relationships with others. (Thomas, 2009: 17)

By the middle of the 19th century the antagonism/*splitting* between the two spirits and its wider social and political implications – not only for the bourgeoisie but also for the lower popular strata – was becoming visible to everybody. Both synchronically and diachronically, different ways of controlling/regulating demand/desire and social hierarchy and rank were employed, ranging from the prohibition of sumptuary laws and ascetic morality to the indirect control implicit in the call to enjoy the emergence of the world of fashion (Appadurai, 1986: 32). And while the overall trend seemed to be in favour of a diffusion of the enforced enjoyment model into wider strata of the population, the ethics of sacrifice was again called to the rescue whenever deemed necessary: 'In a 1849 Commission session on primary education, Mr. Thiers proclaimed: I want to make the clergy all-powerful because I count on it to disseminate the good philosophy instructing humans that life on earth is for suffering, and not the other philosophy that tells humans: "Enjoy"' (Lafargue, 1999: 1).

Although the post-war period has signalled an unprecedented hegemominzation of social life by consumerism and the ethics of enforced enjoyment, this oscillation never ceased. On the one hand, we have witnessed – especially during the last few decades – a cataclysmic diffusion of luxury items. As we read in a case-study involving one such item: 'Like other objects of conspicuous consumption, [oriental] carpets first became luxury furnishings for the elite, and have now gone the way of so many luxuries in recent times and become available throughout the middle class' (Spooner, 1986: 195). In fact, today, even *Ikea* sells oriental carpets! On the other hand, however, the current economic crisis has turned the centre of gravity back to the value of prohibition/sacrifice. When I started writing this essay (June 2008), my newspaper reported the theme of a public discussion organized in the framework of a local book fair, 'Youth and Books: From Obligation to Enjoyment', indicative of the shift in strategies of socialization. Now, that I am finishing it (December 2008) mainstream news web-sites host articles with titles such as 'Recession: How to Talk to your Kids' in which experts provide advice to parents on how to start saying 'no' to their children, something indicative of the reverse trend: 'It isn't always in their best interest to give them everything they want, even if you could, because I think they need to learn that waiting for something, delaying gratification, sacrificing – those are important aspects of character development' (Potter, 2008).

5. Enforced Enjoyments: From Consumption to Workplace Practices

This whole argument pointing to the development of different administrations of enjoyment, different spirits of capitalism, to the dialectics of co-constitution between logics of prohibition and enforced enjoyment and the alternation of the centre of social and ethical gravity – from the one to the other – is not only related to the world of consumption. As we have seen, consumption and production can only be seen as two sides of the same coin. It can also be clearly illustrated through changes marking workplace culture. What one is bound to observe here is that, once more, there is no radical break from prohibition to commanded enjoyment, but a slow passage with many intermediate stations and phases of co-existence, a case of what, in old Marxist jargon, used to be called 'uneven and combined development'. Now, we all know that in order to safeguard and increase productivity, organizations cultivate particular versions of identity by articulating symbolic and fantasmatic frameworks 'through which their values, beliefs, and norms can be conveyed' (Cederström and Grassman, 2008: 41). These frameworks vary from the most strict (such as the openly normative techniques of the Ford era) to the most subtle (characteristic of companies like Google). Here, in this 'neo-normative' universe, 'the accent is no longer placed on a rigid model which promotes the idealized employee, but on a model that takes a more "genuine" interest in the employees as idiosyncratic and individual' (Cederström and Grassman, 2008: 43); for example, rather than promoting a standard template to which employees are expected to converge, Google allows its employees 'to be themselves' (Fleming and Sturdy in Cederström and

Grassman, 2008: 45). By demanding from its employees that they be and enjoy themselves, Google exemplifies the shift from 'raw' prohibition to commanded enjoyment. However, as is the case with society in general and the role of consumerism within it, once more this is a shift that does not signify any kind of emancipation: 'the Googler is in no way "freed" from superegoic pressure but, on the contrary, under the sway of an even more insidious species of normative control' (Cederström and Grassman, 2008: 46). It demonstrates, however, the extent to which the power of the command, symbolic authority, is increasingly being combined with new and more nuanced forms of administering fantasmatic enjoyment.

Today, the command to enjoy is taking even more surprising forms: 'amidst the frenetic attempts to colonize the subjectivity of workers through corporate culture, we find not only systems of identification with the company philosophy, but also practices of subjective distancing, incredulity and disbelief particularly manifest in the form of worker cynicism' (Fleming and Spicer, 2003: 159). It even acquires the cynical form of enjoying one's 'symptom'! Employees in a London firm studied by Cederström and Grassman are even encouraged to 'reflexively' criticize their own work and engage in self-hatred and cynicism (Cederström and Grassman, 2008: 47) – provided, of course, they continue doing their hard work and taking their high salaries. The command to enjoy is still operative here although it moves beyond the 'politically correct' pleasures encouraged by Google, to engage more obscure and masochistic forms of enjoyment (from enjoying fatty food and alcohol to enjoying cynical reflexivity itself). Indeed, within this framework, 'the latest wave of management gurus invites employees to simply be themselves, even if that means being cynically against the values of the firm' (Fleming and Spicer, 2008: 303).

On the one hand, then, we have the Google model of 'neo-normative control', which, by commanding certain forms of enjoyment, introduces 'a human face' transforming the first spirit of prohibition. Following the rules (with all the creative re-interpretation this can entail in certain contexts) is promising a harmonious outcome, an effective functioning of the organization and the satisfaction of its employees: Google's strenuous attempts to offer a balanced, healthy and pleasurable life to their employees are indicative of how they refuse to go beyond a certain limit of the pleasure principle. Transgressions like 'driving scooters in the hallway are confined within a framework of "controlled pleasure"' (Cederström and Grassman, 2008: 45). On the other hand, we have the emergence of a 'masochistic reflexive organization' as Cederström and Grassman call it: here it is already from the beginning openly recognized that the rules and work itself suck and all the employees are allowed to cynically and masochistically discuss that, enjoying their enlightened false consciousness. Different forms of fantasmatic enjoyment are employed by each model. In the first case we have a fantasy *repressing* the lack in the Other and the impossibility of encountering full enjoyment within our social world. In the second case we have a strategy of *disavowal*: the lack is registered and this is what produces the cynical attitude; at the same time people continue to act as if this lack does not affect them. Thus, as is the case with ideological idealizations of societies of commanded enjoyment in general, the romanticization of resistance as transgression of the normative framework fails to understand that cynical transgression often works to 'perpetuate management ideologies' (Hoedemaekers, 2008: 45; Fleming and Spicer, 2003). What is usually seen as a form of transgression of corporate authority does not really affect our attachment to it: 'The ironical distance that subjects take from domination processes is illusory, insofar as it hides their own role in extending the very processes they appear to resist against' (Hoedemaekers, 2008: 36).

Alessia Contu has coined the term 'decaf resistance' to describe such ironic, skeptical and/or cynical instances, which, however, rarely go beyond the dominating logics codifying a given *status quo* (Contu, 2008) and, in effect, fit perfectly the 'new spirit of capitalism' described by Boltanski and Chiapello (Fleming and Spicer, 2008: 303). Contu is right to point out that 'such carnivalesque forms of resistance' not only fail to constitute a threat for the dominant order, but also end up being a crucial support to this order. And indeed, we know how Mikhail Bakhtin has described the medieval carnival as a period of *officially permitted* and *encouraged* transgression entailing a (temporary) suspension of authority but no sustainable change. More recently, in his *State of Exception*, Giorgio Agamben returns to this discussion in a bid to highlight 'the secret solidarity between anomie and law', something directly relevant to our argument. These feasts 'inaugurate a period of anomie that breaks and temporarily subverts the social order' (Agamben, 2005: 71). Agamben's interpretation of this phenomenon is analogous to the highlighting of the relation of mutual engagement between symbolic Law and fantasmatic self-transgression, public ideal and cultural intimacy: here 'law and anomie show their distance and, at the same time, their secret solidarity' (Agamben, 2005: 73). We have to do with two dimensions, which are simultaneously antagonistic and functionally connected. The Law can only apply itself effectively to life and manage its chaotic character only by (partially and periodically) immersing itself into life and living chaos; in Agamben's schema this is precisely the purpose of the *state of exception* (Agamben, 2005: 73).

At this point, however, one should be very careful in order to avoid the 'speculative leftist', quasi-religious, idealization of some kind of radical act of total social refoundation, which – in a Žižekian vein – is often presented as the real radical alternative to 'decaf resistance'. Against the fake promise of 'decaf resistance' the supposedly *pure* radicalism of the 'real act' sounds as the only way to save the lost bite of radical politics and the declining ethical integrity of critical academia. But is the proper way to do this a revival of the old fantasy of a total and miraculous social refoundation through a single apocalyptic cut, 'the act of resistance, qua act of terrifying and unadulterated freedom' (Contu, 2008: 376)? I am afraid that what we have here is a reoccupation of a very old-fashioned theme, combining a gnostic-style rejection of our world *in totto* – as the kingdom of an evil creator (capitalism) – and of its false detractors (decaf resistance), with the millenarian need for an apocalyptic act of pure desire fully transcending it.[19] For those assuming the superiority of such a miraculous act, a clear case of ideological over-investment, every local/partial struggle is found wanting and has to be denounced as worthless.

What is sadly missed here is that all struggle is ultimately an impure process, an 'ongoing, multiple, and unpredictable' dialectic between power and resistance (Fleming and Spicer, 2008: 305). Indeed, it is not only decaf resistance that can be co-opted and operates always in a dialectic of mutual engagement with the forces of order. Revolutionary acts run the same danger and are also subject to the same limits; indeed, seen from the point of view of their long-term institutional effects, revolutions are also marked by an irreducible 'decaf' aspect. But often this works in the interest of socio-political transformation; as is also the case with some acts – quickly and perhaps mistakenly – classified under worthless 'decaf resistance'. As Castoriadis has cogently put it:

> This antinomy between the two main significations of modern society
> has not prevented their multiple mutual contamination… if capitalism

has been able to function and to develop, it is not *in spite of* but *thanks to* the conflict that existed in society and, concretely speaking, thanks to the fact that the workers don't just let things happen [*ne se laissent pas faire*]. More generally speaking, I believe that capitalism's survival can be attributed to the fact that, as the result of historical evolution, revolutions, and so on, society had to institute itself also as a society recognizing a minimum of liberties, of human rights, of legality, and so forth. I spoke of a mutual contamination between two central significations of modern society, but their mutual functionalities must also be underscored. (Castoriadis, 2003: 216)

However, as Lacan reminds us, this mutual engagement/contamination also works the other way round and may entail a more sinister dimension disavowed by *believers* of the 'radical act'. Revolutionary aspiration and/or radical rejection of the *status quo* itself – when it manages to occur – is usually guided by and ends up instituting a new order of subjection[20] and rarely engages in attempts to encircle lack in a radically democratic ethico-political direction.[21] Lacan's reaction to May '68 is absolutely relevant here. During the May events, Lacan observed the teachers' strike and suspended his seminar; it seems that he even met Daniel Cohn-Bendit, one of the student leaders (Roudinesco, 1997: 336). One way or the other, his name became linked to the events. However, the relation was not an easy one. In 1969, for instance, Lacan was invited to speak at Vincennes, but obviously he and the students operated at different wave-lengths. The discussion ended as follows:

[T]he aspiration to revolution has but one conceivable issue, always, the discourse of the master. That is what experience has proved. What you, as revolutionaries, aspire to is a Master. You will have one... for you fulfill the role of helots of this regime. You don't know what that means either? This regime puts you on display; it says: 'Watch them fuck...'. (Lacan, 1990: 126)

To sum up, it is not only that 'radical acts' are far from exempt from a 'decaf' dialectic of mutual engagement with the forces of order; it is also the case that they may even reproduce the most violent, exclusionary, and hierarchical aspects of these forces.

Perhaps the key to real change has to do less with the express intent and magnitude, with the explicit content and ambition of a counter-logic, less with a choice between 'decaf' and 'real' acts, and more with the mode of the subject's engagement with change and activity in general (Glynos and Stavrakakis, 2008: 265). Here, the total rejection of order and the quasi-religious embrace of its guaranteed miraculous transformation both betray a mode of *ideological* over-investment of transgression indicative of the same pursuit of closure and phallic *jouissance* sustaining regimes of hierarchical order; here, the subject remains in the thrall of fantasy 'and thus insensitive to the contingency of social reality' (Glynos and Stavrakakis, 2008: 265; Glynos, 2008a: 277, 291), ultimately unable to deal effectively and productively with the uncertainties and limits of real change (Glynos, 2008a: 288) and to combine energy with modesty. The only thing that can destabilize this mode is the cultivation and investment of an *ethical* stance oriented towards openness and the traversing of fantasies of both subjection and transgression (in their paradoxical mutual engagement), an ethics embracing the *jouissance féminine* of the not-whole: 'It is a matter of showing how the space of the possible is larger than the one we are assigned – that something else is possible, but not that everything is possible' (Badiou, 1998: 121). Only thus can the ever-present dimension of mutual engagement be sublimated from an obstacle or a limit of change to an opportunity for increasing its scope and effectiveness, from a condition of impossibility to a condition of possibility.

Conclusion

I have tried in this essay to briefly outline the ways in which Lacanian theory moves beyond subjectivism and objectivism in illuminating the dialectic between subject and organized Other. By understanding the subject as a subject of lack, Lacan's negative ontology provides a solution to the paradox of a desire for subjection. There is no desire without lack. And the Other – embodied in the symbolic command – is both what consolidates this lack in the symbolic and what promises to 'manage' this lack. At the same time, by understanding the Other as an equally lacking domain Lacan helps us to explain the failure of subjection, the possibility of escaping a full determination of the subject by the socio-symbolic structure. Why is it then that this option only rarely enacts itself? To the extent that the lack marking both subject and Other is always a lack of real *jouissance*, forms of identification offered by the organized Other are obliged to operate at this level also, adding the dimension of a positive – if often obscured – incentive to the formal force of symbolic command and official ideal.

We have thus seen how Lacanian theory illuminates the dialectic between subject and organized Other not only by focusing on the symbolic presuppositions of authority (the irresistibility of the Other's command), but also by exploring the fantasmatic administration of real enjoyment and its lack, which – through cultural intimacy and self-transgression – sustains the credibility of the lacking Other and defers resistance. Only by taking into account all these dimensions, lack and (partial) enjoyment, symbolic command and fantasy, official ideal and self-transgression, can we start to envisage a comprehensive explanation of what drives identification acts sustaining structures of ideological domination.

Far from introducing any kind of a-historical dualism or essentialism, this exploration within the milieu of capitalist societies reveals the mutual engagement between the aforementioned dimensions and permits the formulation of a typology of distinct administrations of *jouissance* (through the social matrices of prohibition and commanded enjoyment and their genealogical association with different but inter-connected and co-constitutive 'spirits' of capitalism). Thus it becomes possible to illuminate the paradoxical dialectic between the ethics of duty and hedonism within modernity – a dialectic that encompasses consumption and consumerism as well as workplace practices and production. A dialectic that can enhance our understanding of power/resistance mechanisms, renew a much-needed dialogue between psychoanalysis, social anthropology, sociological theory and critical management studies, and alert critical academia to the ethical preconditions and difficulties of change beyond the lures of both an idealized (cynical, ironic, etc.) 'micro-transgression' and an equally conformist revolutionary gymnastics.

Notes

1 I am using these two terms in the sense introduced by Ernesto Laclau in his recent work. See, in this respect, Laclau (2004), as well as the relevant discussion in Stavrakakis (2007: 86).

2 In this section I will be drawing on Stavrakakis (2008). Also see Stavrakakis (1999a).

3 At this level, castration is directly linked to the prohibition of incest: "In renouncing his attempts to be the object of the mother's desire, the subject gives up a certain *jouissance* which is never regained despite all attempts to do so" (Evans, 1996: 22).

93

4   As we shall see, fantasy, in this context, signifies a scenario promising to cover over lack or, at any rate, to domesticate its trauma.

5   I am discussing a series of examples – from Milgram's experiment to the iconoclastic activism of the Yes Men – in Stavrakakis (2007, ch. 4) and in Stavrakakis (2008).

6   Here, subordination to an idealized project of miraculous radical change fails to resolve the problem to the extent that it remains fearful and/or dismissive of such a realization/institutionalisation of lack. It fails, in other words, to combine energy with modesty.

7   For a detailed analysis of national identification along these lines, see Stavrakakis and Chrysoloras (2006).

8   If one were to put it in Foucauldian terms, a resistance that is supposed to oppose power as repression is actually 'disguising' the productive aspect of power relations and its own functioning within this same system.

9   Cynical attitudes create a similar picture. Instead of identifying with the organization, some workers dis-identify with corporate culture, distance themselves from company philosophy, and develop a cynical attitude (Fleming and Spicer, 2003: 159). Such cynicism, however, often tends to reproduce relations of power. People dis-identify with the rules but still perform their duties (Fleming and Spicer, 2003: 160).

10 The relation between psychoanalytic reasoning and social anthropology goes back to Freud's work and Lacan's engagement with Levi-Strauss and structural anthropology and has recently been given new impetus. For a review of the relation between psychoanalysis and anthropology, a genealogy of the *anthropological subject* and an attempt to create a certain 'synthesis', see, from the recent bibliography, Henrietta Moore's *The Subject of Anthropology* (2007). James Wiener has also explored 'the possibility of a Lacanian anthropology' by creating a 'meeting point' for parallel psychoanalytic (Freud and Lacan) and anthropological (Strathern and Wagner) interpretations (Weiner, 1995: 3, 5). In an earlier book, Moore is, in fact, focusing on a problematic close to the one explored here, that of resistance and compliance (Moore, 1994: 49) and of instances of simultaneous *consent* and *dissent* (Moore, 1994: 75): 'It often seems that the problem for anthropologists, as for social scientists in general, is to explain how dominant discourses and categories get reproduced when so few people are prepared to acknowledge that they support or believe in them' (Moore, 1994: 51).

11 As we have seen, although two conceptually distinct dimensions are clearly implicated here, this is not a case of a simple binary opposition, rather one of symbiosis and co-constitution. However, in order to capture what in practice functions as a dialectic of co-constitution and mutual engagement it

is necessary to sharpen the conceptual tools so that they are able to account for the (partial) specificity of each dimension. It is in this light that one should read my criticism of Laclau's initial inability to distinguish discourse from affect and enjoyment (Stavrakakis, 2007, ch. 2). Even for concepts whose conceptual specificity relies on such a union, a prior establishment of some difference is necessary. For example, *jouissance* in Lacanian theory embodies the paradoxical union of pleasure and pain. We cannot speak about *jouissance* if one of these aspects is missing. But can one capture the paradox entailed here without a distinct conceptual grasping of 'pleasure' and 'pain' as separate and even as antithetical? In fact, the force and originality of a concept highlighting their indissoluble union relies absolutely on this prior conceptual differentiation. And vice-versa of course. As Freud has shown, even in cases where conceptual opposition is radical (between *Eros* and *Thanatos*, for example) the interpenetration may, in practice, be unavoidable: 'Neither of these instincts is any less essential than the other; the phenomena of life arise from the concurrent or mutually opposing action of both... In order to make an action possible there must be as a rule a combination of such compounded motives' (Freud, 1991: 356).

12 See, in this respect, Stavrakakis (1999b).

13 At the same time the passage into a supposedly 'permissive' society of commanded enjoyment often stimulates a backlash on behalf of conservative forces still attached to the model of open prohibition and resenting the supposed loss of direction in our new 'fatherless' environment. See, for example, the policies directed against 'anti-social behaviour' especially targeting youth. One of the first measures of the new London mayor Boris Johnson was to ban drinking alcohol on London's transport system, while Labour governments have instituted or encouraged a variety of similar initiatives (like ASBOs and 'frame and shame' operations) aimed at limiting the anti-social, excessive enjoyment of youth. In fact, to the extent that commanded enjoyment also involves a command structure, what we always observe is blends of prohibition of certain forms of enjoyment and encouragement of other more domesticated forms (socially acceptable pleasure).

14 For a genealogy of this line of inquiry, see Appadurai (1986: 37), as well as Berg (2005: 26).

15 According to Sombart, who recounts the same story, it is Marechal Richelieu's grandson who is involved (Sombart, 1967: 88).

16 In Mauss's words: 'And how many inclinations do we not satisfy whose ultimate purpose is not one of utility? How much of his income does or can the rich man allocate to his personal utilitarian needs? His expenditure on luxury, on art, on outrageous things, on servants – do not these make him resemble the nobles of former times or the barbarian chiefs whose customs

we have described?' (Mauss, 1990: 76-7). Mauss has also captured the fact that, in our societies, this mode of morality and social organization is affecting both upper and lower social strata: 'Among the masses and the elites of our society purely irrational expenditure is commonly practiced' (Mauss, 1990: 76).

17 This is the hypothesis – related to our discussion – formulated by Keith Thomas: 'Most people bought commodities out of a desire to keep in line with the accepted standards of their own peer group rather than to emulate those of the one above; Similarity in living styles was an important source of social cohesion; and anxiety to do the right thing was more common than the urge to stand out' (Thomas, 2009: 17). Obviously, all these factors played their role and it is futile to search for a *causa causans* of capitalist development, as Sombart (1998) perceptively observes in his *Der Bourgeois*.

18 And this is also the broad framework within which we should interpret the current crisis of capitalism. The crisis results from particular rhythms or tunes this 'cultural tango' has been following and it will only be resolved through a new crystallization of such relations of mutual engagement. Which exact direction these crystallizations will acquire is perhaps the foremost political challenge of our age.

19 I owe this connection to the history of gnosticism to discussions with Thanos Lipowatz. For a critique of Žižek's idealized act along these lines, see Stavrakakis (2007: ch. 3). His reply to this criticism can be found in Žižek (2008b: 304-333).

20 Although this by no means implies that all orders are equally constraining or identical in terms of their implications for our freedom.

21 I am exploring what that (would) involve(s) in Stavrakakis (1999a: ch. 5) and Stavrakakis (2007: ch. 8).

References

Adorno, T. and M. Horkheimer (1997) *Dialectic of Enlightenment*, trans. E. Jephcott. London: Verso.

Agamben, G. (2005) *State of Exception*, trans. K. Attell. Stanford: Stanford University Press.

Appadurai, A. (1986) 'Introduction: commodities and the politics of value', in A. Appadurai (ed.) *The Social Life of Things*. Cambridge: Cambridge University Press.

Badiou, A. (1998) 'Politics and philosophy: interview with P. Hallward', *Angelaki*, 3(3): 113–33.

Barbon, N. (1903) *A Discourse of Trade*. Baltimore: The Johns Hopkins Press.

Bataille, G. (1989) *The Accursed Share, vol. 1*, trans. R. Hurley. New York: Zone Books.

Baudrillard, J. (1996) *The System of Objects*, trans. J. Benedict. London: Verso.

Baudrillard, J. (1998) *The Consumer Society*, trans. C. Turner. London: Sage.

Berg, M. (2005) *Luxury and Pleasure in 18th Century Britain*. Oxford: Oxford University Press.

Boltanski, L. and E. Chiapello (2005) *The New Spirit of Capitalism*, trans. G. Elliott. London: Verso.

Butler, J. (1997) *The Psychic Life of Power*. Stanford: Stanford University Press.

Campbell, C. (2005) *The Romantic Ethic and the Spirit of Modern Consumerism*. Alcuin Academics.

Castoriadis, C. (2000) *The Revolutionary Problem Today*. Athens: Ypsilon (in Greek).

Castoriadis, C. (2003) 'The crisis of the identification process', in *The Rising Tide of Insignificancy*, available at http://www.notbored.org/RTI.pdf (accessed 21 March 2009).

Castoriadis, C. (2005) 'Heritage and revolution', in *Figures of the Thinkable*, available at http://www.notbored.org/FTPK.pdf (accessed 21 March 2009).

Cederström, C. and R. Grassman (2008) 'The masochistic reflexive turn', *ephemera*, 8(1): 41-57.

Contu, A. and H. Willmott (2006) 'Studying practice: situating *Talking About Machines*', *Organization Studies*, 27(12): 1769-1782.

Contu, A. (2008) 'Decaf resistance', *Management Communication Quarterly*, 21(3): 364-379.

Daunton, M. and M. Hilton (eds) (2001) *The Politics of Consumption*. Oxford: Berg.

De Certeau, M. (1988) *The Practice of Everyday Life*, trans. S. Rendall. Berkeley: University of California Press.

Elias, N. (1983) *The Court Society*, trans. E. Jephcott. Oxford: Blackwell.

Evans, D. (1996) *An Introductory Dictionary of Lacanian Psychoanalysis.* London: Routledge.

Fine, B. (2002) *The World of Consumption.* Rev. ed. London: Routledge.

Fleming, P. and A. Spicer (2003) 'Working at a cynical distance: implications for power, subjectivity and resistance', *Organization*, 10(1): 157-179.

Fleming, P. and A. Spicer (2008) 'Beyond power and resistance', *Management Communication Quarterly.* 21(3): 301-309.

Freud, S. (1991) 'Why War?', in *Civilization, Society and Religion, Book 12.* Penguin Freud Library. London: Penguin.

Glynos, J. (2003) 'Self-transgression and freedom', *Critical Review of International Social and Political Philosophy*, 6(2): 1-20.

Glynos, J. (2008a) 'Ideological fantasy at work', *Journal of Political Ideologies*, 13(3): 275-296.

Glynos, J. (2008b) 'Self-transgressive enjoyment as a freedom fetter', *Political Studies*, 56(3): 679-704.

Glynos, J. and Y. Stavrakakis (2008) 'Lacan and political subjectivity: fantasy and enjoyment in psychoanalysis and political theory', *Subjectivity*, 24(1): 256-274.

Goux, J-J. (1990) *Symbolic Economies.* Ithaca: Cornell University Press.

Herzfeld, M. (2004) 'Intimating culture', in A. Shryock (ed.) *Off Stage/On Display.* Stanford: Stanford University Press.

Herzfeld, M. (2005) *Cultural Intimacy.* Second edition. New York: Routledge.

Hirschman, A. (1997) *The Passions and the Interests.* Princeton: Princeton University Press.

Hoedemaekers, C. (2008) *Performance, Pinned Down: A Lacanian Analysis of Subjectivity at Work.* Rotterdam: ERIM.

Jones, C. and Spicer, A. (2005) 'The sublime object of entrepreneurship', *Organization*, 12(2): 223-246.

Lacan, J. (1990) *Television, A Challenge to the Psychoanalytic Establishment*, trans. D. Hollier, R. Krauss and A. Michelson. New York: Norton.

Lacan, J. (1999) *On Feminine Sexuality, the Limits of Love and Knowledge: The Seminar of Jacques Lacan, Book XX, 1972-73*, trans. B. Fink. New York: Norton.

Lacan, J. (2006) *Écrits*, trans. B. Fink. New York: Norton.

Lacan, J. (2008) *My Teaching*, trans. D. Macey. London: Verso.

Laclau, E. (2004) 'Glimpsing the future: a reply', in S. Critchley and O. Marchart (eds) *Laclau: A Critical Reader*. London: Routledge.

Lafargue, P. (1999) *The Right to be Lazy*. Ardmore: Fifth Season Press.

Lipovetsky, G. (1983) *L'Ere Du Vide*, Paris: Gallimard.

Lipovetsky, G. (1992) *Le Crepuscule Du Devoir*. Paris: Gallimard.

Mandeville, B. (1989) *The Fable of the Bees*. London: Penguin.

Mauss, M. (1990) *The Gift*, trans. W. D. Halls. New York: Norton.

McGowan, T. (2004) *The End of Dissatisfaction? Jacques Lacan and the Emerging Society of Enjoyment*. Albany: SUNY Press.

Miles, S. (1998) *Consumerism – As a Way of Life*. London: Sage.

Moore, H. (1994) *A Passion for Difference*. Cambridge: Polity.

Moore, H. (2007) *The Subject of Anthropology*. Cambridge: Polity.

Potter, N. (2008) 'Recession: how to talk to your kids', *ABC News*, available at http://abcnews.go.com/print?id=6339668 (accessed 27 November 2008).

Roudinesco, E. (1997) *Jacques Lacan*, trans. B. Bray. London: Polity Press.

Shryock, A. (2004) 'Other conscious/self aware', in A. Shryock (ed.) *Off Stage/On Display*. Stanford: Stanford University Press.

Smith, A. (2006) *The Theory of Moral Sentiments*. Mineola: Dover.

Sombart, W. (1998) *The Bourgeois*. Athens: Nefeli (in Greek).

Sombart, W. (1967) *Luxury and Capitalism*. Ann Arbor: Michigan University Press.

Spooner, B. (1986) 'Weavers and dealers: the authenticity of an oriental carpet', in A. Appadurai (ed.) *The Social Life of Things*. Cambridge: Cambridge University Press.

Stavrakakis, Y. (1999a) *Lacan and the Political*. London: Routledge.

Stavrakakis, Y. (1999b) 'Lacan and history', *Journal for the Psychoanalysis of Culture and Society*, 4(1): 99-118.

Stavrakakis, Y. (2007) *The Lacanian Left*. Edinburgh: Edinburgh University Press.

Stavrakakis, Y. (2008) 'Subjectivity and the organized Other: between symbolic authority and fantasmatic enjoyment', *Organization Studies*, 29(7): 1037-1059.

Stavrakakis, Y. and N. Chrysoloras (2006) '(I can't get no) enjoyment: Lacanian theory and the analysis of nationalism', *Psychoanalysis, Culture and Society*, 11(2): 144–63.

Thomas, K. (2009) 'To buy or not to buy', *History Today*, 59(2): 12-9.

Weber, M. (2006) *The Protestant Ethic and the Spirit of Capitalism*. Athens: Gutenberg (in Greek).

Weiner, J. (1995) *The Lost Drum*. Madison: The University of Wisconsin Press.

Veblen, T. (2005) *Conspicuous Consumption*. London: Penguin.

Žižek, S. (2008a) *Violence*. London: Profile.

Žižek, S. (2008b) *In Defense of Lost Causes*. London: Verso.

4

The Unbearable Weight of Happiness

Carl Cederström and Rickard Grassman

What do we do now, now that we are happy?

Samuel Beckett, *Waiting for Godot*

The demise of the bureaucratic organization has engendered a new image of the model employee (Sennett, 2006). Unlike the loyal and security-seeking employee found in more traditional work settings, this emerging figure is defined by his 'countercultural subversive edge' (Žižek, 1999; see also Boltanski and Chiapello, 2005). He knows the art of non-conformity; he is creative, entrepreneurial and subversive; and his career is not set in stone or confined to one corporation. To him, organizations are but temporary shelters, or base camps, lined up along the adventurous path towards success and personal fulfilment. In short, today's model worker obeys no other rules than his own: he is his own boss, controlling his own destiny, and his entire being is geared towards happiness and subjective well-being.

Within the contemporary work setting, we find the experience of work articulated in terms of fun, self-expression and personal authenticity (Fleming, 2009) – concepts which are traditionally associated with the pursuit of happiness.

This relatively novel rhetoric, we argue, shifts the focus from the corporation (and its regulative impact) onto the individual (and his or her potential for self-realization). That is, we now go to work not because we necessarily have to but because the workplace is where we might realize ourselves. To illustrate this shift, we need not look any further than Google. With their creative work-politics they have fostered a culture that aims to create the illusion of, precisely, not being at work, but rather 'on some type of cruise or resort' (Vise and Malseed, 2005: 197). Here, employees are not press-ganged into already established roles; they are not forced to give up their idiosyncrasies. On the contrary, they enjoy the right to express who they truly are, warts and all.

The pursuit of happiness through work has gone relatively unchecked. Certainly, organization studies have explored and discussed the possible connection between happiness and productivity at great length. And although some studies have called this relation into question, few have challenged the ideological function of happiness at the workplace. Even philosophy and social theory, areas where we normally expect to find critical analyses, have generally maintained an affirmative perspective. For instance, in Bertrand Russell's classic book on the subject, *The Conquest of Happiness*, we read that engaging in meaningful work is an indisputable avenue for happiness (see also Svendsen, 2008). Our ambition for this chapter is not to oppose this possibility, but to critically examine the novel corporate vocabulary in which happiness holds a prominent place. To this end we turn to what is arguably one of the bleakest analyses available: Lacanian psychoanalysis. It should be stressed that while happiness frequently appears in the pages of Freud (especially in *Civilization and its Discontents*), Lacan remained suspiciously silent on the topic. In fact, happiness is mentioned only on a few occasions in his work, and then in a passing and remarkably dismissive manner. In this sense, it might seem counterintuitive to turn to Lacan. But we will argue that Lacan's violent rejection should also invite some interest. Why did Lacan conceive of happiness as a flawed ideal in the analytic practice? And how would this rejection set Lacanian psychoanalysis apart from other therapeutic practices, notably those that aim to improve the patient's well-being? Indeed, these questions have received little attention in academic debate. It is our wager that a systematic analysis of happiness in relation to the three registers – the imaginary, the symbolic and the real – offers a twofold contribution to the study of Lacan and organization. First, drawing on Lacan's critique of ego-psychology (particularly his rejection of the attempt to restore a strong and potent self), we are able to address the dangers that follow from promoting happiness, in their specificity. Second, teasing out these dangers allows us to level a distinctive critique against the burgeoning ideology of happiness, and how this ideology operates at the workplace.

We begin this chapter with a brief overview of the notion of happiness. After noting its conceptual and historical ambiguity, we explore some of the ways in which happiness is now employed, particularly within the realm of self-help and management literature. We then turn to psychoanalysis and the work of Lacan, where we explore some of the limitations of happiness. Although primarily an imaginary construction, we will argue that happiness might also be conceived from Lacan's other two registers, the symbolic and the real. In the final section we return to the workplace and the prevailing ideology of happiness. Here we will explore three responses to the injunction to happiness – all of which are complicit in a wider ideology of happiness and well-being. We conclude by tentatively pointing to a way forward, defending a subjectivity motivated by partial enjoyment rather than an illusory construction of unbounded happiness.

The Happy Organization

Surely, happiness has a dizzying conceptual history, as it can be conceived of in an almost infinite number of ways. While it is not our ambition to sketch out a conceptual history here (for this see McMahon, 2006), it is important to note that the modern conception of happiness, as an experience of subjective well being, is strongly at odds with earlier understandings, particularly those we find in Classical philosophy and Christianity. For instance, in his *Nicomachean Ethics*, Aristotle connects happiness (or more precisely its ancient Greek equivalent *eudaimonia*) with a virtuous endeavour for the supreme good (*telos*). It is an end rather than a means, always sought for its own sake. Thus, contrary to the contemporary view that happiness is primarily about *feeling* good, Aristotle stressed the importance of *being* good, which, in his view, is a tremendously difficult achievement, available only to the few. While the tragic writers directly restricted happiness to the sphere of the divine, Aristotle maintained that while happiness – like life – belongs to God, it is nevertheless within human reach. In short, happiness relates to what Aristotle calls 'the human good' – that is, the constant struggle to become, not God as such, but a man of virtue and nobility that is worthy of the Gods. So while it would be hubristic to believe that we can *fully* obtain happiness (since it belongs to the Gods), happiness is nonetheless achievable in a limited sense: as a reward in the strenuous struggle to become God-like.

Although Aristotle regarded happiness as an immensely difficult pursuit, restricted only to a select few, he still conceived it as an earthly practice. In Christianity, however, this conception of earthly happiness is replaced by transcendent happiness – one that is obtainable only in the afterlife. Unhappiness was seen as the natural condition of human life in the Middle Ages, a direct outcome of the Fall. And the pursuit of happiness was not so much an attempt to break free from this material condition, as it was the pursuit of an immortal freedom. The latter, in Augustine's words, 'is the happiest of life – who can deny it? – and in comparison with it our life on earth, however blessed with external prosperity or goods of soul and body, is utterly miserable' (1972: 19). Another, more corporeal, way to address the prevailing unhappiness of life was to increase its intensity in the attempt to become unified with the divine. These practices were often masochistic in nature, and presented a sensual and ecstatic picture of happiness, often bound up with pain and suffering, even 'proposing that happiness was not just impervious to pain, but its direct outcome and consequence' (McMahon, 2006: 95).

Following the Middle Ages, happiness undergoes many transformations, not least in the Renaissance. But it is suggested that it is not until the emergence of the Enlightenment that happiness becomes a concept that concerns man, rather than God (McMahon, 2006). Here we find the image of man made independent through reason; an agent who can now pursue happiness and obtain pleasure by his own accord, without being faithful to externally imposed rules. This accent on the freedom of the individual can be found in many places, but it is perhaps most emblematically expressed in the work of Jean-Jacques Rousseau, who famously saw the self as containing an authentic core beyond the labyrinths of the mind (see for example Guignon, 2004). For Rousseau, following one's inner core (as opposed to conceding to the dictates of modern life) was not just the path of the virtuous life, but also the recipe for a happy life. As such, one could argue that Rousseau also anticipated what we might call a modern conception of happiness where the self, by taking up an authentic and harmonious relation to the outside world, is able to experience a pleasurable sense of subjective well-being.

104

Having only briefly described some of the central moments of its conceptual history, we wish to underscore, once more, that this is by no means a comprehensive account. The ambition has merely been to indicate that what we now mean by happiness is something quite different from what was meant in Classical or Christian thought. But again, even these early accounts contained conflicting meanings.

> Since antiquity it [happiness] has been nothing but the history of its contradictory and successive meanings: in his time, St. Augustine already counted no less than 289 differing opinions on the subject, the eighteenth century devoted almost 50 treatises to it, and we are constantly projecting onto earlier periods or other cultures a conception and obsession that belongs solely to our own. (Bruckner, 2010: 3)

Notwithstanding the complex conceptual history attached to happiness, it should be worthwhile to develop a preliminary summary of the various meanings of happiness. A useful entry point can be found in Belliotti's book *Happiness is Overrated*, where he sets out four categories, stretching from purely subjective descriptions to those with a more objective orientation. The first category, *happiness-as-positive-state-of-mind*, makes the case that happiness is a subjective experience that cannot be proved otherwise: 'If I say I am happy, then I am happy'. This view is often associated with philosophers such as G. H. von Wright and Robin Barrow, and conceives of happiness as 'merely introspective and descriptive, an accurate self-report of a person's positive state of mind' (Belliotti, 2004: 69). The second category, *happiness-as-positive-self-appraisal*, claims that mere introspection is an insufficient yardstick for gauging happiness. What is needed in addition, its proponents maintain (e.g. Richard Kraut and Irwin Goldstein), are normative statements and personal evaluative standards. Thus, '[i]f I am deluded and merely think I am living up to my personal evaluative standards while I am not, then I wrongly think I am happy' (Belliotti, 2004: 73). The third category, *happiness-as-accurate-positive-self-appraisal*, goes one step further, claiming with philosophers such as John Kekes and Lyn McFall, that we need to connect happiness not just to our own subjective experiences (even if these experiences include self-appraisal and normative judgment) but also to 'objective standards grounded in shared community' (Belliotti, 2004: 76). This means that our self-evaluation must be based on 'a standard that is valuable' and 'rationally justified' (ibid.) The fourth category, *happiness-as-connection-to-objective-preexisting-good*, represents a more extreme form of objectivism, which links happiness to a greatest good. Philosophers associated with this tradition, such as John Finnis, Josef Pieper and Stephen Feron, argue that shared community and rational values are not objective enough since they ultimately rest on a contingent basis. With more than a nod to Aristotle, they claim that happiness must aim at something more permanent and supreme – namely, our *telos* (Belliotti, 2004: 79).

Happiness remains a central object for philosophical inquiry – as well as economic, political and social theory. Today, we can even find an inter-disciplinary academic journal, *The Journal of Happiness Studies*, exclusively dedicated to the subject. However, it is arguably in the domain of 'up-beat' self-help and management literature where happiness has attained the most central position. The central question here is not about the possibility (let al.one the desirability) of procuring happiness, but rather *how* we should go about attaining it. The typical answer to this question is that we should concentrate our attention, not on the depressing aspects of life, but on those aspects that make us happy. In his *Authentic Happiness*, Martin Seligman explains that psychology – or more specifically what he sees as the depressing version of psychology dating back to Freud – has been occupied with the negative side of human existence in exclusively examining mental illnesses. His wager is that this obsession with 'darkness' has had the undesirable effect of turning psychology into a cynical discipline that considerably undermines the quest for happiness. To restore the possibility of happiness, he continues, we should look into positive psychology (a common source within happiness studies) and its assumption that happiness is ultimately a choice for us to make. This point is mirrored in an endless array of books, from Barry Neil Kaufman's *Happiness is a Choice* to Sonja Lyubomirsky's *The How of Happiness*. These accounts embody a version of subjectivism akin to what Belliotti calls *happiness-as-positive-self-appraisal*. The overarching message seems to be something like the following: 'If I only persuade myself that I am happy, then I am happy; it is *my* choice, and no one can – and indeed shouldn't – call that joyful experience into question'. The general thrust, then, is that 'negative thoughts somehow produce negative outcomes, while positive thoughts realize themselves in the form of health, prosperity, and success' (Ehrenreich, 2009: 5).

Another salient feature of these texts is the importance they attribute to money and work. Typically, the presumed causal relation flows from happiness to money: 'If I am happy I will also be more prone to make money'. In this case, becoming rich is not seen as the ultimate goal, but rather as a pleasant side effect of becoming happy. A case in point here is the story told by business guru Ted Leonsis in his book *The Business of Happiness*. Already a self-made millionaire at the age of 27, he underwent a life-changing event when the plane he was on was forced to make an emergency landing. The poignant aspect of this event was the painful realization that, in spite of all success and money, he could have died unhappy that day. From this point on, he chose to pursue a path in which happiness was the ultimate goal. He began by making a list of things that would make him happier, and then turned that list into a life-plan. The result of his new life-strategy was not just that he became happier – which was his explicit intention – but also richer and more successful.

Another guru, Tony Hsieh, makes a similar point, though more specifically linked to corporations. His far-from-unique argument is that companies should focus their attention on cultivating a strong corporate culture based on the 'science of happiness'. The result, he claims, is that not only will the employees become more happy, but also more productive. It should be noted here that this relation – often tacitly accepted in most self-help books – has been the subject of much academic controversy, dating back at least to the early thirties (Hersey, 1932). Some empirical studies have demonstrated a positive relation between happiness and productivity (Oswald et al., 2010). Others however have pointed in the opposite direction. For instance, in a study of UK's four largest supermarket chains, Rhian Silvestro (2002) reveals an inverse relationship, where the most profitable stores turned out to be those with the least satisfied employees. Whether or not there is a correlation between happiness and productivity (and let us say that we have our doubts), it seems as if this thesis has acquired the dignity of an axiomatic fact in public imagination. In her revealing article 'Why do lay people believe that satisfaction and performance are correlated?', Cynthia D. Fisher claims that the happy/productive thesis continues to exercise a powerful hold over people, despite a lack of substantial empirical support. One of the tentative answers she presents is that people tend to feel happier and more satisfied when they are under the illusion of performing well at work. In this case, it is not that happiness leads to job performance, but rather, the opposite: the mere belief in one's work performance positively impacts one's happiness.

Perhaps a more fruitful way to understand why happiness has become a central focus for work is to examine its ideological flavour. Jean Baudrillard, in *The Consumer Society*, has argued that happiness is part of a bourgeois ideology insofar as it steers our attention away from social and political questions towards personal ones. It acts, he says, as a 'vehicle for the *egalitarian myth*'; but it is a myth that is 'removed from any collective "feast"' since it is ultimately 'based on individualistic principles' (1998: 49). Thus, the ideology of happiness employs egalitarian values as an alibi. As he explains:

> The revolution of well-being is heir, or executor of, the Bourgeois Revolution, or simply of any revolution which proclaims human equality as its principle without being able (or without wishing) *fundamentally* to bring it about. (Baudrillard, 1998: 50)

This lesser revolution wishes to bring about, Baudrillard continues, a form of socio-historical amnesia, which eliminates 'the objective, social and historical determinations of inequality' (ibid.). This means that the ideology of happiness has the ulterior aim of glossing over inequality and other depressing aspects of late-modern capitalism.

If we recall the message from positive psychology – that positive thoughts can overcome the most tragic situations – we can begin to see how Baudrillard's idea about an ideology of happiness functions in relation to work. If the focus is exclusively put on the individual and his quest for well-being, then organizations are not seen as perpetrators. As Barbara Ehrenreich (2009) notes in her critique of positive psychology, motivational exercises and team building are often used to divert the attention from the corporation to the individual, particularly in bad times with radical downsizing. Again, *happiness-as-the-possibility-for-each-and-everyone* has the effect of placing the responsibility upon the individual, thus reproducing the motto 'every man for himself' (cf. Mackay, 1988). In the present work-situation, defined among other things by a low degree of job-security, we find a vocabulary that is increasingly structured around the authentic, entrepreneurial and anti-authoritarian individual (Fleming, 2009). Here, the model employee is not the dutiful and loyal employee, who diligently acts in accordance with externally imposed norms and rules. On the contrary, today's model employee acts on his or her own accord, constantly seeking new opportunities and adventures (Sennett, 2006). We will come back to these issues in the final section, where we will ask how happiness can be understood in relation to a new vocabulary of authenticity and individuality. For now, however, it suffices to note that happiness, in spite of its complex conceptual history, has become a key ingredient in contemporary work-politics, functioning not only as a vehicle towards increased productivity, but also as a way to conceal socio-political conditions of work.

The Trouble with Happiness: Enter Lacan

One of the most pressing problems that happiness studies are forced to address is that of methodology. Given that a substantial part of these studies are quantitative in character, ultimately aiming to render happiness measurable, they face at least two mounting tasks. First they need to establish a working definition of happiness, and this is often built around a set of related emotions, such as well-being, life-satisfaction, etc. (see Fordyce, 1988). Second they need to craft a reliable and valid research method. The question of method has provoked much controversy, and continues to hold a central position in debates within the social sciences, at least in those academic domains where positivism reigns. However, these questions are only of secondary importance to this chapter. For our purposes here, it is enough to note that these studies – driven as they are by the desire to operationalize emotional categories – rely on the contestable assumption that happiness is a discrete and measurable concept of which we now know a great deal. In the words of Fordyce, '[m]uch is now known regarding the nature of happiness, the factors which contribute to it, and the attributes of happy individuals' (1988: 373).

Leaving aside the methodological problems iterated above, the question of happiness remains highly problematic. In what follows we wish to point to some of these problems from a psychoanalytic viewpoint, more specifically through the work of Lacan. We do this by following Lacan's three registers: the imaginary, the symbolic and the real.

Imaginary Happiness

With very few exceptions, happiness studies presuppose a coherent and transparent self, equipped with an introspective faculty. In studies aiming to measure happiness we often find the assumption that a self can accurately report on its current state of happiness. Self-help authors could be said to go even further; for, in addition to assuming that we can accurately measure the state of our present situation, they also assume that we are able to 'engineer' ourselves in intentional and desirable directions. Lyubomirsky (2008), for instance, claims that when biological and circumstantial aspects are set aside, we have at least 40 percent left of ourselves that we can change. Happiness, from this viewpoint, is not only something we can constantly monitor and get adequate information about (as if checking the balance of our bank account), but also something we can actively change through thinking more positively.

Psychoanalysis, however, is less optimistic about the prospects of valid self-evaluation, let al.one the prospects of self-engineering. In his 1917 text, *A Difficulty in the Path of Psycho-Analysis*, Freud famously states that '[t]he ego feels uneasy; it comes up against limits to its power in its own house, the mind' (1958: 141). Reflecting and further reinforcing the limitations of the ego set out by Freud, Lacan – from his early text 'The Mirror Stage' from the 1930s, all the way through to his final seminars in the early 1980s – argues that the autonomous ego belongs to the register of the imaginary. For Lacan, the imaginary feeds on and reproduces the illusory image of a sovereign and likeable self, what he (following Freud) calls the ideal ego. In childhood this ideal image takes shape through the identification with the mirror image, and allows the ego to delineate the inside and outside of its own being. As such, imaginary identification begins with a jubilant moment of recognition and satisfaction, as the child becomes aware of its own image. But what then happens is that the subject begins to develop a sense of alienation *vis-à-vis* the image ('This is not me!'). And this is a painful experience, marked by a nagging sense of frustration and narcissism. As Lacan put it, in *Seminar II*, 'the human being has a special relation with its own image – a relation of gap, of alienating tension' (Lacan, 1991b: 323). What happens ineluctably then is that the ego puts his identity outside himself, since it attempts to become an image, which, by definition, remains out of reach. To link this argument more directly to happiness, we could say that the specular image of happiness produced by our consciousness is one that will always be alien to us, because we could not construct an external image of happiness and at the same time be integral to it. As Giorgio Agamben puts it in a different context: 'Someone who is happy cannot know that he is; the subject of happiness is not a subject per se and does not obtain the form of a consciousness' (2007: 20).

The danger of alienation following the identification with a specular image has been demonstrated also in the workplace. Drawing on Lacan's early writing on the mirror stage, John Roberts (2005) has pointed out how employees who identify with particular ideal images become vulnerable to control. Like the child in front of the mirror, the employees first develop a sense of satisfaction when they recognize themselves in an idealized image, but then begin to experience a sense of alienation – realizing that they are trapped in an image which is not their own.

Lacan's early theory of the mirror stage constitutes a first articulation of identification. But perhaps more importantly, this theory can be read as a critique of what Lacan saw as an erroneous interpretation of Freud's work, an interpretation that would legitimize a practice directed towards strengthening the analysand's ego. According to Lacan, this was a futile practice, since privileging the patient's ideal self-image amounted to either an illusory narcissism or a sense of alienation – the felt disparity between one's actual self and their idealized image. Moreover, the apparent self-mastery of the strengthened ego was in fact dependent upon the analyst, and in order to maintain it, the subject begins to act and desire not of his own accord but as a prolongation of the analyst's desire. For this reason, Lacan warned that the analyst must always be attentive to the presence of transference, due to the consequences of bringing his or her own ego into play:

> And that is precisely what is so serious. Because we have [as analysts] effectively allowed ourselves – to bring our *ego* into play in the analysis. Since it is argued [by ego-psychologists] that one is trying to bring about the patient's readaptation to the real, one really ought to find out if it is the analyst's *ego* which offers the measure of the real. (Lacan, 1991a: 18)

Precisely because the analytic situation involves transference, the analyst must never promote the advancement of happiness and well-being, let al.one authenticity and independence (Nobus, 2000: 76). Not only are these promises delusional; they are also measured by the analyst's ego. The dream of obtaining happiness lies in the deceitful prospect of usurping the identity of someone else. And in the analytic session, this 'someone else' is typically the analyst, who is glorified as the person who both leads a happy life and holds the key to our own happiness.

Promoting the advancement of happiness outside the clinic has arguably a similar effect. As Barbara Ehrenreich (2009) points out in her critique of the growing happiness industry, it is impossible for the individual to live up to the demand of constant and unbounded happiness. Rather than producing the intended experience of harmony and satisfaction, it becomes a tyrannical imperative. Thus, when we are commanded to enjoy and be happy, we suddenly seem paralyzed, nervously looking around for some authority to help us out.

This paradox seems to lie at the heart of self-help literature. On the one hand we find the celebration and promotion of the autonomous ego ('I am myself the source of my happiness.'). On the other hand we find prescriptive guides to happiness ('If I only copy the life of a happy person then I, too, should become happy.'). In *Seminar II,* Lacan makes a rare comment about happiness, which points to this paradox:

> So when am I really me then? When I'm not happy, or when I'm happy because the others are happy? This relation of the subject's satisfaction with the satisfaction of the other – to be understood, please, in its most radical form – is always at issue where man is concerned. (1991b: 236)

The ambiguous relation between the self and others is precisely what the imaginary ego tries to deny – hence its narcissistic and delusional predisposition. In the next section, however, we will investigate this ambiguity from a symbolic viewpoint, which draws attention to the close interrelation between the subject and the Other, and how the idea of happiness is realized, or more accurately preserved, through displacement.

Symbolic Happiness

While the imaginary ego is trapped in the illusion of its own autonomy, the symbolic subject is defined by an insurmountable lack. As such the symbolic subject is conceived as an inherently split entity – though not split into two halves, as in the case of Aristophanes' classic description of the human being (from Plato's *Symposium*). Rather, it points to the fact that the subject is incapable of ever coinciding with itself. That is, the subject remains *ex-centric* in relation to itself insofar as the core of its self-identity remains blocked, located outside of its reach. This ex-centricity can be noted not just in analytic practice, but also in everyday situations. Consider the following example, borrowed from Alenka

Zupančič, which neatly describes the ambiguity inherent in the everyday-question: 'How's it going?'

> The greatness of this formula resides in the fact that the usual answer (*Very well, thank you*) leaves wonderfully intact the ambiguity of this question, its two possible 'subjects'. In order to see this, it is enough to shift the accent a little and to emphasize the 'it' in 'How's it going'. What I have in mind is that the full answer to the question *How's it going?* might very well be something like: It is going very well. But me – well, that's another matter. I'm tired, I'm depressed, my back aches… (2008: 63)

When responding to the question of our own happiness we can note a similar divide. Are we speaking about the imaginary constructions of ourselves (ideal ego) or about the symbolic place from where we are being observed (ego ideal)? The *you* in the question 'Are you happy?' does not point to a coherent subject, but a subject that is inherently split, unable of introspection and incapable of directly speaking about itself. As we have already pointed out, there is no such thing as an unambiguous *I* in Lacan's work. In the sentence 'I am happy' for example, *I* could refer to what Lacan calls the subject of the statement – that is, the narcissistic misrecognition of the ego. But it could also point to the subject of enunciation, which is 'an ambivalent speaker who says yes and no at the same time, who while saying one thing, insinuates another' (Fink, 1995: 40). What we have here are two different subjects: the imaginary ego (subject of statement), who would find the question of happiness unproblematic and likely respond in the affirmative; and the unconscious subject (subject of enunciation) who would either say yes and insinuate no, or say no and insinuate yes. To be more precise: while the former remains in the illusion of autonomy and self-potency, thus remaining cut off from the symbolic universe, the latter acquires its identity by way of sacrificing its phallus (or illusion of self-potency). Such a subject of enunciation exists in a situation defined by the constant presence and absence of the Other – that is, an indeterminable situation with regard to one's own self-identity.

There are many reasons as to why Lacan opposed the doctrines of ego-psychology, particularly their uncritical assumption of an autonomous ego. For instance, the assumption of a strong ego downplays the extent to which the subject is dependent on other human beings and their desires. Not only are we taught to perceive ourselves from the viewpoint of others; we are also prone to transfer our emotions to other people (and even objects). While the ego constructs its identity by distinguishing its sense of self from others, thus producing the illusion of possessing its own autonomy, the symbolic subject unwillingly sacrifices its core of self in order to acquire an identity.

Now, to begin elaborating what we wish to call 'symbolic happiness', we must first consider the significance of this sacrifice, which in Lacan's view is the sacrifice of one's *jouissance*, or, seen from a slightly different angle, the sacrifice of phallus (castration). One of the cornerstones of Lacan's work is that the subject first needs to sacrifice something in order to appear in the symbolic (as a signifier).

This indeterminable something that has to be forsaken can be described as the idea of 'full being' or the signified, which both represent the illusion of possessing one's own *jouissance* (or enjoying direct access to one's self-identity). Whereas the imaginary ego refuses to let go of this dream, thus remaining in a perpetual state of misrecognition and alienation, the symbolic subject has to surrender, distinctly cutting itself off from this dream – that is, forsaking the phallus and becoming castrated. But what we gain in return for this sacrifice is the signifier, which makes *jouissance* possible in another, more circuitous, way. As Lacan put it: 'Castration means that jouissance has to be refused in order to be attained on the inverse scale of the Law of desire' (2006: 700).

If, hypothetically, we were to assume a formula for happiness in Lacan's teaching it would be something like getting hold of an uncontaminated form of *jouissance*, and consequently receiving the undivided love and appreciation of the Other. But as we have already made clear, attaining this complete form of *jouissance* is, by definition, impossible. As Lacan put it in an oft-cited line: 'jouissance obtained is distinguished from the jouissance expected' (Lacan, 1999: 35). This means that the 'jouissance obtained' fails to meet the splendour that has been fantasmatically attributed to the 'jouissance expected'. To illustrate how *jouissance* appears first and foremost as an ultimate yet impossible fantasy of fullness, Bruce Fink distinguishes between what he calls *jouissance* before the letter and *jouissance* after the letter. The first-order *jouissance* can merely be presupposed as an imagined primordial state, prior to the subject's castration, where happiness and well-being would abound. Lacan is careful to point out that no such state has ever existed. There is no lost object that, if were we only able to find it again, would put an end to all our suffering and throw us into an existence of unlimited joy. As he put it:

> [S]ince it is a matter of finding it again, we might just as well characterize this object as a lost object. But although it is essentially a question of finding it again, the object indeed has never been lost. (Fink, 1998: 58)

Important to note in this regard is how the lost object, in spite of being purely imaginary, continues to haunt us, as an invented possibility. And this is what Fink means by *jouissance* after the letter, where *jouissance* persists in two incomplete forms: as a reminder (of a lost state), and a remainder (as a vague feeling of something still being there).

It is in this light that we could understand Lacan's notion of desire, not as a desire for what is possible, but a desire for that which is located beyond the Law. However, as desiring and castrated subjects, we are still dependent on the Law. This means that while we seek to retrieve the blocked object of our innermost desire, beyond the Law, we also need to maintain the function of the Law, simply because it is this instance that upholds the illusion of the lost object. That is to say, without the support from the Law, desire would lose its orientation and aim. This is also why Lacan, from *Seminar X* onwards, conceived of the Law and desire as two sides of the same coin, arguing that their circuitous relation should primarily be understood as an attempt to shield the subject from directly confronting its own *jouissance* – an experience which, as we will soon see, is defined by an unbearable anxiety rather than satisfaction.

Desire is anything but a straightforward enterprise. Far from the lessons found in some self-help books, where it is assumed that our desires can be translated into checklists, psychoanalysis maintains that desire is not a strictly private engagement. This is illustrated by Lacan's famous declaration that 'man's desire is the desire of the Other', which in its most straightforward interpretation implies that we desire what others desire, but can also mean that we desire to become the object of the Other's desire. Another specific feature of desire worth noting at this point is the fact that it is never geared towards a concrete empirical object, but always towards something else or something more. Drawing on structural linguistics, and especially the work of Roman Jakobson, Lacan illustrates this point by associating desire with metonymy, which implies that desire is defined by a continual deferral, perpetuating itself in a never-ending fashion.

From this perspective, the prospect for symbolic happiness is bleak. If desire lacks a specific object that could bring about its satisfaction – and if, in addition, a complete and pleasurable sense of *jouissance* can never be obtained – then wherein lies the possibility for happiness? The only possible answer would be that happiness, like *jouissance*, exists only as an impossible object, displaced onto the Other. More specifically, happiness could be displaced onto the Other, either as the 'good' Other, or the 'bad' Other. The 'good' Other is that of the primordial Other (from which the subject has involuntarily been torn away); and the 'bad' is that of the obscene Other (which is held as responsible for the subject's castration). These two faces of the Other are complementary: while the primordial Other is associated with an ultimate object of desire, the obscene Other is an instantiation of the Law, which renders the retrieval of our lost *jouissance* impossible.

We arrive here at two complementary versions of happiness, both of which are supported by fantasy. The first of these versions has a predominantly protective structure, aiming to fill in the lack of the Other, thus creating the illusion of unity and harmony. Happiness, in this particular sense of the word, amounts to little more than the experience of *status quo*, where the social nature of things appears as stable and predictable. It does not signify a direct experience of happiness, and does not actively challenge the Law. Rather, it produces a sense of mild contentment insofar as the symbolic Other functions largely according to our expectations. To illustrate this, we might here invoke Voltaire's Candide. After coming home from a long adventure, and suffering from bereavements and disappointments, Candide famously says: 'let us cultivate our gardens'. Symbolic happiness could be understood as that: as the desire to keep disturbing events at bay and to restore a harmonious and naturalized order of social reality.

The second version of symbolic happiness is even more obscure than the first, although they are closely related. Here, happiness appears first through its privation, as something that we have lost. Although it might seem that happiness is a strange word to use in this context, it is relevant in that a certain sense of satisfaction occurs. And this sense of satisfaction relieves the subject from pursuing his own happiness. All failures and miseries can then be blamed on external circumstances, as we can see for example in racist fantasies of an obscene Other, stealing our jobs and molesting our beloved ones. Both these versions of 'symbolic happiness' border on the imaginary insofar as they seek to avoid the unpleasant experience of castration as well as the unbridgeable lack of the Other. Thus, symbolic happiness is closely linked to imaginary happiness. But symbolic happiness is not exactly the thought that one is actually happy (as in the case of imaginary happiness), but more humbly, the disavowal of the unpleasant knowledge of one's own castration. As Lorenzo Chiesa has previously remarked:

> Indeed, happiness amounts to the stupidity of 'not wanting to know' the truth about symbolic castration, the inconsistency of the Other, and the actual lack of *jouissance*. (2007: 361)

Chiesa points to the impossible nature of happiness, and how the failure to acknowledge this impossibility is tantamount to a bovine contentment. It suggests that happiness is about denying castration, which by extension sustains the illusion of (at least vicariously) possessing the phallus. This also mirrors Lacan's curious statement from *Seminar XVII* that '[t]here is no happiness besides that of the phallus' (2007: 360). We should note that the phallus is associated with the register of the real. It is conceived as a partial object, which means that it is impossible to obtain, but at the same time impossible to evade.

Real Happiness

Together with the imaginary and the symbolic, the real also maps human experience in Lacan's work. But whereas the two former registers primarily seek to restore a sense of continuity, endowing the subject either with an image (the imaginary) or a place (the symbolic), the latter has a disruptive function, suspending all certainties. In one of the most common interpretations of the term, the real denotes an insurmountable impossibility, described by Lacan as 'that which resists symbolization absolutely' (1991a: 66). In this respect, the real cannot be integrated into the symbolic, and can only be represented in a distorted manner through the imaginary. Far from denoting a higher form of objectivity or a 'realist turn', the real has a monstrous element to it, in that it inexorably intrudes into the constitution of reality and introduces a radical indeterminacy at the level of being.

> The Real is not some authentic Beyond, constituting the truth of the reality. The Real is not the Beyond of reality, but its own blind spot or dysfunction – that is to say, the Real is the stumbling block on account of which reality does not fully coincide with itself. The Real is the intrinsic division of reality itself. (Zupančič, 2003: 80)

Already here we can see how 'real happiness' is a contradiction in terms. If happiness, as construed in self-help literature, relies on an experience of harmony and joy, then its relation to the real can only be that of denial or escape. Another way of understanding this antithetical relation between the real and happiness is to consider the relation between *jouissance* and Freud's thesis about the pleasure principle (see Freud, 1920; 1930). The original thesis that Freud presented was that man, in his pursuit to attain happiness, tried to avoid pain and gain pleasure – an idea close to the Epicureans. The happy man is the one who steers clear from pleasures that are too excessive, in order to avoid the inevitable backlash of suffering. Such an individual focuses on the small immediate things, such as taking care of the body, seeing friends and indulging in yoga, or other spiritual activities – anything that would keep suffering at bay.

Now, if the pleasure principle is characterized by its calculative and rational nature, where expected pleasure is always carefully weighed against anticipated sufferings, then *jouissance*, as it appears in the work of Lacan, represents an oppositional tendency, knowing no boundaries and certainly not paying any heed to instrumental calculations. In Lacan's words:

> One only has to begin with the pleasure principle, which is nothing other than the principle of least tension, of the minimum tension that needs to be maintained for life to subsist. This demonstrates that in itself *jouissance* overruns it, and that what the pleasure principle maintains is a limit with respect to *jouissance*. (2007: 46)

The *jouissance* that we find here is not the *jouissance* described in the previous section, which is displaced on the Other and manipulated into something merely pleasurable. Directly confronting our own *jouissance* is a terrifying experience of the real, akin to the experience of anxiety, where 'all words cease and all categories fail' (Lacan, 1991b: 164). In that sense, it is distinctly separated from pleasure as it 'goes beyond the limits imposed, under the term of pleasure, on the usual tension of life' (Lacan, 2007: 49).

Jouissance can now be understood in a different way, as opposed to pleasure. Rather than denoting the possibility of happiness, as we suggested in our previous discussion, it signifies the impossibility of happiness, not because it is itself an impossible object, but because it is an object that never ceases to haunt us, constantly appearing in undesired situations and guises.

> For Lacan, the trouble with *jouissance* is not only that it is unattainable, always already lost, that it forever eludes our grasp, but, even more, that *one can never get rid of it*, that its stain drags on forever. (Žižek, 1999: 291)

This reading of (late) Lacan indicates that the subject is not reducible to the subject of the signifier or the subject of desire, which is caught in the circuitous loop of Law and desire. Because the subject is also the subject of the drive, which, in Copjec's words, is 'riveted to *jouissance*' (2006: 102). Again, *jouissance* in this particular meaning of the word is dissociated from the presupposed *jouissance* of uncontaminated pleasure that the subject displaces onto the Other in order to shield itself. Rather, it appears involuntarily without the subject being able to pre-empt the monstrosity of the encounter. It arrives, like the real, without warning and without representation. This is not to say, however, that the real, *qua jouissance*, is experienced directly, in a positive form. What it means is simply that the real is experienced through a rupture in the symbolic, as an unsettling reminder of reality's *non-coincidence with itself* (Zupančič, 2008: 80).

We should now be in a position to understand Lacan's ambiguous formulation in *Seminar VII* concerning happiness, where he states that 'nothing is prepared for it, either in macrocosm or the microcosm' (1992: 13). Nothing is prepared for it, because we are ultimately incapable of confronting our own *jouissance*. *Jouissance* does not bring well-being or happiness, nor does it make our lives more harmonious. Rather, it inexorably intrudes into our lives, making itself present in the form of an indivisible remainder, leaving us in a state of terrifying anxiety. When Lacan says that there is no happiness besides the phallus, he points to the fact that happiness belongs to the register of the real:

while it is a foreclosed object, it nonetheless makes itself felt and refuses to leave us alone.

To summarize: happiness is primarily an imagined object that pertains to the ego. Here, happiness appears in the form of a bodily pleasure of unity, based on the false experience of autonomy. In addition to its imaginary appearance, happiness could also be conceived as a symbolic entity, but only in an indirect form, as something in the field of the Other – beyond the reach of the subject. Finally, real happiness should be regarded as a contradiction in terms, since the real pays no attention to the subject's well-being, but provokes an experience of anxiety that originates in the unbearable confrontation with *jouissance*.

Happiness as a Moral Obligation

With this in mind we may now return to what was briefly described in the earlier part of this chapter as an ideology of well-being. As it was described, this ideology draws on an egalitarian vocabulary while nevertheless propagating individual principles (Baudrillard, 1998; cf. also Bauman, 2008). As such, it is not so much the image of an egalitarian socialist community that is being promoted. Rather, it is the glorified image of the happy and healthy individual: he or she who strenuously engages in the business of self-expression and life-style entrepreneurship; who cultivates his or her own personal brand; and who perceives the new conditions of work not as a threat but as an opportunity for constant self-renewal (Sennett, 2006). This is the image promoted by self-help books, life-style magazines, and the preaching of management gurus – the prevailing image of the happy and self-empowered individual, driven by no other ethos than to be themselves. Indeed, as Renata Salecl describes, this individualized image of authenticity and well-being makes itself present at every turn in our daily lives:

> Traveling around London, during a single tube ride, I was reminded many times that I am totally free to make whatever I want out of my life: a university encouraged me with the advertising: 'Become what you want to be'. A beer company was addressing me with an ad: 'Be yourself'. A travel company was seducing me to take a new trip with the saying 'Life – book now', and on the cover of Cosmopolitan, I read: 'Become yourself – only a better one'. (2009: 157-8)

Whether the accent is placed on well-being, authenticity, happiness or health, these commandments rest on the same assumption: that we have now moved away from a society based on prohibition and entered a new economy of enjoyment (McGowan, 2004). Whereas previous generations enjoyed little choice with regard to their future occupation, often socially compelled to walk in the footsteps of their parents, we now experience an unprecedented opportunity to realize our own dreams (Csikszentmihalyi, 1997). And it is precisely this assumption that we find in the ideology of well-being: since we now enjoy the freedom of choice (even the choice to be happy) we have a moral obligation to face up to these demands.

This moral dimension of happiness can be found in Dennis Prager's book, *Happiness is a Serious Problem*, in which he makes the claim that happiness should not be perceived as a private business. Rather, we must consider how our moods influence the moods of others: if we go around the world with a depressive countenance and repeatedly complain about our lives, we inevitably affect those around us, contaminating our fellow beings with negative energy. Hence, happiness is a moral problem. A critical account of this argument can be found in Alenka Zupančič's *The Odd One In*, where she associates the moral dimension of happiness with an ideology of bio-morality, in which an unhappy (and unhealthy) person is perceived as morally flawed. What this moralization of happiness entails is the culpability of the subject, where the failure to be happy and healthy – not to mention the failure to be yourself – is seen as a corruption at the level of being.

From a psychoanalytic point of view, enjoyment cannot be produced on command, especially not when expressed by the superego. In his extensive studies on the effects of a society of commanded enjoyment, Todd McGowan writes that the 'problem with the society of commanded enjoyment – what constitutes its danger for us – is not the enjoyment that it unleashes, but the barrier that it proves to enjoyment' (2004: 192). When we face the demand to maximize our enjoyment, compelled to wear a happy smile, and morally obliged to make the most out of our situation, we do not automatically become happier and more fulfilled. Rather, we become oppressed, and stagger under the weight of these commands. Freedom of choice has the unintended result of morphing into what Salecl calls an 'anxiety of choice', leaving us perplexed with regard to what we might and might not do with our lives. This line of though is neatly expressed by Lacan in *Seminar II*, where he takes up the famous line from Dostoevsky's *The Brothers Karamazov*, in which the father says to his son, 'If God doesn't exist... then everything is permitted', to which Lacan comments, 'Quite evidently, a naive notion, for we analysts know full well that if God doesn't exist, then nothing at all is permitted any longer. Neurotics prove that to us every day' (1991b: 359). When God is dead, or the Other's demand has been eradicated, the individual is not free to choose what he desires, but is crushed under the weight of free choice (Salecl, 2010). In other words, when the externally imposed demand is no longer in place, we become compelled to invent it anew. But then it is no longer an external demand, against which we could shield ourselves, but one that has become integrated with our person and as such much more difficult to oppose.

How is this related to life in the workplace? In Peter Fleming's recent analysis of the 'just be yourself' ideology we find a vivid description of the post-modern firm and its prevailing work-politics. Distancing themselves from the strong cultural programs found in the large corporations of the 1980s and 1990s, these firms draw on a seductive vocabulary of individual emancipation, anti-corporate sentiment and the freedom 'to be yourself'. Here, authenticity, happiness, difference and conspicuous self-expression are key. Together, they constitute the central features of the young progressive employee, who, in expression and behavior, is closer to a radicalized entrepreneur wearing Che Guevara t-shirts than an old and boring clerk wearing suits. To attract this generation of underground slacker cool, the post-modern firm now offers a new vocabulary, shot through with liberalist catchwords:

> Unlike earlier generations of workers, they are less willing to forget their countercultural attitudes in the workplace. Overlaying this disposition are ideological changes in the organizational form marked by the transposition of liberalist values into the sphere of work: life, liberty, and happiness ought to be found at work too and not only at the weekend or when one finally escapes into the leisure industry. (Fleming, 2009: 80-1)

Of course there are a number of limitations to this up-beat management babble. For sure, the radical who is not complicit in the wider ideology (working long hours to produce what he or she is actually supposed to) is kicked out. In this respect, the expressionistic culture of 'just be yourself' must 'rest upon a structural political economy of the firm for it to be congruent with the accumulation process' (Fleming, 2009: 89). Another related effect of this rhetoric is that the employee, contrary to experiencing a greater sense of satisfaction and freedom, ends up being more alienated, caught in a disciplinary process that is far more totalizing (insofar as it hegemonizes more aspects of life) than more traditional forms of control.

Along similar lines, Žižek has argued that postmodern subjectivity – as for example those produced in corporations like Google, where the employees are 'under the injunction to be what they are' (1999: 368) – faces an even stronger superego pressure than that of Weber's Protestant work ethic. Again, the breakdown of paternal authority does not signal a new era of freedom. Instead, Žižek argues, it has two facets: 'On the one hand, symbolic prohibitive norms are increasingly replaced by imaginary ideals (of social success, of bodily fitness…); on the other, the lack of symbolic prohibition is supplemented by the re-emergence of ferocious superego figures' (1999: 368).

Against this background we can begin to see what we mean by the unbearable weight of happiness in the context of work. Facing up to the constant demand of self-realization and the pursuit of happiness is, we ague, more complicated and indeed more counterintuitive than the self-help industry would admit. Rather than opening up new avenues for obtaining pleasure, the ideology of happiness produces an anxious subjectivity. Whether we steadfastly hold on to the ideal of happiness or look upon it with ridicule and contempt, it has become a defining feature of present-day work-politics. But how does this ideology operate? What are the viable responses to the injunction of happiness? And wherein lies the possibility of resistance? With no intention to be exhaustive, we can see at least three responses – all of which are complicit with the ideology of happiness, and which might be described as different versions of what Simon Critchley has called passive nihilism (see Critchley, 2007).

The first response is that of fetishizing the image. Here, the subject takes the ideology of happiness at face value, identifying with the illusory image of autonomy and self-realization. The new condition of work is largely seen as an endless source of fascinating adventures, providing the opportunity for a life defined by unlimited freedom, fun and happiness. Although this message can be found literally everywhere, it is most conspicuously expressed in the growing literature on personal branding and life management. In the recent work of Chris Guillebeau (2010), one of the more prominent preachers of personal branding, we find recipes for how to lead an exciting life, filled with adventurous travels, unconventional work and other stimulating life-enriching activities. Portraying himself as a fighter of *status quo*, he wishes to teach the art of non-conformity, according to which we can lead a flourishing life outside the repressive functions of society. The prospect of happiness resides in pursuing your own projects, rebelling against obsolete authorities and reaping the benefits from today's unpredictable yet challenging environment. Briefly recalling the four dimensions of happiness offered by Belliotti, we might say that the happiness found in personal branding is a paradoxical mix between two extremes: the purely subjective (*happiness-as-positive-state-of-mind*) and the purely objective (*happiness-as-connection-to-objective-preexisting-good*). Given the accent placed on individuality (and the individual's alleged struggle against repressive social orders), happiness is construed as an inherently subjective state, which can only be directly experienced by each individual self. But at the same time happiness is supposedly something we can learn from others (personal branding gurus, for instance). It is by imitating the happy life of other people that we can make ourselves happy – that is to say, by elevating externally promoted ideals and morphing them into our own *telos* we are assumed to become happy. Indeed, if we usurp the life of the successful bobo (bourgeois bohemian) or the rebellious gyp-set (Gypsy Jet-set), we too can join the club of the happy non-conformists. It should come as no surprise that this version of happiness is seen as purely imaginary from a psychoanalytic viewpoint. As we already know, Lacan's claim is that the imaginary ego, which has surrendered to the ideology of happiness and believes itself to be in possession of the phallus, is ultimately caught in its own mirror image, defined by misrecognition and a lingering sense of alienation. The more the ego engages in the doctrine of self-management and personal branding, the more alienated and frustrated it will become – tortured by the inexorable experience of being outside itself. Moreover, the more the ego pursues the project of 'radicality' (refusing to conform to social order), the more it becomes ensnared and complicit in the prevailing ideology of capitalist accumulation – which, quite evidently, *is* the dominant social world order (McGowan, 2004: 193).

The second response to the ideology of happiness is what Adorno (1973) has called a cult of inwardness (see also Fleming, 2009). Unlike the buoyant optimism of the first response, we find here a deep-seated worry about late capitalism and its impact on everyday life, from the increased speed of life to the mounting pressure at the workplace. The message goes something like the following: To pursue happiness, we need first to shield ourselves from the pressing artificiality of modern life. We should not listen to the externally imposed demands we constantly face. Instead we should look inside ourselves; find the unchanging core of our inner being; and organize our lives accordingly. Only then can we become truly happy. From Dr. Phil and Deepak Chopra to Mihaly Csikszentmihalyi we find this notion of inward happiness. It is a bodily notion of happiness, where our selves seem to be one with the world around us, and where our entire organism experiences a pleasurable sense of wholeness, what Csikszentmihalyi calls *flow*:

> Imagine, for instance, that you are skiing down a slope and your full attention is focused on the movement of the body, the position of the skis, the air whistling past your face, and the snow shrouded trees running by. There is no room in your awareness for conflicts or contradictions; you know that a distracting thought or emotion might get you buried facedown in the snow: And who wants to get distracted? The run is so perfect that all you want is for it to last forever, to immerse yourself completely in the experience. (Csikszentmihalyi, 1997: 28-29)

The same experience of flow is to be sought also at work. Ideally, we should engage in the sort of purposeful work that directly resonates with our inner core of being. The classical distinction between work and non-work is dismantled, as work is now seen as an extension of our authentic selves. From a Lacanian viewpoint this is the classic example of a protective fantasy, where the subject is not necessarily convincing himself of possessing the phallus, but where all conflicts and contradictions arising from the experience of a lacking Other are glossed over. Happiness is here closely associated with maintaining a sense of unity and harmony, which is meant to produce a bodily sense of pleasure. In this sense, it is a purely subjective notion of happiness, where the appraisal of others is ignored. This cult of inwardness is part and parcel of the ideology of happiness. It embraces the individualistic focus of the ideology, while at the same time withdrawing from actively engaging with it. In this particular respect, the cult of inwardness produces the symptom that Critchley has described: '[r]ather than acting in the world and trying to transform it... [the passive nihilist] simply focuses on himself and his particular pleasures and projects for perfecting himself' (Critchley, 2007: 4).

The final response is cynicism – a subjective position that has been explored at great length elsewhere (Žižek, 1989; Sloterdijk, 1988; Fleming and Spicer, 2003). For the cynic, the present situation is not just difficult and somewhat artificial, but a fraudulent spectacle. The imagery of the autonomous life-style entrepreneur is looked upon with contempt, and the cult of inwardness is simply written off as delusional new-age sophistry. At the workplace the cynics silently laugh at what they see as preposterous group exercises and phony management gibber.

If the two previous responses have an ambivalent relation to the Other, manifested either by internalizing its demand or filling in its lack, the cynic believes himself to have complete knowledge of the Other. In short, they know that the Other sucks, and that it won't provide them with happiness. However, the cynics' mockery does not so much undermine the ideology of happiness as reproduce it. For even though they take pains to exhibit their disdain, they nevertheless act according to the rules. Thus, their knowledge is merely theoretical, and never put to work. As McGowan explains: 'All of the cynic's knowledge does not help the cynic escape the determinations of the symbolic order: the cynic remains a perfectly obedient and docile subject' (2004: 121). Which is also why Sloterdijk (1988), in his treatise on the subject, calls cynicism an *enlightened false consciousness*.

It is perhaps difficult to see how happiness comes to the cynic. But as we described in the previous section of this chapter, we might think of the paranoid fantasy of a happiness stolen from us by an intruding Other. This is obviously not a direct form of happiness, as in the case of the bodily happiness previously described. Instead it is a happiness based on (delusional) knowledge and certainty; more specifically the certainty that happiness will not disruptively enter into our lives. Recalling Lacan's curious statement that 'there is nothing prepared for happiness', we might say that the cynic has internalized this message, blocking any possibility of directly confronting their own *jouissance*. At this point we can also see some affinities with both the previous positions. Similar to those cultivating their personal brands, the cynic perceives himself as acting beyond social structures, while at the same time remaining true to its ideological content. Like those searching for an authentic experience of inward happiness, the cynic has no ambition to act or transform the world, but prefers to observe it from a safe distance. In short, the cynic accepts abstract knowledge instead of seeking real change.

None of these responses are particularly hopeful, at least not from an ethico-political point of view. Not only do they maintain the ideological basis of happiness; they also seem to produce subjectivities that are incapable of action. Indeed, merely declaring one's own happiness is by no means producing the condition for transformative action. As Beckett's character Estragon says in *Waiting for Godot*, after declaring both himself and his friend Vladimir happy, 'What do we do now, now that we are happy?' This is a an aspect of happiness that is rarely addressed in the field of self-help, namely what the acquisition of happiness produces beyond the mere experience of subjective well-being, and the ability to be 'nice' to our fellow beings. Indeed, the pursuit of happiness, as expressed in this literature, steers clear of the call for political or ethical engagement. On the contrary, it celebrates an inward turn, whereby the obsession with subjective well-being, and the concomitant desire to improve oneself, becomes the sole object of interest, thus glossing over the ethical demand to engage with and ultimately affect the world.

By way of conclusion, we wish to briefly point to a way forward, beyond the pursuit of happiness. Another possible model can be conceived of on the basis of what Lacan (1998) calls a 'subjectivity of the drive', or a 'headless subjectivization'. Contrary to the subject of desire, the subject of the drive transcends the circular movement of desire and Law. The subject of the drive does not merely escape desire, but insists on desire to the point where the dialectic of Law and desire breaks down. Here, a partial *jouissance* rather than any complete and pleasurable form of *jouissance*, becomes the motivation for ethical action. This implies that society of enjoyment, apart from tyrannizing the subject (as we have described in this chapter), might also provide novel avenues for what we could perhaps call an ethical enjoyment:

127

> [T]he emergence of the society of enjoyment produces a window of opportunity: we might obey the command to enjoy in a way that frees us from its superegoic compulsion and opens enjoyment as such. We can only do so if we reject the image of completion – and of complete enjoyment – that this command proffers. As long as we pursue and defend an image of total enjoyment, we remain within the domain of the superego. Accepting the partiality of enjoyment is the path to freedom that the contemporary world offers us. (McGowan, 2004: 196)

An enjoyment of not-All would retain the motivation for political transformation, while at the same time abandoning any utopian projects of completion. It would demand the subject confront his own finitude and limitations, rather than seek self-perfection. By extension, it would demand that the subject acknowledge the irreducible contingency underlying social relations, the radical alterity of the Other, and the ontological dimension of the political. Such a program would stress the ethical dimension of subjectivity, where the subject could work to reactivate the historical contingency of socio-political situations and open up new spaces for political articulation.

The ethico-political dimension of Lacan's work has been extensively discussed elsewhere and provides, in our view, a fruitful alternative to thinking about politics. It remains relatively unclear, however, how these thoughts would operate in the context of work and organizations. There is insufficient space to discuss these issues here, but let us reemphasize that happiness, particularly in the ideological form found in management doctrines, is a dangerous ideal that effectively sutures over the inconsistencies of late-capitalist ideology. If we think of the heroes in Lacan's work – from Antigone, to Sygne de Coufontaine to James Joyce – each was fundamentally motivated by the task of radically suspending the basic co-ordinates of the situation in which they found themselves. Could these structural models for ethical subjectivity perhaps be thought within the context of work? And how, in that case, could they undermine some of the more bizarre (and oppressive) permutations of today's work-politics (such as commanded enjoyment and compulsory fun)? These are questions we will leave unanswered here, but which might be explored in future studies aiming to critically investigate the relation between ethical engagement and work.

References

Adorno, T. (1973) *The Jargon of Authenticity*, trans. K. Tarnowski and F. will. Evanston: Northwestern University Press.

Agamben, G. (2007) *Profanations*, trans. J. Fort. New York: Zone Books.

Aristotle (2003) *The Nichomachean Ethics*, trans. J. A. K. Thompson. London: Penguin Classics.

Augustine, St. (1972) *The City of God*, trans. H. Bettenson. Harmondsworth: Penguin.

Baudrillard, J. (1998) *The Consumer Society: Myths and Structures*, trans. C. Turner. London: Sage.

Bauman, Z. (2008) 'Happiness in a society of individuals', *Soundings*, 38: 19-29.

Belliotti, R. (2004) *Happiness is Overrated*. Lanham: Rowman and Littlefield.

Boltanski, L. and E. Chiapello (2005) *The New Spirit Of Capitalism*, trans. G. Elliott. London: Verso.

Bruckner, P. (2010) *Perpetual Euphoria: On the Duty to Be Happy*. Princeton: Princeton University Press.

Chiesa, L. (2007) *Subjectivity and Otherness: A Philosophical Reading of Lacan*. Boston: MIT Press.

Copjec, J (2006) 'May '68, the emotional month', in S. Žižek (ed.) *Lacan: The Silent Partners*. New York: Verso.

Critchley, S. (2007) *Infinitely Demanding: Ethics of Commitment, Politics of Resistance*. New York: Verso.

Csikszentmihalyi, M. (1997) *Finding Flow: The Psychology of Engagement with Everyday Life*. New York: BasicBooks.

Ehrenreich, B. (2009) *Smile or Die: How Positive Thinking Fooled America and the World*. London: Granta.

Fink, B. (1995) *The Lacanian Subject*. Princeton, NJ: Princeton University Press.

Fisher, C. D. (2003) 'Why do lay people believe that satisfaction and performance are correlated? Possible sources of a commonsense theory', *Journal of Organizational Behavior*, 24(6): 753-777.

Fleming, P. (2009) *Authenticity and the Cultural Politics of Work*. Oxford: Oxford University Press.

Fleming, P. and A. Spicer (2003) 'Working at a cynical distance: implications for subjectivity, power and resistance', *Organization*, 10(1): 157-179.

Fordyce, M. A. (1988) 'A review of research on happiness measures: a sixty second index of happiness and mental health', *Social Indicators Research*, 20: 355-81.

Freud, S. (1917) *A Difficulty in the Path of Psycho-Analysis. The Standard Edition of the Complete Psychological Works of Sigmund Freud, Volume XVII (1917-1919)*. London: Penguin.

Freud, S. (1920) *Beyond the Pleasure Principle. The Standard Edition of the Complete Psychological Works of Sigmund Freud, Volume XVIII (1920-1922)*. London: Penguin.

Freud, S. (1930) *Civilization and its Discontents. The Standard Edition of the Complete Psychological Works of Sigmund Freud, Volume XXI (1927-1931)*. London: Penguin.

Guignon, C. (2004) *On Being Authentic*. London: Routledge.

Guillebeau, C. (2010) *The Art of Non-Conformity*. Berkeley: Berkeley Trade.

Hersey, R. B. (1932) *Workers' Emotions in Shop and Home: A Study of Individual Workers from the Psychological and Physiological Standpoint*. Philadelphia: University of Pennsylvania Press.

Kaufman, N. B. (1994) *Happiness is a Choice*. New York: Fawcett Columbine.

Lacan, J. (1962-1963) *Anxiety: The Seminar of Jacques Lacan, Book X, 1962-1963*, trans. C. Gallagher. Unpublished.

Lacan, J. (1991a) *Freud's Papers on Technique: The Seminar of Jacques Lacan, Book I, 1953-1954*, trans. J. Forrester. New York: Norton.

Lacan, J. (1991b) *The Ego in Freud's Theory and in the Technique of Psychoanalysis: The Seminar of Jacques Lacan, Book II, 1954-1955*, trans. S. Tomaselli. New York: Norton.

Lacan, J. (1992) *The Ethics of Psychoanalysis: The Seminar of Jacques Lacan, Book VII, 1959-60*, trans. D. Porter. London: Routledge.

Lacan, J. (1998) *The Four Fundamental Concepts of Psychoanalysis: The Seminar of Jacques Lacan, Book XI*, trans. A. Sheridian. New York: W. W. Norton.

Lacan, J. (1999) *On Feminine Sexuality, the Limits of Love and Knowledge: The Seminar of Jacques Lacan, Book XX, 1972-73*, trans. B. Fink. New York: Norton.

Lacan, J. (2006) *Écrits*, trans. B. Fink. New York: Norton.

Lacan, J. (2007) *The Other Side of Psychoanalysis: The Seminar of Jacques Lacan, Book XVII, 1969-70*, trans. R. Grigg. New York: Norton.

Leonsis, T. (2010) *The Business of Happiness: 6 Secrets to Extraordinary Success in Life and Work*. Washington, D.C.: Regnery.

Lyubomirsky, S. (2008) *The How of Happiness*. New York: Penguin.

Mackay, H. B. (1988) *Swim With the Sharks Without Being Eaten Alive*. New York: Ballantine Books.

McGowan, T. (2004) *The End of Dissatisfaction: Jacques Lacan and the Emerging Soceity of Enjoyment*. Albany, NY: SUNY Press.

McMahon, D. M. (2006) *Happiness: A History*. New York: Atlantic Monthly.

Nobus, D. (2000) *Jacques Lacan and the Freudian Practice of Psychoanalysis*. London: Routledge.

Oswald, A. J., E. Proto, and D. Sgroi (2008) 'Happiness and productivity', Working Paper, Warwick Economic Research Papers No. 882.

Prager, D. (1995) *Happiness is a Serious Problem: A Human Nature Repair Manual*. New York: Reagan Books.

Roberts, J. (2005) 'The power of the Imaginary in disciplinary processes', *Organization*, 12(5): 619-649.

Russel, B. (1996) *The Conquest of Happiness*. New York: Norton.

Salecl, R. (2009) 'Society of choice', *Differences*, 20(1): 157-180.

Salecl, R. (2010) *Choice*. London: Profile Books.

Seligman, M. (2002) *Authentic Happiness: Using the New Positive Psychology to Realize Your Potential for Lasting Fulfilment*, New York: Free Press.

Sennett, R. (2006) *The Culture of the New Capitalism*. New Haven, CT: Yale University Press.

Silvestro, R. (2002) 'Dispelling the modern myth: employee satisfaction and loyalty drive service profitability', *International Journal of Operations and Production Management*, 22 (1): 30-49.

Sloterdijk, P. (1988) *The Critique of Cynical Reason*, trans. M. Eldred. Minneapolis, MN: University of Minnesota Press.

Svendsen, L. (2008) *Work*. Stocksfield: Acumen.

Vise, D. A. and M. Malseed (2005) *The Google Story: Inside the Hottest Business, Media and Technology Success of our Time*. London: Pan MacMillan.

Voltaire, F. (2003) *Candide*, trans. H. Morley. New York: Barnes and Noble Classics.

Weber, M. (2001) *The Protestant Ethic and 'The Spirit of Capitalism'*, trans. A. Giddens and T. Parsons. New York: Routledge Classics.

Žižek, S. (1989) *The Sublime Object of Ideology*. London: Verso.

Žižek, S. (1999) *The Ticklish Subject: The Absent Centre of Political Ontology*. London: Verso.

Zupančič, A. (2003) *The Shortest Shadow: Nietzsche's Philosophy of the Two*. Boston: MIT Press.

Zupančič, A. (2008) *The Odd One In: On Comedy*. Boston: MIT Press.

5

For the Love of the Organization

André Spicer and Carl Cederström

Buzzing computers accompanied by low groans of worn-out white-collar workers and the relentless sound of customised ring-tones: the office would seem to offer the worst possible soundtrack for a romantic scene. Not surprisingly, classical accounts of the modern workplace often banish emotions like love. As we all know, the founding fathers of organization theory were careful to draw the line between love and work. For instance, Max Weber (1947) thought that love could endanger the rule of impartial bureaucracy in the workplace. The whole history of organization studies after Weber has instead largely focused upon the rational and cognitive aspects of organizational life in that setting (Fineman, 2000). A search of any major journal or textbook in the field of organization studies will yield little on the theme of love. If one were to give a talk on the topic at an academic conference, people would likely produce an embarrassed smile and quietly return to their fantasies about the upcoming luncheon. The more serious minded scholar might consider toying with the themes of emotion, attachment, or perhaps even desire. However, academics working with organization theory most often relegate love to their private calamities. This silence about love has come at a great cost – that of ignoring the battered hearts of those who work in such fundamental institutions. As passions and attachments are what ignite and motivate people in the workplace, being blind to these influences is extremely problematic.

Despite our stopped ears, love continues to call out within the wastelands of the post-modern workplace. In a recent investigation into the coldness of modern life, Eva Illouz (2005) has argued that contemporary societies are characterised by a curious movement: our private and intimate life – which once served as a welcomed escape from the calculations of modernity – has become increasingly rationalised. This means that our families and personal relationships are no longer the seat of love, intimacy, and emotion, but rather a sphere for trade, exchange, and emotional management (see also Tyler and Hancok, 2009; Zelizer, 2000). Just consider, for example, the rise of internet dating services that create a brutal spot market for romantic liaisons; or, on the other hand, the plethora of emotional techniques that are now offered for managing your children. And of course, our relationship with ourselves – that is, our own intimate life – has become one of the primary targets for self-management techniques. As our private lives have become emotional deserts, we have been driven to search for a place where we can experience authentic feelings and passions. For many people, this desperate search for an emotional space has led them to their own workplaces. After all, many people now spend more of their time at work than at home. It is no coincidence then that the workplace has begun to offer itself up as a place where employees can experience many of the emotions that are usually limited to the private sphere. Many workplaces now positively encourage experimentation with the following: sexuality (Fleming, 2005), exploration of personal authenticity (Fleming, 2009), experiences of fun and jocularity (Fleming and Sturdy, 2008), expressions of being 'hip' and 'cool' (Ross, 2004), new articulations of one's identity (Sveningsson and Alvesson, 2003), and individual connections (Boltanski and Chiapello, 2005). This reminds us that today's workplace does not just demand a technocratic regulation of actual activities – they also demand a more profound and deeper regulation of our very sense of self (Alvesson and Willmott, 2002; Ekmann, 2010). The result is that the workplace has now become the space where we are allowed to 'authentically' express ourselves (Fleming, 2009).

Given the increasing 'emotionalisation' of the workplace, it is not surprising that love, to an increasing degree, is played out in this context. Of course we know that the workplace is a hotbed of affairs and romantic liaisons (Thompson and Ackroyd, 1999). In some ways, a romantic affair might function as a dangerous transgression that clearly cuts against the grain of workplace rules. On the other hand, they can also be seen as one of our last desperate attempts to find something genuine in the increasingly meaningless world of office cubicles. However, we can ask if love is the only real 'event' or 'act' through which we redeem the disillusion of our pathetic worn-out selves and experience a re-birth or more genuine way of life?

Putting these points of speculation aside, the increased presence of romance in the workplace is paralleled by a distinct rise in the expectation by employers that employees should 'love their company'. Indeed it has been widely noted that many firms have sought to engender emotional commitment on the part of employees (e.g. Barley and Kunda, 1992). A number of studies exploring knowledge-intensive firms have pointed out how these organizations seek to engender a deep commitment from employees through the development of a corporate culture. For instance, Catherine Casey (1995) looks at how an electronics firm encouraged employees to experience the same kinds of intimacy and attachment to the company that they might have previously experienced towards their family.

The results may seem ideal for management gurus: employees who are prepared to work endless hours and gleefully spout the company line. However, some of the more unsavoury effects of such attachments are neglected in this perspective. For instance, Casey found that some employees became obsessional and engaged in all sorts of strange acts, in order to protect their special relationship with their love object (that is, their work). Others have pointed out that the deep emotional bond encouraged by corporate culture has disastrous consequences for individuals if they are 'abandoned' by the beloved organization during downsizing (Sennett, 2006). In these cases, workers loose more than their main source of sustenance and income; they lose their most precious relationship. For some individuals, this can be a deadly blow from which they cannot recover. This demand for commitment, along with the consistent threat of withdrawal of that commitment, often means employees become increasingly plagued by a sense of anxiety (Salecl, 2004). Others still have pointed out that talk about love and long-term commitment to the firm are increasingly being replaced by 'one-night stands' and loose patterns of attachment among many employees (Barley and Van Maanen, 1999).

Given the importance of encouraging love in contemporary management, it is indeed surprising that so little has been written on the subject. In this chapter, we would like to stop skirting around the subject and go directly to the question of love. In particular, we would like to ask how we might understand love? How does this love work?

What is specific about the kind of love that companies seek to engender? Does it create actors who are tied to the organization by their heartstrings? Is love a kind of violent interruption in rational modern organizations or is it simply a fact of life to be carefully inspected empirically and lived through without the elated sense of worth we usually experience?

In order to address these questions, we begin by looking at a handful of existing accounts of love. We then seek to develop what we see as the most promising of these accounts – namely the work of Jacques Lacan. We take the following Lacanian slogan as our starting point: 'I love you, but because inexplicably I love in you something more than you – *objet petit a* – I mutilate you' (Lacan, 1998: 268). This recalls one of the crucial questions involved in taking love to heart: namely, how does the lover relate to his or her love object. Since, in Lacan's view, there is no symmetry between the lover and the beloved, nor between the sexes, there can be 'no such thing as a sexual relationship' (1999: 34). This provocative statement suggests that we need to look for strategies in order to overcome this impasse. We suggest that there are at least four ways in which we might do this: through *obsessional* love, indicating how the lover identifies with a particular ideal or rule which must not be transgressed; *hysterical* love, where the subject identifies with the love object; *platonic* love, where the subject de-sublimates the love object in order to enjoy it in an impersonal and calculative manner; and *cynical* love, where the lover not just distances him or herself from the love object but disavows it. We explore how each of these forms of love may be at work within the workplace through a consideration of the sitcom *The Office*. In particular we consider the relationship of four characters to their workplace, in a forlorn paper company in Slough, England. By theoretically exploring and empirically illustrating the multifaceted nature of love, we argue that attentiveness to the complex and paradoxical character of love opens up novel avenues for understanding the importance of emotions in relation to control and resistance. In particular, it provides a sense of how we can 'fall for our work' and how we deal with our increasingly intense attachments to the places in which we work.

Theorizing Love

Love is a central category in Western culture. We often justify our own acts with appeals to love (for instance the extreme lengths that parents will go to for their children). Our life histories are often marked by the vital moments associated with falling in love, loosing love, or coping with it. Advertising agents frequently appeal to love in order to sell everything from breakfast cereal to vacations. It seems that every second song on pop radio stations is about love. We voraciously consume films that show people falling in and out of love. If we just cast our mind across the history of Western literature we recognise that many of the great stories have been driven forward by love: Antigone's love for her brother; Romeo and Juliet's adolescent love; Werther's broken love for the inaccessible lost Charlotte. In each of these cases, we notice that love is the force driving characters forward, often into crazed and destructive acts. It is something that overwhelms them and eventually leads to their undoing. But at its most elemental, the love we notice in each of these representations is an intense attachment – typically between one person and their beloved. However, it can also involve an intense attachment to a thing (such as a beautiful painting) or to an idea (freedom, one's country, the Truth).

The experience of Goethe's sorrowful Werther is painfully familiar: readers often feel as if they have heard the story a thousand times before. Indeed, some evolutionary theorists would argue that love is an emotional reaction that helps to ensure the survival of our selfish genes (e.g. Buss, 1994). By loving our offspring, we are driven to invest additional effort and energy in their upbringing. By loving our partner, we protect them, nourish them and bind them to us. This ensures that they will help to nurture fit offspring who will carry our selfish genes forward in the great Darwinian struggle for survival. However, any serious investigation of love will often quickly chance upon the fact that we use the word love to describe many relationships, ranging from experiences ('I love listening to the Opera, *Le Nozzi de Figaro*'), to objects ('I love monster trucks'), to people ('I love Valeria'). It would only be the most blinkered evolutionary theorist who would seek to explain our love affairs with objects, experiences and ideas as being strictly driven by the desire to reproduce our own sad selves. Even if we focus on the love we feel for other people, we notice that many of these relationships of love are not about procreation at all. Rather, they seem to be about something else altogether.

Perhaps the first meaningful step in theorizing love involves thinking about its different forms of appearance. Classical accounts of love usually make a distinction between three forms of love: *eros, agape,* and *philia* (see: Soble, 1998). Typically *eros* is thought of as a passionate response to a desired object such as a particularly attractive person. In contrast, *agape* involves a kind of love that is completely independent of the qualities of the loved object and may in fact create those very qualities that are adored in that object (for instance, the love of God is often described in terms of *agape*). Finally, *philia* involves a sense of friendship or attachment towards members of a group, family, or even a city.

However, many philosophers and cultural theorists have pointed out that although love may seem like a universal experience, what it means to us has profoundly changed throughout history (e.g. Singer, 1984a; 1984b; 1987; Armstrong, 2003; Wagoner, 1997). For instance, today we treat love as the product of the relationship between two adults rather than, say, a relationship between an adult and God. However, these old ideas about love and attachment continue to colour much of our thinking about what love is and the way that we love. For this reason, it is worthwhile to briefly consider some of the basic ideas concerning love in the Western tradition (for more extended accounts see: Armstrong, 2003; Wagoner, 1997; Kristeva, 1987; Helm, 2005).

One common view is that love is the desire for wholeness. The roots of this conception can be found in ancient Greece where love was largely understood as the desire for a perfect union with our ideal, lost sense of self. We find this very clearly in the speech that Aristophanes gives in Plato's *Symposium*, where the comic playwright proposes that we were originally born as a single creature that had two faces, two backs, four legs, four arms, and so on. Due to the strength, vigour, and hubris of these unusual multimodal beings, they posed a threat to the Gods. To weaken them, Zeus cleaved them in two with a thunderbolt. The result was that human beings were left incomplete, continually searching for their 'other half'. When we meet someone who forms this other half, they are said to complete us – to make use whole. In this case, love is represented in terms of an original cleavage or as the return to a lost unity. Moreover, the lost self who we were once unified with is utterly singular – they are *the* one for us. Indeed, that we desire another because they have characteristics that we ourselves lack, is indicative of such a lost unity. For instance, our lover may be socially gregarious while we are shy. Through providing those things that we don't have, our lover is said to complete us.

Another conception of completion, however, is the idea of completion via recognition. Perhaps the best contemporary example of this claim can be found in Axel Honneth's (1995) argument that the foundational recognition that we gain from the other comes in the form of love. This involves being seen as a worthwhile and emotionally viable human being. We gain this in the experience of primary relationships, such as with a parent or lover. By recognising us, our lover bestows a sense of integrity and goodness to our identity. Thus, according to this tradition, love is seen as *eros*, the desire for what we lack – whether this lack concerns our other half, the complementary abilities of our lover, or their reassuring gaze of recognition.

A second major tradition understands love as a sense of selfless desire. This approach to love can largely be found in Christian conceptions of love. The best representative of this tradition is St Augustine's *Confessions* in which he tries to distinguish love from incessant desire (see Arendt, 1996). He pointed out that worldly love involves the constant nagging of our desires: achieving career goals, accumulating material possessions, possessing the people we lust after, or in Augustine's case refusing the temptation of his concubine. This kind of love Augustine calls *Cupiditas*. However, Augustine is careful to distinguish this from an unworldly love that he calls *Charitas*. In *charitas* we do not seek to vainly possess the things that move us to desire and want. Rather, it involves an unworldly desire or craving for God. By falling in love we gain a sense of worldless possession that makes everything else that we strive for seem less important. This longing can become transformed into the possibility for giving. In this case, the most profound act of love turns out to be when we seek to give everything to our lover. Love is therefore not a moment where we seek to gain recognition for our self – as others like Honneth have suggested. Rather, love involves a selfless act of dissolving our self through giving everything that we have to the loved one. Thus, love is a kind of annihilation of the self, achieved by dissolving ourselves into the wants, needs, and appetites of the other (in the case of Augustine this is God). Thus it is the act of giving more than mere gifts. It also involves giving our whole sense of self. However, this unworldly dwelling with our loved one can lead to a somewhat lonely existence where we become utterly withdrawn from the rest of the world. By dwelling in this lonely world, the lovers try to create a private sphere safely sheltered from the noisy world outside. The result is what Hannah Arendt (1958) would later call 'world alienation', which involves an utter withdrawal from the harmful outside world and a turn inwards. Arendt argues that any interactions with the outside world are done only to serve the higher good of the relationship demanded by our love (for instance the Christian gives charity because God demands that we love thy neighbour as thyself). The result is that when we engage in the social world, we only do so in a mechanistic and distanced way. To get out of this trap, Arendt suggests that we need to recognise our common fallenness or distance from our loved one. In the Christian context, this involves our common fallenness from God through sin. And this shared distance provides a common basis through which we might share the world. Thus, we might love our neighbour not because of our love for the other, but because we both share the common experience of being distanced from our lover.

A third major approach conceives love as the creation of a union. This can be found in Romantic accounts of love. According to this view, love is a kind of magical, idealist fusion of two bodies into one soul (e.g. Solomon, 1988). The realization of this union presupposes the willingness to utterly deliver our selves to the other, no matter what the consequences are. The two 'I's involved in this love relationship heedlessly submit themselves, while at the same time, each retains the intense desire for the other. The result is that two divisible individuals become one. This happens 'just as soon as reciprocity becomes community: that is, just so soon as all distinction between my interests and your interests is overcome' (Scruton, 1986: 230). When we become fused with the other in this way, our interests, delights and longings become theirs, and vice-versa. That is, each individual adopts a kind of collective identity and begins to 'pool' their rights, concerns, and interests together (Nozick, 1989). In order to achieve this sense of perfect union, huge sacrifices are often required on the part of each of the lovers – they are required to do almost anything for the other person. To gain this perfect union one has to unselfishly sacrifice resources, ways of life, and even one's sense of identity. Through this sense of sacrifice, we literally come to be reborn as another more unified being, a being-in-common, a 'we'. But as much romantic literature reminds us, this rebirth often comes with terrible costs.

Love and the Economy

One of the tacit, yet striking, lessons that can be drawn from these three approaches is that love is usually attributed to a sphere outside the formal economy. For the classical Greeks, love is something one might experience through friendship; for Christian thinkers it might be experienced through our relationship with God; and for the Romantics it involved an intense erotic attachment. As such, the modern economy has been seen as a place bereft of love. For Romantics, the factory or other appendages of industrialism were loveless places. Even thinkers profoundly influenced by individualistic economic relations such as Robert Nozick (1989) saw love as a kind of escape from this – for them it was the moment when the interests of two autonomous individuals become merged. The resulting relationship created a sense of oneness, and in this sense of oneness there can be no properly economic relations. The truck and barter of commerce were typically thought to be absolutely devoid of any true human emotion, in particular love. For instance, Stendhal (1915) argued that the habits acquired in the course of doing business often mean that we seek to see the world in terms of facts and categorization rather than attending to the wonderful transubstantiation and follies that our romantic imagination can introduce.

To see this traditional opposition between the economic world and the world of love (a consistent thesis which ran throughout many romantic works), we have to look no further than Marcel Proust's *À la recherche du temps perdu* (In Search of Lost Time). In the first volume, the young Proust obsessively follows the love life of the dashing entrepreneur and dandy Monsieur Swann. A key theme in this story is Swann's obsessional love for his mistress. To express this love, Swann dashes around the restaurants of Paris searching for her. He buys her all manner of expensive items. He listens to her endless discourse on nearly any topic imaginable. And we, as readers, realise long before poor Swann that he is seeking to buy the love of this beautiful courtesan, but that in trying to buy it, he has turned it (and indeed her) into a kind of commodity, which will never yield the mystical value he seeks. When she begins to loose interest, Swann doubles his efforts, spending more, but ever more fruitlessly. As she moves on to another supporter, we recognise the painful truth that in seeking to buy love Swann actually destroyed it.

This age-old lesson about the cleft between love and the economy has been called into question recently. For instance, economists will assess the efficiency of a romantic interlude by developing a pay-off matrix by comparing the amount invested vs. outcomes gained (leading some sad utility maximizers to the inevitable conclusion that prostitution is far more efficient than dating!). Others have begun to develop economic market models for love (for babies, children, spouses, etc.) and the inevitable free-market policy recommendations that accompany them.

Whether the economy has a natural relation to love or not is a staple concern. Some have argued that the economy is generating a complete genre of work relying on staging emotions. Typical examples of these works are service-oriented occupations, like call-centre work, flight attending, hospitality, care work and so on (Hochschild, 1983). Thus, the economy establishes an inauthentic relation between people, where emotional expressions may flow in abundance as long as they are part of a business contract. Others, however, have shown how the economy is increasingly becoming driven by love. This has been argued by Kevin Roberts (2004), who claims that the future of marketing will be characterized by consumer's genuine love towards a brand rather than beguiling marketing tricks.

Love and Organizations

Whether organizations are hospitable soil for love or not, it is clear that they have become places where a large portion of the population engages in intimate relations. Kakabadse and Kakabadse (2004), in their survey of the sex lives of people at work, found that 60% of their 200 respondents had had an intimate experience of some kind at work. Other surveys have pointed in the same direction. Reportedly, 40% of British workers look for love in the office, 43% have set up business meetings to have a night away from home, and 33% of men would take a job if they saw someone attractive at an interview (as cited in Vernon, 2005). While this might give the impression that love is a natural part of the organization, this is not the full story. In fact, the idea that economy and love can form an unproblematic whole is a rather novel conception. Traditionally, the organization has been conceived as a cold and barren place, in which employees are constrained and suppressed. But as we have already pointed out, this conception has gradually been replaced with a novel conception of the organization as a site in which one can authentically express oneself. Instead of obeying rigid military-style rules, imposed by stiff, one-dimensional managers, the employee is now expected to express their true selves, 'warts and all' (Fleming, 2009).

These liberal organizations should not be regarded as an isolated phenomenon, but rather expressions of what Todd McGowan (2004) has called an emerging society of enjoyment. What distinguishes this form of society from earlier ones, McGowan claims, is its ideological rhetoric. If the accent used to be on prohibition and the danger of giving full weight to one's inner desires, it is now obsessively concerned with the freedom-loving individual and her supposed power to enjoy. This gradual shift towards a more liberal work-politics can be seen also in the literature on office romances. While traditionally regarded as having a negative impact on work-productivity, office romances have increasingly been conceived as an asset to the organization, infusing motivation and thus creating a more productive workforce (Williams et al., 1999). Building on this assumption, Lobel et al. (1994) have set out the curious argument that a good manager is distinguished by his ability to manage love romances.

The belief that romances would have a desirable effect on work is based on two assumptions. The first is that love and romance create an inspiring and creative atmosphere, in which people are likely to be more productive. Some have taken this assumption surprisingly far, claiming that a good manager must openly embrace the message of love (Maniero, 1986). Others have been less enthusiastic, arguing that romance at work may come with some undesirable side-effects, such as laziness and scandal (Anderson and Hunsaker, 1985). The most sensitive love-affairs are those that cut across power hierarchies. If, for example, a manager starts an affair with a subordinated employee, this might be problematic for a variety of reasons (see Powell, 2001). How would we know that the manager is not taking advantage of his or her power position? Will the lover receive benefits and perks beyond his or her colleagues? And how do we conceive of sexual harassments if we liberally accept all forms of hierarchical sexual relation?

The second assumption, underpinning the conception that the organization is the natural habitat for love, is that we now live in a post-private age, where intimate emotions can be publicly displayed. This assumption is part of a wider trend in which employees are encouraged to take small items from one's home and bring them to work. Contrary to the old doctrine according to which the employee had to adopt the ideals of the corporation, and even bring them back to their private sphere, this new ideology of work encourages the individual to do the opposite, to bring their private, true selves to work. This new ideology of capitalism takes its cue from the private sphere (the home, etc.) and extends it into others spheres, like the workplace. There are numerous ways through which this trend is expressed. Imagine, for example, an employee who feels depressed after having been dumped. Instead of keeping these emotions to herself (on the basis that a private matter should not take focus away from work), the employee is now encouraged to sit down, take her time, and openly share her grief and emotions with her colleagues. She might even be encouraged to use these emotions as a source of inspiration for her work. This is supposed to bring a more homely and loving feeling of togetherness, where people's emotional needs are respected and affirmed.

The idea that love and the economy are Siamese twins reaches its apogee in leadership discourse (particularly in popular airport 'literature'), where business gurus proclaim new lessons with intense enthusiasm. For example, in his book, *Love and Profit: The Art of Caring Leadership,* James A. Autry claims that loving leadership is the royal road, not only to a more happy organization, but also to increased profitability. The underlying message of these books boils down to the following maxim: a good leader must understand, appreciate, and even love the differences of their employees. If they fail to do so, they will also fail to locate and harness any hidden talent within the organization. Books like *Love 'em, Lead 'em* (Malone, 1986) and *Love 'em or Lose 'em* (Kaye and Jordan-Evans, 2008), tell us that love is the indispensable tool for creating, cultivating and safeguarding talent. 'Lovin' leaders' must abandon military tactics and one-size-fits-all reasoning, and get to know the differences and deviant behaviours of their employees. In getting to know them on a personal level, they can create an atmosphere of intimacy.

This obsession with love in the contemporary workplace has also been diagnosed in more critical, nuanced texts. In a series of analyses, Andersen and Born (2007, 2008) point out that the code of passion has become a widespread way of sorting and organizing people in the workplace. For them, love is a 'second order observation' or way of understanding an organization and placing it into particular categories. They point out that '[e]mployees are now being urged to win the "love" of their organization through an incessant anticipation of its needs' (2008: 326). Through a study of change within Danish public administration (often a leading test-bed for many 'new' ideas about public administration) they show how there is a gradual move towards a code of commitment and love that is used to understand employees' participation. They point out that this code of love-based communication is an attempt to recognize the individual in a highly personal and indeed risky way. The result is that there is an increasing expectation that the employee will be ready and willing to consider the organization's needs (perhaps above their own) in all decisions that are made. In addition, organizations create opportunities for employees to express their love. For Andersen and Born, the code of love – the ability to love and be loved – becomes one of the central bases on which people are included or excluded in organizational life. The result is that the ability, or indeed failure, to be included in organizational life is seen as the consequence of one's personal ability.

Building on these insights, Bojesen and Muhr (2008) point out that management strategies in contemporary firms seek to kindle love in employees. New ways of managing people such as coaching, employee engagement, and corporate cultural programmes encourage staff to fall in love with their company. The love demanded by many organizations often involves 'a unifying act of assimilation – that wants to own you; absorb you, direct you to its needs' (2008; 84-85). They point out that this unifying force of love manufactured by companies is not a cuddly feeling of harmony, intimacy, or general happiness; rather, it is a vicious and sometimes overwhelming force that incorporates the person no matter what the external cost. It is possible that falling in love with the company can, in fact, derail one's personal life, rather than provide a much longed-for sense of connection. Although they point towards the disturbing impact of this desire, they also highlight how it may serve as a source for ethical action. For them, nurturing a space for confrontation is the way ethics is lived and indeed experienced. They argue that this ethical experience of love takes place, not when a company brings us close to its bosom and makes us feel complete, but when the experience of love comes from exposure to the other and exposure to a sense of being pulled apart and absolutely called into question. In short, they are clear that love is not something that can be carefully plotted through techniques such as Human Resource

Management. Rather, it is something that fundamentally disturbs and questions us.

So in attempts to get employees to love the company, organizations seem to be doing two very different things. On the one hand, they are seeking to create the utmost sense of intimacy and attachment on the part of employees. On the other, they are creating a fundamental disturbance in people's relationship to their work. Instead of simply seeing work in a fairly utilitarian fashion, work becomes a place where we might also experience love. But what is the nature of this love? Bojesen and Muhr point out that love is far from cuddly because it is a profoundly interrupting and disturbing experience. What they don't explain however is how this generates different modes of being in love or how this interrupting experience is routinely circumscribed either by destroying the love object, or making it inaccessible. In an attempt to further understand the role of love at the workplace we will now turn to Jacques Lacan and his theory of love. We will begin with a brief theoretical discussion of Lacan's conception of love, after which we will tease out four modes of love – all of which attempt to circumscribe the impasse of love.

Lacan and Love

Love is one of the questions that Lacan studied most closely. In *Seminar XX* he even suggested 'I've been doing nothing but that since I was twenty, exploring the philosophers on the subject of love' (1999: 76). Among the most well-known passages are his exploration of love in relation to transference in *Seminar VIII*, which he primarily illustrates through Plato's *Symposium*; his analysis of love in relation to sublimation, antiquity and ethics in *Seminar VII*; and his notion of *feminine jouissance* and transgressive love in *Seminar XX*. Apart from these in-depth analyses, love also appears in numerous other places, where it is described as an active and crucial aspect of the analytic treatment. For instance, the demands that the analysand addresses to the analyst 'boil down, according to Lacan, to one and the same thing: the demand for love' (Fink, 1995: 89). Hence, the 'analyst has to be the perfect love object, neither smothering, nor absent' (Ibid.).

As with so many other of Lacan's concepts, love undergoes a conceptual transformation over the years. Aiming to capture some of the broader significations, his interpreters often point to three distinct meanings – each of which can be traced to one of the three registers

(Restuccia, 2001; Žižek, 1996). The first meaning of love is situated in the imaginary and concerns loving oneself through an object. This kind of love is a narcissistic form of love relation, where the love object is operating first and foremost as a screen, onto which the ego attempts to projects itself. The lover sees in the love object, not another human being, but a glorified self-image. As Lacan repeatedly points out, this form of identification with a specular image is predicated on a serious *misrecognition*, where the subject fails to acknowledge its full dependence on the other. In this sense there is no clear separation between the ideal image of the ego and its love object, as they have both become trapped in a specular image – an image to which the ego remains exterior, in spite of being its originator. The result of this love is ultimately alienation, narcissism and aggression.

The second meaning of love appears in the symbolic. Here the lover seeks to obtain an object located in the sphere of the Other. Like desire, love is directed towards an inaccessible object, the object-cause of desire. This object is not so much an empirical and tangible object, which could be isolated from other objects and ultimately obtained, but an object that signifies something beyond its own symbolic specificity. In Lacan's words it is an object that provokes an uncanny feeling on the part of the lover insofar as the love object emits something enigmatic, beyond its mere semblance. The subject trapped in this love of desire is the radically decentered subject, who has accepted that the love object is impossible to directly obtain, but nevertheless engages in creative activities directed towards the Other – with the aim to reanimate the object. We will come back to these strategies in the next section, where we explore the ways in which employees might express their love for the corporation.

The third version of love pertains to the real, and signals a transgressive form of love, beyond the Law. These thoughts were chiefly developed in *Seminar XX*, where Lacan separates the *jouissance* of the phallus (love based on the male fantasy) from Other *jouissance*, or what he also calls feminine *jouissance* (a divine love that traverses the fantasy). This form of love has been a central object to many Lacanians (for example Žižek, 1996; Copjec, 2002; Zupančič, 2000) as it involves a radical transformation of the subject – from the register of desire to drive.

It is clear that each of these versions of love sets itself apart from the more hopeful vision of two becoming one (as in Aristophanes' description). Lacan's first notion of narcissistic love does – at least on the surface – involve two becoming one. The specular image becomes fused with the ego. However, what is involved here is not two human beings coming together and forming a unified and harmonious entity. Rather, it is a relationship completely overdetermined by the image of one ego, where the other is subsumed in that image.

The second kind of love is also distinct from the idea of a harmonious relationship. Given that the love object always remains indeterminable and ambiguous, signifying something more than itself, there can be no union between the lover and the beloved. This is also what is implied in Lacan's statement that there is 'no such thing as a sexual relationship' (Lacan, 1999: 34). By that, Lacan is certainly not implying that there are no sexual liaisons or that people don't fall in love with one another. Rather, he suggests that love is an inherently asymmetrical, knotty affair where the lover and the beloved never meet. It is a love predicated on the insatiable desire for something more. It is geared exclusively towards the impossible kernel that the lover presupposes to be hidden within, and beyond, the beloved. As such, the lover (*qua* subject of desire) can never be satisfied. Even if love does happen to chance his way, he fails to see and appreciate such an idiosyncratic kernel within the other. For as soon as the object is revealed to the lover, the magical attraction fades away. The result is that he or she quickly grows disheartened, pushes his or her loved one away, and starts the search for the non-existent desired object once again. To illustrate this we could turn, once more, to Monsieur Swann's hysterical relation to Odette in Proust's work. On the one hand, Swann never figures out what it is in Odette that he so strongly desires. He doesn't respect her intellectually. He doesn't even find her particularly attractive. But nonetheless he completely subordinates himself to the search for her affections, as if his heart had been delivered to an external power. However much he tries to escape her influence, he cannot help but continue his effort to envelope – or symbolize – Odette's escaping spirit and puzzling desires. But ironically, the more he tries the more distant she becomes. And when Swann, by the end of the first volume, has finally won her heart, he laconically declares:

> To think that I have wasted years of my life, that I have longed for
> death, that the greatest love that I have ever known has been for a
> woman who did not please me, who was not in my style! (Proust, 1957:
> 229)

The third version of love is even more antithetical to the illusion of two
becoming one, as it transgresses the circular logic of Law and desire. As
Žižek describes, such transgression involves 'asexual sublimation of
drive', 'ecstatic surrender', and 'subjective destitution', where the subject
'is no longer bothered by the Other's desire' (Žižek, 1996). Thus,
contrary to the subject of desire (assumed in symbolic love), who is
determined by the decentred cause of the Other, the subject of drive
causes itself. The result is a corporeal and often masochistic relation to
love, where the aim of finding an inaccessible object is replaced by a
nonsensical loop of repetition.

These differences aside, this dimension of love in Lacan's thinking
can be clearly distinguished from what we might call a 'Meg Ryan
approach to love', where we find a cute and harmonious unity between
two longing souls. In place of these reconciliatory love stories, Lacan
proposes a notion of love where two excluding realities become one,
but a 'one' that can never coincide with itself – what he describes as an
'intersection of two substances that have no part in common' (1999:
17). This implies that love involves the madness consisting in the
creation of 'two' where there never was one and which is not itself one
(Copjec, 2005).

However, what will concern us here is neither love as the creation of
two, nor love as a transgressive act of feminine *jouissance*. Such Lacanian
analyses often concern ethical subjectivity and political resistance –
questions, which, in spite of being important, are not immediately
addressed in the present chapter. Rather, we will concentrate on the
second version of love, which begins with an exploration of the
subject's desire for love, and continues with an analysis of the various
strategies that subjects employ in order to retain the glory of the love
object. Renata Salecl's (1998) work on love is key here. The starting
point for her analysis is that love does not flourish in a context of
boundless freedom, but instead requires restrictions, prohibitions and
strict boundaries. In the case of Swann and his hysterical love, we can
see how it is precisely the obstacle (Odette's evading and capricious
character) that ignites his desire. If she would suddenly throw herself in

Swann's arms, and stop seeing other men (and women), we could be quite sure that his desire would gradually evaporate (and possibly even be replaced by a feeling of disgust). This argument puts the organization, as a possible site for experiencing love, in a different light. It indicates that the organization could be a site for experiencing love not in spite of – but because of – its suppressive and regulated character. In short, this would imply that the organization, with its regulatory norms and disciplinary rules, invites the lover rather than pushing him or her away.

Building on this assumption we suggest that love operates in the organization in a number of ways. First, and as already mentioned, love might appear between different people in the organization, in the form of romances or love affairs. The second form of love is closely associated with care, respect, empathy, and altruism. It is based on the assumption that management has much to learn from spiritualism and that these lessons, if incorporated, would have a desirable impact on the corporation. The third form of love concerns the employee's attitude towards work, captured in the expression: 'I love (or hate) my work'. The fourth form, which is of particular interest in this chapter, brings us to the more complex relation between the employee and the organization. In contrast to the other forms of love associated with work, this form concentrates not on how the employee may derive a balanced and happy life from working in an organization. Rather, it concentrates on the asymmetrical relation between the employee, as lover, and the organization, as simultaneously a love object and the barrier that prevents access to love objects. In this respect, we would argue that the organization has a dual function. The first function is to make the illusion of love feasible. This could be done through career ladders, where the employee is being inspired to believe that they may reach a desired point, and thereby acquire a sense of satisfaction. The second, complementary function of the organization is that it keeps the object, not completely out of sight, but out of reach. Given the impossibility of obtaining this love object, the lover can take on a number of strategies. He may destroy it (as in the case of the hysteric), idealize it (as the obsessional), negate it (as the cynic), or domesticate it (as the platonic). In the remaining part of this chapter we will attempt to describe these varying strategies. In order to illustrate these positions we will turn to the sitcom *The Office* and four characters who, each in their own way, represent the impossibility of becoming One with the organization.

Love at the Office

David Brent

In Ricky Gervais and Stephen Merchant's comedic mockumentary, *The Office*, we follow the decline and fall of David Brent (played by Gervais), a regional manager for the paper manufacturer Wernham Hogg. When we first get to know the middle-aged, schlubby David he is doing pretty well. The employees clearly have their reservations, but they also seem to have learnt how to deal with his clumsy ways and bad jokes. In his own, slightly exaggerated, words:

> People say I'm the best boss. They go, 'Oh, we've never worked in a place like this before, you're such a laugh. You get the best out of us'. And I go, you know, 'C'est la vie'. If that's true – excellent. (Season 1, Episode 1)

These self-asserting declarations are more than characteristic. Whenever the chance arises, David tries to convince the camera (and himself) that he's not only a popular office humourist, who makes his colleagues burst into laughter, but also an influential figure at the workplace, from whom the employees have much to learn. He is equipped with a practically inestimable absence of self-reflexivity, and he acknowledges his lack of popularity only on occasion:

> People could come to me, and they could go, 'Excuse me, David, but you've been in the business twelve years. Can you just spare us a moment to tell us how to run a team, how to keep them task-orientated as well as happy?' But they don't. That's the tragedy. (Season 1, Episode 1)

What people make of him is more important to him than anything else; his desire to be liked knows no limits. Do they think he's funny or popular? David enacts a frenzy of failed attempts to capture his colleagues' attention, which only testifies to his decentred desire: he 'accidentally' reveals that he once appeared in 'Inside Paper' (Wernham Hogg's internal newspaper); he casually mentions that he used to be a popular singer-songwriter and then delivers a few songs; or he tries to excel during the company quiz night. That is to say, his desire consists in his perception of being loved. It is a desire that has to be reciprocal in that it only counts if he is recognized. Even though Lacan's idea that 'desire of man is the desire of the Other' applies to every subject, he points out that this is more true of the hysteric than anyone else (Evans, 1996). The hysteric is exclusively guided by the question, 'what am I to the Other?' This question is rooted in sexuality, and the uncertainty as to whether one is a man or a woman. Now, we are not suggesting that David mistakes himself for a woman, is driven by repressed homosexuality, or longs to become a suburban drag queen. Such suggestions, besides appearing as cheap pop-psychological banalities, are moreover, downright erroneous. What we suggest is something different; namely, that David suffers from an anxiety as to how he, as a sexed being, is perceived (and hopefully loved) by the Other. This anxiety is visible in a number of ways. It is visible in David's assiduous attempts to appear indispensable, claiming that the organization would not survive without him. But it is also visible in his numerous attempts to be regarded as attractive, even sexy (such as when he dresses up in a brown Shamarni leather jacket and high-heeled boots). These attempts may produce the image of a completely self-absorbed, inveterate boaster – and this does hold true to some extent. But we must also register that in his zealous struggle to appear likeable, he attributes an even stronger importance to the organization and the people therein. For if the organization did not constitute a mirror in which he could detect his own image in a desirable light, his vanity would find no form.

What the hysteric ultimately desires is an unconditional love that could finally make him or her whole. But the hysteric does not try to reach an unattainable love object for this end. Instead, he or she identifies with the unattainable love object. In this sense the hysteric attributes considerable importance to herself, making up fantasy scenarios in which the other would be left in paralyzed sorrow if he or she would suddenly decide to disappear. If we think of David in these terms, we might say that he, too, is convinced that the organization would collapse, were it not for his presence.

Gareth Keenan

We will return to David and his hysteric relation in a moment, but let us first introduce his second in command, Gareth Keenan. He is both similar to and different from his boss: similar insofar as he shares the same desire to be loved and recognized, and different insofar as he employs different means to this end. If David constantly challenges the rules, taking on rather extreme measures to be recognized and beloved, then Gareth maintains a low-key attitude, taking pride in following the formal regulations of the organization. In this sense, Gareth constitutes the model of an obsessional, since nothing is more important to him than rules, order, or discipline.

This passion for the rules is constantly manifested in Gareth's behaviour. When, for example, a few papers happen to slide over to his desk, Gareth aggressively demarcates his desk with a ruler, pushing all papers back to the adjacent desk. When asked what he's doing, Gareth snaps back, in an exasperated yet calm tone: 'It was overlapping. It's all coming over the edge. One word, two syllables – demarcation. All right?'

Following the code of the organization is Gareth's mantra. Positions, ranks, titles, and practically any other manifestation of formal order do not simply represent social relations. To him they signal something much more profound, almost the essence of life. This fetishization of social rules becomes obvious on a number of occasions. For example, after David found a compromising photomontage of himself as an eroticized nude woman, he gives Gareth the mission to find the culprit. Gareth takes on this mission with a childish enthusiasm. He brings the 'suspects' to his 'interrogation room', one by one, asking what he believes to be cunning questions. The scene is absurdly theatrical. It shows Gareth in his grey shirt and mobile-phone holster, walking back and forth in the room in his (hilarious) attempt to resemble a detective. He even peers through the Vienesse blinds at one point, projecting a mysterious glance out the window. The seriousness with which he undertakes the mission is displayed in numerous signs he hangs on the door of his interrogation chamber, which include: 'Interrogation Room', 'Investigation Room', 'Investigation Office', 'Quiet please Investigation in process', 'Investigation and Meeting room' and 'Gareth Keenan Investigates!'

There is certainly something sad about Gareth's attempts to find consolation in the ideals of the organization. When, for example, his co-worker, Tim, says that his official title, 'team leader', is nothing but a cover-up for the unexciting nature of the work he has been given, we learn that Gareth's attempt to assume different roles goes back a long time:

153

Tim: Team Leader don't mean anything mate.

Gareth: Excuse me, it means I'm leader of a team.

Tim: No it doesn't. It's a title someone's given you to get you to do something they don't want to do for free – it's like making the div kid at school milk monitor. No one respects it.

Gareth: Er, I think they do.

Tim: No they don't Gareth.

Gareth: Er, yes they do, cos if people were rude to me then I used to give them their milk last… so it was warm. (Season 2, Episode 1)

One way of interpreting Gareth's naive behaviour is that he has no other choice; that being perceived as a div kid (pejorative slang for a slightly retarded kid) is his tragic faith. It is truly difficult to imagine Gareth suddenly becoming cool, but we should not jump to conclusions. Gareth's well-organized world, with his like-minded friends, and many rituals do in fact bring him some pleasure. In this way, his desire is always kept in check by his repetition of rituals and he escapes being confronted with his own desire. As Salecl notes:

Lacan characterizes the obsessional as one who installs himself in the place of the Other, from where he then acts in a way that prevents any risk of encountering his desire. That is why he invents a number of rituals, self-imposed rules, and organizes his life in a compulsive way. (Salecl, 1998: 9)

Again, Gareth attempts to escape his desire by way of speaking or acting compulsively. But it is slightly more complicated than that. On the one hand he hints at his true desire – as for example when he speaks about his 'adventurous' past, supposedly filled with intense love affairs and other excesses – which would indicate that he actually desires something more than what he presently enjoys. On the other hand he seems amazingly content. When he is asked about office romances, he says:

Yes I've had office romances. Loads. Not here, another place I worked at. Good looking ones as well. But it's not a good idea. Office romances. Like shitting on your own doorstep. (Season 1, Episode 3)

Lacan's point is that by blocking the love object, the subject tries to retain the illusion of love. If David's strategy for keeping the illusion alive is to become the love object, then Gareth's is to completely submit himself to the Other. In so doing, Gareth keeps the unattainable love object at a safe distance, blocking any possible form of union. What Lacan maintains, however, is that these constraints are not just necessary means to block the love object, but rather the end in themselves, which produce enjoyment. Thus, submitting himself to the theatrical performance of rituals, Gareth takes on an identity which blocks the love object but at the same time allows him to enjoy it, in an idealized form. This is why the office seems to fit Gareth so well.

> It's all right here. But people do sometimes take advantage because it's so relaxed. I like to have a laugh, just as much as the next man, but this is a place of work. And I was in Territorial Army for three years and you can't mock about there. (Season 1, Episode 1)

Gareth's mask, we argue, is not just mannerism or a compulsive way to block the love object. More profoundly, he *is* the mannerism. This means that the passion does not lie beyond the mask, but in the mask itself. It is precisely through the performance that Gareth experiences passion.

Tim Canterbury

If Gareth and David strike us as exceptionally non-reflexive, mindlessly going on with their awkward businesses, then their co-worker Tim Canterbury represents the enlightened 'college boy', who constantly distances himself from work. He makes no illusions as to what his work comes down to:

> I'm a sales rep, which means that my job is to speak to clients on the phone about quantity and type of paper and whether we can supply it with them and whether they can pay for it and – I'm bored even talking about it. (Season 1, Episode 1)

He sees himself as a failure that has traded in his youthful aspirations for an adult life pervaded by a permanent boredom. Nonetheless, he constantly reminds himself of the outside world, fervently trying to convince himself that there is still time to go back to university: 'I'm not thinking about it. I'm doing it. I'm leaving, to go back to university to learn about more than the price of Optibright's laser copy paper' (Season 1, Episode 5). But there is always something that prevents him from leaving. In fact, Tim never goes back to university. He stays at Wernham Hogg. When he, by the end of the second season, is given the offer to replace David as regional manager, he politely turns it down. The obvious question that follows is: why? What is it that makes him want to stay? Is it his love for the office secretary, Dawn, that is decisive? And if he for some reason decides to stay at the office, why doesn't he at least accept the offer to advance?

In the context of organization studies it has been widely argued that employees may protect what they see as their authentic selves through engaging in cynicism and dis-identification (Fleming, 2009; Fleming and Spicer, 2003). In other words, conceiving oneself as outside the spectacle of the corporation – as Tim clearly does – is a way to endure an otherwise unbearable situation, and at the same time retain a private sense of self. When Wernham Hogg has a comic relief day, Tim expresses his discontent saying: 'I just don't want to have to join in with someone else's idea of wackiness, okay? It's the wackiness I can't stand' (Season 2, Episode 5). Moreover, his cultural preferences are sophisticated and very far from those of his closest colleagues. When he is asked to join a booze marathon with Gareth, David, and Finchy (David's rather coarse friend), Tim ironically comments:

I don't know where we're going tonight. Obviously Finchy's a sophisticated guy, and Gareth's a culture vulture, so you know, will it be opera, ballet? I don't know. I know the RSC's in town, so er… having said that, at Chasers, it's Hooch for a pound and Wonderbras-get-in-free night tonight. So I don't know, I don't know who'll win, it's exciting. I'm staying out of it. (Season 1, Episode 5)

But the discrepancy between Tim's 'authentic persona' and his 'designer self' is not confined to his life in the workplace.

I'm thirty today. My mom got me up really early this morning to give me my present. Yes this is it. It's nice. I like ballet. I love the novels of Proust. I love the work of Alain Delon. [*With irony.*] And that I think is what influenced her buying me Hat FM. I like the radio too. (Season 1, Episode 3)

The question persists, however. Why does Tim stay in what seems a miserable existence? Why does he not leave Slough behind to go back to university? An obvious guess would be that he has become comfortable in his work and simply couldn't be bothered to turn his life around. While this might have some truth in it we would like to posit an alternative hypothesis. Staying at the soul-destroying drudgery of Wernham Hogg gives Tim a definite place and a solid identity that would be painful to lose. Rather than being excluded from the organizational scene, as one could argue, Tim has successfully managed to include himself as an outsider. Far from being a passive victim of circumstances, Tim has arranged his world such that nothing could really go wrong. His recurring failed attempts to snare Dawn should be seen in precisely this light, as a form of unburdening failure. It is precisely this failure that gives Tim an identity. What's more, it is an identity that cannot easily be challenged or called into question. In fact, perhaps the only way it might in fact be destabilised is if he actually succeeded (with Dawn, took up the promotion, returned to university).

These three characters – David, Gareth and Tim – form an interesting union. In the eyes of Gareth, David is impeccable, not because David is the perfect boss, but because he *is* the boss. Even though Gareth constantly tries to amplify his authority (e.g. presenting himself as assistant regional manager instead of assistant *to* the regional manager) he would never stoop to do anything that would compromise the hierarchical relation he has to his superior. David, in turn, needs Gareth. When everyone turns against David, Gareth loyally stays by his side, confirming David's self-declared excellence. The less obvious question, however, is why Tim would need both David and Gareth. To find this answer one needs to recognize Tim's desire to retain a sense of dignity, even authenticity, beyond his organizational persona. When Gareth and David indulge in one thing more stupid than the other, and Tim stays at the level of the spectator, his experience of inauthenticity becomes so overwhelming that he never has to doubt as to whether he has anything in common with these people. In this sense they form the antithesis to his identity, and as such become constitutive, that is to say, the driving force of his own self-image. At a training day, when they are asked about their ultimate fantasies, we can see how this functions: David is excruciatingly difficult by questioning the assumptions of the query (he asks whether one could also pick impossible fantasies such as immortality or time travel). Gareth plays by the rules perfectly and gives an overly candid response ('Two lesbians, probably. Sisters. I'm just watching.'). Tim, instead adopts the position of the cynical outsider ('I never thought I would say this but can I hear more from Gareth please?').

Neil Godwin

The fourth character worth mentioning, perhaps not because he makes a particularly interesting case, but because he constitutes a kind of mirror in which we can more clearly see the other characters, is the former regional manager at the Swindon branch of Wernham Hogg, Neil Godwin. Neil is everything David isn't. He takes his job seriously and knows the art of setting limits. Moreover, he is delicate and knows how to charm his staff. When introducing himself to the new staff Neil strikes the right chord, making the staff laugh. 'I'm a man of simple pleasures', he begins:

> I don't need lovely houses, beautiful girls or classy restaurants – so it's a good draw I moved to Slough. No it's great to be in Slough, really it is, I just spent a year in Beirut. (Laugh). Now, I know David is a bit worried taking on all this new staff. Because, as manager, it's going to be a lot more responsibility – he now has to delegate twice as much work. But there will be perks for him. I'm sure he's looking forward to having a whole new group of men underneath him. Here's the man at the top of the pile, David Brent. (Season 2, Episode 1)

David, who is supposed to say a few words after Neil, completely looses himself, cracking one joke after the other, each one worse than the last, until he has literally emptied the room. David's hysterical wish to be loved is never so conspicuous as when Neil is around. The idea that someone would be more cherished and appreciated is just too torturous for David to face up to.

Neil seems to have a very 'rational' and 'emotionally balanced' relation to Wernham Hogg. He never crosses the line of unacceptable work behaviour, and does not reveal more about himself than necessary. But we don't get the experience that he deliberately tries to conceal a true self, behind the mask. In this sense we would suggest that he has a *platonic* love relation to the organization. He makes sure that the organization becomes a serious and productive, yet hospitable, place to work at. What Neil brings to the office is a well-configured cultural system of norms and values, where boundaries are clearly drawn. Under Neil's supervision, employees know what they can and cannot do. This was never the case during David's halcyon days, when there were no clear regulations except 'having a laugh'.

The conflict between David and Neil rapidly intensifies, and it is not before long that David has been offered a 'generous redundancy package'. We have already mentioned that the hysteric is obsessed with the question of what will happen to her partner if she leaves him: in her imagination the partner will not manage one day without her. In this precise manner, David constructs a scenario of having captured the heart and soul of his employees. He says, for example:

> I'm an educator. I'm a motivator of people. I excite their imaginations.
> It's like bloody *Dead Poet's Society* sometimes out there. You know at the
> end, where they all stand on the tables? (Season 2, Episode 4)

So when David knows that his time is over, and that he has no other option than to accept the redundancy package, he takes comfort in his unshakable belief that all employees – his loyal partisans – will stand up for him, and create havoc. He tells Neil that if they force him to go, 'you'll have a mutiny in your hands. They will go berserk' (Season 2, Episode 5). But when he goes out to the staff and publicly announces his resignation, he realizes to his great despair that no one intends to go berserk, not even Gareth.

Albeit very differently, we argue that all of these four characters form emotional bonds with the organization, and that these bonds could be understood with regard to love. David's hysterical relationship to the office is one that is doomed from the outset. His indefatigable endeavour to be liked, together with his constant questioning of authorities and regulations, turn him into a hopeless case. But what makes David most troubling for the organization is that he is something of a truth-teller. By identifying with the good-hearted, funny, and free-minded leader in too literal a manner, without retaining any distance to this image, he reveals many of the absurdities of the organization. His babble about team-individuality, not to mention his conviction that a tiny bit of fun(d) raising would save the world, becomes an unsettling satire of contemporary 'compassionate' work-politics. Tyler and Cohen (2008) have argued that David is a parody of the 'heterosexual matrix' and as such a powerful critique of male-dominated work-politics. Taking this one step further, we would argue that both David and Gareth (although in different ways) push the logic of the relation between love and work to its extreme, thus revealing how this relation is first and foremost a construct of mythical management jargon. As such, they can be said to constitute a firm critique of seemingly liberal work-politics. In an age of cynicism (see Sloterdijk, 1988), where we tend to believe only vicariously, characters like David and Gareth are hard to come across. Identifying too much with the organization and its ideological content, they reveal the unsustainability of management practices. For instance, the flora of titles, ranks, and buzz-words – which pass unnoticed in most other contexts, given that no one *really* believes in them – become painfully comic when Gareth picks them up. Similarly, when David engages in what he perceives as real ethical responsibility, it becomes abundantly clear that what ethical responsibility often comes down to in the context of the corporation is a narcissistic desire to appear in an attractive light.

If Gareth and David may become something of a threat to the organization then Tim and Neil retain precisely the proper amount of distance that contemporary work cultures seem to require. At the comic relief event Neil dresses up as John Travolta, from *Saturday Night Fever*, and delivers an impeccable dance, which both amuses and impresses the staff. For sure, Neil strikes a perfect balance between fun and work: he high-mindedly tolerates employee's attempts to express themselves – they're even allowed to pull half-obscene jokes – as long as they never cross the invisible line. Neil's intuitive flair for rules and regulations is reminiscent of Gareth's, but with the important difference that Neil refrains from fetishizing rules.

Now, the final question we wish to ponder is why it seems so easy for people like Neil and Tim to keep a lofty and dignified sense of detachment. We believe that in order to find the answer to this question we have to look not at their innate gifts or individual disposition but, rather, how their withdrawn identities rely on the not-so withdrawn identities of Gareth and David. This, we think, is particularly true with regard to Tim, who seems to vicariously derive pleasure from the absurd craziness that occurs in the comical rampages of Gareth and David. We might thus say that Gareth and David are perfect subjects on to which the cynic might displace his own beliefs. Instead of having to shoulder the beliefs themselves, they (Tim, and to some extent also Neil) can sit back and enjoy the show.

This dignified resignation should now appear in a slightly different light. Rather than having only platonic or cynical love for the organization, Neil and Tim vicariously love their work, through the figures of David and Gareth.

Conclusion

In this chapter we have explored the vital, yet stunningly under-researched relationship between love and work. Classic accounts of the 'modern' workplace see it as a place dominated by cold technical rationality and bereft of love and emotion (e.g. Weber, 1947). The ideal modernist worker has a technical mind-set and a heart of stone. In contrast, more recent accounts of the 'post-modern' workplace have pointed out that companies now seek to bring love into the centre of company life (e.g., Casey, 1995). The result is that the perfect post-industrial worker is the one who is passionately 'in love' with their company and burns with a passion for their work (Ekman, 2010). In this chapter, we have tried to move beyond these two positions by arguing that those who succeed in this contemporary workplace are in love with their work, but remain able to retain a certain distance from their object of desire. Figures who are completely subsumed and passionately attached to an organizational love object can prove to be a serious risk for the organization. This is because they see no boundaries to the love relationship and will frequently engage in excessive behaviour that disturbs the smooth functioning of the organizational machine. David's hysterical need to be loved results in embarrassing situations which waste company time and destroy his relationships. Gareth's neurotic love of rules creates what can sometimes be highly inefficient and certainly alienating situations.

The failings of such excessive love for the organization are by no means limited to the fictional world of *The Office*. Many empirical studies of 'loved up' organizations reflect the pathologies that result from people becoming too passionately attached to their organizations. We have already mentioned the neurotic engineering employees studied by Catherine Casey (1995). Their bizarre activities, like obsessively collecting golf balls while on a Sunday walk, might seem to belie some kind of cute syndrome or even a touch of creative genius. However, such neurotic compulsions could easily spill over into working life and begin to make an individual unmoveably attached to highly inefficient and ineffective practices. There is always a danger that their love of the rules could become a serious impediment to the organization. Hysterical desire for love in organizational life is an equally troubling case. Research on media work by Susanne Ekman (2010) identified many extremely successful individuals who exhibited a hysterical need for love and recognition from their organizations and managers. These 'creative class' employees constantly doubted their abilities and their validity to the organization. To assuage the constant and nagging doubts, these employees demanded constant praise and recognition from their managers. Often times this was a highly productive dynamic, as it lead employees to constantly push boundaries and work ever-increasing hours. But at the same time this hysterical dynamic came at a high price – the employees felt constantly anxious, on edge, and stressed out. At times, when they really began doubting their self-worth in the eyes of their love object, they could slide into depression. And their managers were constantly taxed with the need to nurture and support their fragile egos.

It therefore appears that excessive love for an organization or one's work can come with significant baggage. In contrast, love that involves a certain touch of distance seems to be more sustainable. Cynics are able to distance themselves from their love object, see the faults in it, and treat it 'objectively'. But far from completely rejecting their love object, cynics remain reliant on the organization to give them a sense of meaning and an identity. This kind of detached attachment creates a relationship between the organization and the employee that is both objective and avoids excessive demands at the same time as facilitating attachment. We find a similar functionality at work in what we have called Platonic love. Unlike the cynic who negatively marks the object of detached attachment, the platonic lover sees their object in a positive or perhaps more accurately ideal light. However, they recognise this idea as always being necessarily unreachable. But due to this necessary distance, Platonic attachment does not lead to the same kind of pathological acting out to reaffirm the love object. Rather, it allows the platonic lover to be attached but to also keep a kind of safe distance.

Our argument – that the detached attachment of cynical or platonic love is the desirable form of love on the part of organizations – has some interesting implications. At the most simple level, it reminds us that when business gurus cry out that employees should love their organization, then they expect to find neither David nor Gareth. Instead they rely on figures like Tim and Neil who, instead of taking management babble literally, retain an appropriate distance from their work. It is not that this distant love follows representations of the cold, calculating employee. After all, it most certainly involves a note of passion and attachment – even if this involves some degree of distance. Nor do corporate love relationships allow all aspects of human emotions and expression back into the workplace. We have argued that some of the more passionate attachments that are routinely urged by proponents of corporate love can actually result in destructive relationships with work. In order to get out of this bind between a soul-destroying lovelessness and the destructiveness of passionate attachment, we have explored the possibilities of a kind of detached attachment to the organization. This stance certainly creates many problems: it can practically bind people to organizational activities, which they do not necessarily agree with; it can create painful mismatches between espoused ideology and actual practices; and it can also create a sense of self-alienation. However, it is also important to recognise that this paradoxical kind of attachment can bring with it certain benefits: it could be more sustainable because it does not require the same kind of obsessive acting out or seeking recognition, which drives neurotic or hysteric love. It is also more 'realistic' insofar as it recognises the inevitable imperfection of one's relationship with an organization and allows an individual to do the best with what is there. But, perhaps most importantly these kinds of patterns of attachment allow a way for the passionate worker to 'traverse the fantasy', which is implicit within so many contemporary workplaces (i.e. that it can provide a perfect, all-fulfilling and inspiring life, if only we try hard enough). Detached attachment involves seeing organizations for what they are, seeing how our fantasy structures our work, and recognising the inevitable distance which we will have from our fantasy of a perfect working life. By recognising our innate distance from the corporate love object, we become able to deal with it on less weighty terms.

References

Alvesson, M. and H. Willmott (2002) 'Identity regulation as organizational control: producing the appropriate individual', *Journal of Management Studies*, 39(5): 619-643.

Andersen, N. A. and A. Born (2007) 'Emotional identity feelings as communicative artefacts in organizations', *International Journal of Work, Organizations and Emotions*, 2(1): 35-48.

Andersen, N. A. and A. Born (2008) 'The employee in the sign of love', *Culture and Organization*, 14(4): 325-343.

Anderson, C. I. and P. L. Hunsaker (1985) 'Why there's romancing at the office and why it's everybody's problem', *Personnel,* 62: 57-63.

Arendt, H. (1958) *The Human Condition*. Chicago: University of Chicago Press.

Arendt, H. (1996) *Love and Saint Augustine*. Chicago: University of Chicago Press.

Armstrong, J. (2003) *The Conditions of Intimacy: The Philosophy of Love*. London: Penguin.

Barley, S. and G. Kunda (1992) 'Design and devotion: surges of rational and normative ideologies of control in managerial discourse', *Administrative Science Quarterly*, 37(3): 363-399.

Barley, S. and J. Van Maanen (1999) 'Changing scripts at work: managers and profesionals', *Annals of the American Academy of Political and Social Science*, 561(1): 64-80.

Bojesen, A. and S. L. Muhr (2008) 'In the name of love: let's remember desire', *ephemera*, 8(1): 79-93.

Boltanski, L. and E. Chiapello (2005) *The New Spirit of Capitalism*. London: Verso.

Buss, D. M. (1994) *The Evolution of Desire: Strategies of Human Mating*. New York: Basic Books.

Casey, C. (1995) *Work, Self and Society: After Industrialism*. London: Routledge.

Copjec, J. (2002) *Imagine There's No Woman: Ethics and Sublimation*. Cambridge, MA: MIT Press.

Copjec, J. (2005) 'Gai savoir sera: the science of love and the insolence of chance', in G. Riera and R. Gasche (eds) *Alain Badiou: Philosophy and Its Conditions*. New York: SUNY Press.

Ekman, S. (2010) *Authority and Autonomy: Paradoxes of Modern Knowledge Work*. Doctoral Thesis, Copenhagen Business School.

Evans, D. (1996) *An Introductory Dictionary of Lacanian Psychoanalysis.* London: Routledge.

Fineman, S. (ed.) (2000) *Emotions in Organization.* London: Sage.

Fink, B. (1995) *The Lacanian Subject.* Princeton: Princeton University Press.

Fleming, P. (2005) 'Workers' playtime? Boundaries and cynicism in a "culture of fun" program', *Journal of Applied Behavioral Science*, 41 (3): 285-303.

Fleming, P. (2009) *Authenticity and Cultural Politics of Work.* Oxford: Oxford University Press.

Fleming, P. and A. Spicer (2003) 'Working at a cynical distance: implications for subjectivity, power and resistance', *Organization*, 10 (1): 157-179.

Fleming, P. and A. Sturdy (2008) '"Just be yourself" – towards neo-normative control in organizations?', Working Paper, Queen Mary College, University of London.

Helm, B. (2005) 'Love', *Stanford Encyclopedia of Philosophy*, available at http://plato.stanford.edu/entries/love/ (accessed September 2010).

Hochschild, A.R. (1983) *The Managed Heart: Commercialization of Human Feelings.* Berkley, CA: University of California Press.

Honneth, A. (1995) *The Struggle for Recognition.* Cambridge: Polity.

Illouz, E. (2005) *Cold Intimacies: The Making of Emotional Capitalism.* Cambridge: Polity.

Kakabadse, A. and N. Kakabadse (2004) *Intimacy: An International Survey of the Sex Lives of People at Work.* New York: Palgrave MacMillan.

Kaye, B. and S. Jordan-Evans (2008) *Love 'Em or Lose 'Em: Getting Good People to Stay.* San Francisco: Berrett-Koehler.

Kristeva, J. (1987) *Tales of Love.* New York: Columbia University Press.

Lacan, J. (1998) *The Four Fundamental Concepts of Psychoanalysis: The Seminar of Jacques Lacan, Book XI*, trans. A. Sheridian. New York: W. W. Norton.

Lacan, J. (1999) *On Feminine Sexuality, the Limits of Love and Knowledge: The Seminar of Jacques Lacan, Book XX, 1972-73*, trans. B. Fink. New York: Norton.

165

Lobel S. A., R. E. Quinn, L. St. Clair, and A. Warfield (1994) 'Love without sex: the impact of psychological intimacy between men and women at work', *Organanizational Dynamics*, 23(1): 4-17.

Mainiero L. A. (1986) 'A review and analysis of power dynamics in organizational romances', *Academy of Managemenet Review*, 11(4): 750-62.

Malone III, P. B. (1986) *Love 'Em and Lead 'Em*. Annandale: Synergy Press.

McGowan, T. (2004) *The End of Dissatisfaction? Jacques Lacan and the Emerging Society of Enjoyment*. Albany: SUNY Press.

Nozick, R. (1989) 'Love's bond', in *The Examined Life: Philosophical Meditations*. New York: Simon and Schuster.

Powell, G. N. (2001) 'Workplace romances between senior-level executives and lower-level employees: an issue of work disruption and gender', *Human Relations,* 54(11): 1519-1544.

Proust, M. (1957[1922]) *Remembrance of Things Past, Vol. 1: Swanns Way*, trans. C. K. Scott Moncreiff. London: Chatto and Windus.

Restuccia, F. L. (2001) 'Impossible love in *Breaking the Waves*: mystifying hysteria', *Literature and Psychology,* 47(1-2): 34-54.

Roberts, K. (2004) *Lovemarks: The Future Beyond Brands*. Auckland: Reed.

Ross, A. (2004) *No-Collar: The Humane Workplace and its Hidden Costs*. Philadelphia: Temple University Press.

Salecl, R. (1998) *(Per)Versions of Love and Hate*. New York: Verso.

Scruton, R. (1986) *Sexual Desire: A Moral Philosophy of the Erotic*. New York: Free Press.

Sennett, R. (2006). *The Culture of the New Capitalism*. New Haven: Yale University Press.

Singer, I. (1984a) *The Nature of Love, Volume 1: Plato to Luther*, 2nd ed. Chicago: University of Chicago Press.

Singer, I. (1984b) *The Nature of Love, Volume 2: Courtly and Romantic*. Chicago: University of Chicago Press.

Singer, I. (1987) *The Nature of Love: The Modern World*. Chicago: University of Chicago Press.

Sloterdijk, P. (1988) *The Critique of Cynical Reason*, trans. M. Eldred. Minneapolis, MN: University of Minnesota Press.

Soble, A. (ed.) (1998) *Eros, Agape, and Philia: Readings in the Philosophy of Love*. New York: Paragon House.

Solomon, R. C. (1988) *About Love: Reinventing Romance for Our Times*. New York: Simon and Schuster.

Stendhal (1915[1822]) *On Love*, trans. P. S. Woolf and C. N. Sidney. London: Duckworth.

Sveningsson, S. and M. Alvesson (2003) 'Managing managerial identities: organizational fragmentation, discourse and struggle', *Human Relations*, 59(10): 1163-1194.

Thompson, P. and S. Ackroyd (1999) *Organizational* Mis*behaviour*. London: Sage.

Tyler, M. and L. Cohen (2008) 'Management in/as comic relief: queer theory and gender performativity in the office', *Gender, Work and Organization*, 15(2): 113-132.

Tyler, M. and P. Hancock (2009) *The Management of Everyday Life*. Buckingham: Open University Press.

Vernon, M. (2005) 'Love at Work', *Management Today*, December: 54-57.

Wagoner, R. (1997) *The Meanings of Love: A Introduction to the Philosophy of Love*. Westport, CT: Praeger.

Weber, M. (1947) *The Theory of Economic and Social Organization*. New York: Free Press.

Williams, C. L., P. A. Giuffre and K. Dellinger (1999) 'Sexuality in the workplace: organizational control, sexual harassment, and the pursuit of pleasure', *Annual Review of Sociology*, 25: 73-94.

Zelizer, V. A. (2000) 'The purchase of intimacy', *Law and Social Inquiry*, 25(3): 817-848.

Žižek, S. (1996) 'Love beyond law', available at http://www.lacan.com /zizlola.htm (accessed September 2010).

Zupančič, A. (2000) *Ethics of the Real: Kant, Lacan*. London: Verso

6

You Are Where You Are Not: Lacan and Ideology in Contemporary Workplaces

Peter Fleming

Lacan's psychoanalytic insights regarding identification, the subject and the unconscious hold much promise for extending important themes in critical organization studies. This has been demonstrated by, among others, Roberts (2005) in his analysis of power and in the work of Jones and Spicer (2005) in relation to entrepreneurship. This chapter aims to show how some of Lacan's most interesting translations of Freud can further our understandings of *ideological power* in organizations. Ideology has long been a staple concern in organization theory – best summed up in Burawoy's (1979) classic question about behaviour on an shop floor: 'Why do these workers work so hard?' This question is animated by a crucial absence: the level of work conducted betrays an excessive enthusiasm that cannot be explained by the whip of economic necessity alone. Following the post-Marxist tradition, ideology is defined as 'reasons for participating in the accumulation process that are rooted in quotidian reality, and attuned to the values and concerns of those who need to be actively involved' (Boltanski and Chiapello, 2005: 21). In other words, all is not what it seems, and it is this appearance of discourse that covers up, displaces and structures the social mechanics of domination lying behind and under official accounts of reality. Such a discursive attuning is constitutive also, co-ordinating the energies of people through the subjectification of certain desires, needs, ideas and so forth. While ideology may involve force and coercion, ideological domination secures subordination through the constitution of the subject and their bodies (Eagleton, 1991; Žižek, 1997).

The implications that Lacanian psychoanalysis has for understanding ideology can be found in the extremely influential writings of Žižek. While Žižek draws upon the Lacanian *oeuvre* in a varied and diverse manner, his use of it to understand ideology is particularly powerful. His approach consists of an unconventional and unintuitive blend of Lacanian psychoanalysis, Hegelian dialectics and Althusserian structuralism. It is not only via the ego that subjects become constituted as believing bearers of ideology, but also through the transference of belief, identification and desire onto the 'external' world of practice, objects and others (who do the work of believing in our place). Following Lacan's infamous re-reading of Descartes datum, '*cogito, ergo sum*' ('I think where I am not, therefore, I am where I do not think'), the ideological constitution of the subject is characterised by a radical alterity. The subject is a *symptom* of processes that take place elsewhere within the signifying chain of believing rituals, object and other agents (Grosz, 1990). Žižek's well-known example of the modern cynic is exemplary here: the cynical bureaucrat, lawyer or corporate accountant dis-identifies with the dominant ideology of capitalism (perhaps reading *Marx for Beginners* on the weekend), but still acts *as if* they are stalwarts of the free market, and it is in the realm of social practice that the politics of belief and obedience really take hold (see Fleming and Spicer, 2003; 2005).

This approach to ideology is a political corollary of Lacan's displacement of the subject. The ego is always in secret communication with its absent other onto which it projects its own image. For it is the division between elements that indexes the signifier rather than the signified itself. Žižek transposes this positive symbolic absence into a material absence. It is not only the symbolic Other that stands in for us, but *presupposed* others insofar as we transfer the labour of identification onto people, rituals and practices within a social network. In this sense, ideology in work organizations today uncannily follows the favourite management strategy of out-sourcing: others (who do not necessarily exist) conduct the labour of our ideological beliefs (that we may never have actually held) since the psychic costs of such beliefs are reduced through externalization. This consequently frees an inner sphere of subjectivity where we can indulge in fantasies of compassion, philanthropy and the obscene. Or, as Žižek puts it, we can simply 'take a rest' (Žižek, 1997: 109).

Why might the outsourced subject be a prime manifestation of ideological power in today's organizations? I think it relates to the emergence of a management trend that actually encourages dis-identification, tempered radicalism and creative criticism among employees. In the last part of this chapter I will suggest that Žižek's reading of ideological displacement highlights developments in capitalist organizations and a new spirit of capitalism in managerial discourse (Boltanski and Chiapello, 2005). With the failure of the mono corporate cultures of the 1980s and 1990s, management are increasingly mobilizing neo-normative controls in which so-called authentic expressions of self ('warts and all') are encouraged (Fleming and Sturdy, 2009). Management gurus now argue that 'liberated firms' ought to employ free-radicals, dissenters and freaks who in actual fact conform to the logic of production in very specific ways. Underlying the promotion of such designer resistance is the mantra to 'be yourself', often expressed in the anti-corporate and anti-hierarchy ethos of hackers, IT-heads and dot.com engineers (Ross, 2004). I will maintain that the ideology of dis-identification and its function of displacing belief onto the external Other fits very well with this emerging form of identity regulation.

Lacan's Displaced Subject

As is well known, Lacan makes a major contribution to the tradition of thought that has aimed to decentre the subject, demonstrating how he/she is not the master of his or her own home. The notion of displacement and the stand-in (or substitute), of course, goes back to Freud's analysis of hysteria (displacement of the symptom) and dream-work (displacement of the unconscious through association). While displacement features in much of Lacan's work, it is particularly prominent in his analysis of the so-called split subject that can never coincide with itself. The common theme here is that once the subject enters the symbolic it foregoes the signified and becomes fundamentally divided from itself. This division is a lack we desire to fill but cannot since this lack *is* the very subject and was always there from the start (we were never whole). Important for this chapter is Lacan's argument that the subjective apparatus is something that is forever displaced beyond itself, determined by what it is not and has never been (hence the importance of retroactive psychic work). Indeed, so important is the idea of this lack or breach, that the subject can only be supposed or assumed (hence the importance of barring the ~~subject~~). As Lacan puts it, 'once the subject himself comes into being, he owes it to a certain nonbeing upon which he raises up his being' (Lacan, 1988: 192). Let's unpack this notion in more detail so that we can demonstrate how Žižek utilizes it in his materialist theory of ideology.

In his classic paper discussing the 'The Mirror Stage', Lacan (1977a) identifies an image of self that is differentiated from the world in the dissolution of the primary narcissism of the pre-symbolic subject. The small child laughs and enjoys the accomplishment of the unity that it mis-recognises in the ideal-image of itself. This imaginary represents an alienating split between the ego and the specular image, setting into play expectations and desires that operate both in and outside of us through a kind of autoscopy. The image that the ego identifies with and fixates on is something that is very recognisably us but at the same time alien since it is never attainable and always one step ahead or behind us. In this sense, Lacan's notion of displacement reconfigures the Cartesian cogito of primary doubt by revealing the tautological basis of its founding axiom ('I think therefore I am'). The basis of self-recognition cannot be completely in-itself since this is akin to pulling ourselves up by our own bootstraps – the cogito requires something beyond itself that cannot figure within its own self-reflection (just as Plato considered the conundrum of why the eye cannot see itself seeing). The Lacanian subject is thus symptomatic of the alienating split brought about by a foreign imaginary that creates an exterior view. This foreignness cannot be escaped since it is the self in proper terms, although it is never truly ours either; hence, our vacillation between inner and outer mental spheres and the desire to return to the pre-mirror stage.

The radical alterity of the subject is explored in the paper, 'The Agency of the Letter' (1977b). Here Lacan deals directly with the idea that the psychic apparatus is a function of an Other language. While this alienation through language paradoxically affords a degree of presence and fullness, it is always lacking given the displacement that makes it possible. When the Other of language (the unconscious in this case) speaks, of course, the subject is then nothing but a signifier. As explained nicely by Fink (1995):

> By submitting to the Other, the child nevertheless gains something: he or she becomes, in a sense, one of language's subjects, a subject 'of language' or 'in language'. Schematically represented, the child,

submitting to the Other, allows the signifier to stand in for him or her... The child coming to be as a divided subject, disappears beneath or behind the signifier, S. (Fink, 1995: 49)

Further, in the seminar on the 'Purloined Letter' (1972), the idea of the signifier over the signified gives predominance to the operative relationship between the signifiers of any given chain. Thus, not only is the subject 'lost' to the letter, but a mere relationship between signifiers since, following de Saussure, langue is structured by difference and displaced presence. The signifier 'slides' over the signified and is lacking in any central anchor or defined place. What some have called the constitutive lack of the signifying chain suggests that the subject is defined by what it is not, a set of displaced signifiers that can never be gathered within itself (Grosz, 1990). It is this vacillation between the concentric and excentric, the signifier and signified 'I' that underlies the substituted ego. Once again, this stance echoes with the Cartesian *cogito, ergo sum*:

Is the place that I occupy as subject of the signifier concentric or eccentric in relation to the place I occupy as subject of the signified? That is the question. The point is not to know whether I speak of myself in a way that conforms to what I am, but rather to know whether, when I speak of myself, I am the same as the self of whom I speak. (Lacan, 2006: 430)

The field of the Other spreads the subject along the sliding signifying chain, revealing a lack that we narcissistically desire to close. Hence Lacan's strange phrase mentioned above, 'I think where I am not, therefore, I am where I do not think'. Indeed, note the topological meaning of this re-interpretation of *cogito, ergo sum* whereby space becomes an important index. As the great tradition of structural anthropology (Levi-Strauss) and linguistics (Saussure) suggests, the structure of language is one of symbolic space, of relations, demarcations, differences and distances. I will propose next that Žižek reads this approach to displacement through the socio-geography lens of Marxian political economy.

Žižek, Displacement and Ideology

Žižek develops his notion of the displaced ideological subject through a novel blending of Marx, Hegel and Lacan (see also Fleming and Spicer,

2003; 2005). Two important displacements are evident in his reading. The first is that which is proper to historical materialism, the sphere of contextualized practice. Here, the centred inner seat of belief is unwittingly transferred onto the subject's practice – with the modern cynic who dis-identifies with the dominant ideology as the most obvious example. The second displacement enlists other people who are within the imaginary network of social relations in any given political milieu. The important aspect of this type of displacement, of course, is that these believing others might not even exist, since it is enough to *presuppose* that there are others who will believe for us. This approach to ideological displacement has significant implications for how we understand power in contemporary organizations where dis-identification and anti-hierarchical coolness are encouraged.

1. Displacement onto Practice

The displaced subject in the symbolic order bears a striking resemblance to the ideological secret of the commodity fetish outlined by Marx (1976) in *Capital*. The simple and unassuming commodity is but a manifestation of a complex social apparatus operating behind the scenes. Marx's theory of the commodity fetish suggests that relations between people – intimate exchanges of discourse and identification and most importantly, co-operative labour – are displaced onto objects that then go to work in the marketplace, as if endowed with 'metaphysical subtleties and theological niceties' (Marx, 1972: 163). Such a displacement is 'interpassive' in the sense that when I interact with objects, rituals and others, 'the object itself takes from me, deprives me of, my own passive reaction of satisfaction (or mourning or laughter), so that it is the object that "enjoys the show" instead of me, relieving me of the superego duty to enjoy myself' (Žižek, 2006b: 5). In relation to practice, key here is the opening of a gulf between the formal subject of belief and the objective practices that believe in our place. The objectivity of practice – the rituals, routines and mind-numbingly ordinary vagaries of everyday life in the marketplace of commodities and employment – becomes the index of ideological devotion to the dominant economic order.

In *The Sublime Object of Ideology* Žižek applies this formula to the quintessential post-modern figure of the enlightened cynic. The cynic found in today's skeptical Western culture (see Sloterdijk, 1988; Bewes, 1997), is immune to the typical charge of commodity fetishism. The disillusioned cynic is well aware there is nothing mysterious about the commodity form, that it is merely the symbolic manifestation of social relations that have become dead labour. But herein lies the potential ideological function of cynicism. As Žižek argues, 'cynical distance is just one way to blind ourselves to the structuring power of ideological fantasy: even if we do not take things seriously, even if we keep an ironical distance, *we are still doing them*' (Žižek, 1989: 32). Žižek accordingly reformulates the Marxian idiom, 'they know very well what they are doing and do it anyway' (see also Žižek, 1991). Furthermore, the illusion of the commodity is 'at the level of what the individuals are doing, and not only what they think or know they are doing... the problem is their social activity itself' (Žižek, 1989: 31).

According to Žižek, the fetishistic fantasy props up the commodity form in a two-fold manner: first, by infiltrating our practices so that we act as if we are fervent believers in capitalist relations. Second, by perpetuating the error that ideology only works on our internal thoughts and opinions: 'what they do not know, what they misrecognize, is the fact that in their social reality itself, in their social activity – in the act of commodity exchange – they are guided by a fetishistic illusion' (Žižek, 1989: 31). Amidst the structuring fantasy of the marketplace, Žižek suggests, the subject is completely free to have all the radical and deviant thoughts he or she wants because, in their actions and institutional supports, they are still identifying with the commands of authority. What we see at work here is a process of ideological transference in which identification in an authority is placed onto a set of objects that perform the necessary rituals of submission for us. Žižek uses the example of the movie *MASH* (an army field hospital) in which the antiwar cynicism and cheeky fooling around of the doctors actually allows them to work more efficiently. In elaborating this idea, Žižek mentions Althusser's (1971) celebrated reference to Pascal's Jansenist meditation on religious devotion: if you do not believe in God, then 'kneel down, move your lips in prayer and you will believe' (Althusser, 1971: 168). Act *as if* you believe in God and you will then believe. Here the dialectic of belief subverts the common rationalist fallacy that action is a product of cognition – indeed, the opposite is just as true, belief is a corollary of action. For Althusser, ideological belief takes hold of the subject in a manner analogous to Pascal's (1966) depiction of religious belief because the external ritual of ideology has a material element that

175

precedes our subjective identifications, or in Žižek's case, dis-identifications (cynicism, satire, humour, etc.).

2. Displacement onto Others

What we can call the 'vertical' displacement of the subject onto material practice has an even more unsettling 'horizontal' counterpart, the displacement of the labour of belief onto supposed others. Not only can our identification with a system be displaced onto objective practice, but also onto other actors and agents who believe for us in our place. Žižek is fond of emphasising just how radically exterior our most personally experienced sensations are. For instance, enjoyment and laughter might be experienced for us by canned laughter on television sitcoms. When we slip over on a wet footpath, our companion exclaims 'oops!' instead of us. In some cultures mourners are hired to do the wailing for the bereaved at the funeral of a loved one. Žižek gives a very humorous example by way of a famous joke that circulated in the former Yugoslavia. In the USSR, the party officials drive in luxury limousines and workers must walk. In Yugoslavia, however, it is the workers who drive in the limousines, *via* the party officials.

There are two important caveats regarding the idea that belief might be displaced onto external others. First, as far as Žižek is concerned, the subject who believes through others should not be conceptualized in terms of reification because 'there are some beliefs which are from the outset "decentred" beliefs of the Other' (Žižek, 1997: 41). Indeed, he attempts to avoid the humanist error of positing an original or *a priori* agent of belief behind the event of transference. Žižek's (1997) concept of displacement is qualified thus:

> the crucial mistake to be avoided here is, again, the properly 'humanist' notion that this belief embodied in things, displaced onto things, is nothing but a reified form of direct belief, in which case the task of the phenomenological reconstitution of the genesis of 'reification' would be to demonstrate how the original human belief was transposed onto things. The paradox to be maintained... is that *displacement is original and constitutive*: there is no immediate, self-present living subjectivity to whom the belief embodied in social things can be attributed and who is then dispossessed of it. (Žižek, 1997: 44)

Here, the 'dis' of displace is misleading since there was never an original place of belief that was subsequently transferred onto the subject. This is the paradox of holding beliefs that we have never personally held. The second point is that those who believe in our place do not have to actually exist – they can be merely supposed. This is because the displacement of belief onto others involves a minimal *belief in the belief of the other*. To paraphrase Žižek, when I say 'I believe in the corporate culture', what I really mean is 'I believe there are some people who might believe in the corporate culture'. This is the function of the guarantor: 'yet this guarantor is always deferred, displaced never present in persona... the point of course is that the subject who directly believes, needs not exist for the belief to be operative' (Žižek, 1997: 44).

This barring of both the original subject of belief and the Other who does the work of believing in my place is the ultimate example of the signifier replacing the subject. It is now more the radically de-centred subject that is at work than any psychologically centred ego. In *The Parallax View* (2006a), Žižek provides yet another example of the Other believing in our place that reveals the important ideological consequences of presupposing others who identify for us. The example is framed with a discussion of why it is difficult to be Kantian or at least 'enlightened' in the Kantian sense. For Kant, the mature citizen (enlightened and autonomous) does not fear their freedom – they do not rely on an external or natural master who sets the limits to their bad and unruly behaviour. The mature individual realises that there is no natural master to provide this limit, since we are free to decide for ourselves what this might be. As a result, 'a truly enlightened mature human being is a subject who no longer needs a master, who can fully assume the heavy burden of defining his own limitations' (Žižek, 2006a: 90). According to Žižek, it is the inability to act maturely that fuels a particular type of ideological transference in today's promiscuous post-modern society. Underlying the chic transgressions of the avant-garde consumer culture, the ideological support of supposed *non-transgression* is never far away. In terms of Kantian immaturity, much pop-radicalism relies upon an external guarantor, another who represents pure conformity and lawfulness. As Žižek explains:

> a promiscuous teenager may engage in extreme orgies with group sex and drugs, but what he cannot bear is the idea that his mother could be doing something similar – his orgies rely on the supposed purity of his mother which serves as the point of exception, the external guarantee: I can do what ever I like, since I know my mother keeps her place pure

for me... The most difficult thing is not to violate the prohibitions in a wild orgy of enjoyment, but to do this without relying on someone else who is presupposed not to enjoy so that I can enjoy... the same goes for belief: the difficult thing is not to reject belief in order to shock a believing other, but to be a nonbeliever without the need for another subject supposed to believe on my behalf. (Žižek, 2006a: 91)

This turns on its head the usual Žižekian argument regarding the obscene underbelly of the Law (see Contu, 2006). Rather than resistance being the deferred precondition for the operation of a dominant ideology, it is the presupposition of a reliable conformity that underlies a particular type of pseudo-subversive activity (in terms of popular culture, see Frank, 1998). In the context of the corporation, we might get up to all sorts of tricks in terms of sabotage, lampooning the corporate culture and farting as the CEO drives past in his antique Porsche, but the meaning of that resistance must be gauged in terms of the presupposed limitations displaced by the act. Does my dis-identification in the corporate context use the ideological prop of actual or imagined others who will (and indeed must) believe in my place? If so, it is not only my practice that identifies for me, but extended others (be they team members, managers, consumers or whatever). In this sense, the labour of identifying with an ideology of enterprise, culture, innovation and so forth is effectively outsourced. And as Žižek nicely maintains, the ideological importance of such outsourcing is not the displaced Other (the person who believes in my place) but the cipher of inner freedom that this generates in me.

Designer Resistance and the New Spirit of Capitalism

Žižek's reading of Lacan is important for understanding ideology in contemporary organizations because it seems to resonate with permutations in contemporary forms of managerial control (in core employment situations of the West at least). Indeed, I will suggest that the ideology of false dis-identification fits the new spirit of 'binge capitalism' in that the bleeding-edge software company or consulting firm desires the flexible and innovative cynic, rather than the conformist 'organizational man'. A number of recent studies have identified a novel form of identity regulation emerging out of the failed projects of culture regulation and normative control popularized in the 1980s and 1990s. Rather than exhorting employees to subjectively conform to a unitary set of values *à la* cultures of commitment, workers are invited to simply 'be themselves'. Here, in addition to task empowerment, recruits should be existentially 'empowered' in that they should not share the organization's values, and should even oppose them (or at least within the limits of continued productivity). Moreover, today's employees ought to break the traditional work/non-work boundary by 'having fun' at work and express more of their true selves – be this tempered radicalism, disagreement or discretion. Diversity and incongruence with (traditional) organizational norms is key (Florida, 2004). In Tom Peter's (2003) latest series of offerings, for example, he argues that managers should hire the young, imaginative, underground type, who despise managerial hierarchies, display generation-Y characteristics and follow individualist portfolio-careers. From a more humanist perspective, Meyerson (2003) celebrates the tempered radical as the youthful postmodern organizational leader that will render for-profit firms as spheres of virtue. Opposed to the fake presentations of self engendered by patently bogus culture programmes, life-style, chic radicalism, authenticity and difference are encouraged instead (also see Foster and Kaplan, 2001). I suggest that this shift represents a form of managerial identity control that is perhaps more insidious than its predecessor; it is the self behind the faux displays including cynicism, irony and 'warts and all' expressions of self that is now targeted by organizational control systems. This development maps almost perfectly onto broader trends associated with industrializing bohemia and anti-capitalist sentiments among young professional knowledge workers.

In much of this trend, as Ross (2004), Fleming and Sturdy (2009) and Boltanski and Chiapello (2005) note, there is a strategic promotion of a particular kind of designer resistance associated with distancing, dis-identification and so forth. It is in this way that the dynamics of this new spirit of capitalism (and its attendant management techniques) displays fundamental aspects highlighted in Žižek's Lacanian analysis of ideological control. We can see this in relation to the two kinds of displacement outlined above. In relation to displacement onto practice, we can extend our earlier analysis regarding the ideology of cynicism to indicate how novel management techniques may actually encourage 'designer resistance' in order to enhance the labour process. That is to say, in our earlier article on cynical dis-identification (Fleming and Spicer, 2003), we positioned the ideological effects of distancing selfhood from culture as an *inadvertent* outcome of shifting workplace politics. But now I think that a degree of designer resistance is promoted, especially in the sense of cynical cool, the slacker ethic and bohemian distance – as I have indicated in empirical examples elsewhere (Fleming, 2009). This is no more evident than in Frank's excellent *The Conquest of Cool* (1998) where he shows how the corporate machine attempts to appropriate the production of cool, something that is usually borne in the exploited classes and anti-establishment sentiments.

In terms of this extremely circumscribed 'be yourself' ethos, the cynical ideology formula becomes even more embedded: 'I know very well that culture management is a pile of shit, but I act as if I firmly identify with it'. Here the typical displacement of identification occurs. But the dis-identification that smooths the road for the objectivity of belief is not an inadvertent outcome of disgruntlement or well-founded mistrust; it is now an important dimension of the official discourse of cultural regulation that short-circuits real insubordination. It adheres to the philosophy of *employable* authenticity, anti-authoritarianism, life-style diversity and self-fashioning that we now see being articulated as a work ethic in more and more organizations (e.g. Foster and Kaplan, 2001). Returning to Burawoy's (1979) still pertinent question ('why do they work so hard?'), in this case it is because it is easier to put in long and creative hours when one is no longer required to devoutly internalize a unitary belief in exploitation (via a flimsy culture management programme). The internal space created by the displacement of identification onto external practices, rituals and significant others allows respite from the 'siege and assault' of corporate life. Further, in the case of Ross's (2004) youthful anti-capitalist hackers recruited by a dot.com company called Razorfish, the culture of 'being yourself' subtly articulates the anti-conformist ethos to the goals of the company. As a result of cynical outsourcing of belief to objective practices, an unlikely congruence is established between underground sentiments (e.g. coffee infused late nights in a dark warehouse environment which is expressly anti-commercial) and the extraction of surplus value (what Ross calls 'Geekploitation').

Now to the second kind of displacement in which others are posited as the believing agents that under-write the dis-identification process. It can be recalled how Žižek highlighted how much of the pseudo-transgression encouraged by the post-modern super-ego supposes a pure and believing other. It is this external Other that sets the limits for the transgression to produce meaning. Parallels can be found in the anti-establishment bohemian youth culture quietly filling the ranks of leading-edge capitalist firms. Ross's (2004) study provides an excellent example of this in which computer hackers espouse all sorts of subversive anti-corporate sentiments in the name of integrity and authenticity, even though the guarantor-image of their upper-middle class parents is obvious. The transgressive life-style of the creative class is supported by the knowledge that they are both defying and reinforcing their investment savvy parent/accountants who believe in their place. Of course, such a displacement imposes a strong limit to the 'freedom' of the enlightened cynic – transgress up until the point that income and future returns of investment might be jeopardised. The mature resistor, in Kantian terms, would perhaps not enter such an environment in the first place, as I will suggest below.

Resistance after Lacan

In using Lacan's analysis of displacement, Žižek has opened up some counter-intuitive features of ideological domination in contemporary organizations. We work hard because of our career, our identifications and consumption patterns. However, we also work hard not necessarily because we believe in the source of our domination, but because we have externalized the labour of belief to others who believe for us. The ideological illusion that keeps capitalism going is an objectively necessary one rather than one that gains positive endorsement among the workforce. Overall, the message is somewhat pessimistic from a progressive political standpoint. Indeed, the preoccupation is with manifest resistance: dis-identification and critique might be but a symptom of a more sophisticated mode of domination. In unpacking the Kantian notion of maturity and transgression without the supposition of an external Other who conserves the ideals of domination, Žižek approvingly quotes Lacan's criticism of the students involved in the '68 Parisian uprising; so often the pin-up ideal for the radical left: 'What you aspire to as revolutionaries is a master. You will get one' (Lacan, 2007: 207). It is surely worth noting, as shown in Boltanski and Chiapello's (2005) excellent analysis, that Lacan's admonition is germane to the successful incorporation of 1960s radicalism (or artistic critique as opposed to social critique) by a re-organized capitalism (see also Latour, 2004). But what would a mature resistance look like in this regard? Well, it is certainty not our job to ascertain some kind of authentic subversive space, especially following the important criticisms of this task levelled by Kondo (1990) and Collinson (1994) among others. But it is fair to ask how contemporary modalities of oppression that condone or even favour the tempered radical might be undermined. Given the above argument, one would expect that a non-reproductive resistance would entail distancing that fundamentally *includes practice, objects and others*. That is to say, counter-designer resistance would not distance itself from domination whilst presupposing an external guarantor of identification. It would adhere to a praxis of distance where practices, objects and others are enrolled in the radicalism rather than transferred.

For example, the ideological trope of cynical distance is undermined by connecting the radical cogito to practice by a) exiting the organization in question or b) never entering it in the first place. The importance of exit as a modality of protest has been well documented in sociological and organization thought (see Hirschman, 1970; Gabriel, 2006). Here, ideological displacement is foregone for material distance – literally leaving the organization. Perhaps more important are those instances where people choose not to enter the organizational sphere in the first place. Rather than focus on resistance that occurs within the firm, what about the multitude who make an ethico-political decision not to enter the ranks of corporate life? Another way in which the ideological effects of displaced identification might be short-circuited is through believing too much. Such 'in-sourcing' of belief has already been explored elsewhere in the literature – if a certain distance is actually necessary for the smooth functioning of the organization. As Gouldner (1955) and Blau (1955) highlighted in relation to the dysfunctions of bureaucracy, strict adherence to the principles contained in culture management, innovative flexibility and so forth, are potentially disruptive. Indeed, a major weakness of the culture management movement in the 1980s and 1990s was the ridiculous claims *apropos* participation, democracy and equality. Such claims were never really to be taken seriously – but when they were by subordinates and trade unions, they contradicted and confounded an important dimension of managerial control.

Finally, the ideological features of displacement might be confounded by not necessarily acting without the guarantor of an external limit as Žižek's reading of Kant might imply, but by enrolling the guarantor into the practice of dis-identification. That is to say, rather than relying on an Other who believes full-heartedly in the commodity, investment packages and management prerogative, the material other might be persuaded to follow the practice of disbelief. This is the basic process of recruiting others to join a counter-organization of resistance, be it an informal group (Roy, 1952; 1958), underground network of like-minded people (Collinson, 1994) or formal trade union (Edwards, 1979). There are many dangers associated with such a strategy, of course. But in a system in which the individualization of employees is a fundamental principal of domination (e.g., 'just be yourself'), the accentuation of solidarity over difference among cohorts may be more effective in transforming the social structures of exploitation that currently under-labour capitalism.

References

Althusser, L. (1971) 'Ideology and ideological state apparatuses (notes towards an investigation)', in L. Althusser *Lenin and Philosophy and Other Essays*. London: New Left Books.

Bewes, T. (1997) *Cynicism and Postmodernity*. London: Verso.

Blau, P. (1955) *The Dynamics of Bureaucracy*. Chicago: University of Chicago Press.

Boltanski, L. and E. Chiapello (2005) *The New Spirit of Capitalism*. London: Verso.

Burawoy, M. (1979) *Manufacturing Consent: Changes in the Labour Process Under Monopoly Capitalism*. Chicago: University of Chicago Press.

Collinson, D. (1994) 'Strategies of resistance', in J. Jermier, D. Knights and W. Nord (eds) *Resistance and Power in Organizations*. London: Routledge.

Contu, A. (2006) 'A question of resistance?' Paper presented at the Critical Management Studies Research Workshop, 11-12 August, Atlanta.

Eagleton, T. (1991) *Ideology: An Introduction*. London: Verso.

Edwards, R. (1979) *Contested Terrain: The Transformation of Workplace in the Twentieth Century*. New York: Basic Books.

Fink, B. (1995) *The Lacanian Subject: Between Language and Jouissance*. Princeton: Princeton University Press.

Fleming, P. (2009) *Authenticity and the Cultural Politics of Work*. Oxford: Oxford University Press.

Fleming, P. and A. Spicer (2003) 'Working at a cynical distance: implications for subjectivity, power and resistance', *Organization*, 10(1): 157-179.

Fleming, P. and A. Spicer (2005) 'How objects believe for us: applications in organizational analysis', *Culture and Organization*, 11(3): 181-193.

Fleming, P. and A. Sturdy (2009) '"Just be yourself!": towards neo-normative control in organizations?', *Employee Relations*, 31(6): 569-583.

Florida, R. (2004) *The Rise of the Creative Class*. North Melbourne: Pluto Press.

Foster, R. and S. Kaplan (2001) *Creative Destruction: Why Companies That Are Built to Last Underperform the Market – And How to Successfully Transform Them*. New York: Currency.

Frank, T. (1998) *The Conquest of Cool: Business Culture, Counterculture and the Rise of Hip Consumerism*. Chicago: University of Chicago Press.

Gabriel, Y. (2006) 'Spectacles of resistance and resistance of spectacles', Paper presented at the Critical Management Studies Research Workshop, 11-12 August, Atlanta.

Gouldner, A. (1955) *Wildcat Strike*. London: Routledge and Kegan Paul.

Grosz, E. (1990) *Jacques Lacan: A Feminist Introduction*. London: Routledge.

Hirschman, A. (1970) *Exit, Voice, and Loyalty: Responses to Decline in Firms, Organizations and States*. Cambridge, Mass: Harvard University Press.

Jones, C. and A. Spicer (2005) 'The sublime object of entrepreneurship', *Organization*, 12(2): 223-246

Kondo, D. (1990) *Crafting Selves: Power, Gender and Discourse of Identity in a Japanese Workplace*. Chicago: University of Chicago Press.

Lacan, J. (1972). 'Seminar on "the purloined letter"', trans. J. Mehlman, *Yale French Studies*, 48: 39-72.

Lacan, J. (1977a) 'The mirror stage as formative of the function of the I', in J. Lacan *Écrits: A Selection*, trans. A. Sheridan. London: Tavistock.

Lacan, J. (1977b). 'The agency of the letter in the unconscious or reason since Freud', in J. Lacan *Écrits: A Selection*, trans. A. Sheridan. London: Tavistock.

Lacan, J. (1988) *The Ego in Freud's Theory and in the Techniques of Psychoanalysis: The Seminar of Jacques Lacan, Book II, 1954-1955*, trans. S. Tomaselli. New York: Norton.

Lacan, J. (2006) *Écrits,* trans. B. Fink, New York: Norton.

Lacan, J. (2007) *The Other Side of Psychoanalysis: The Seminar of Jacques Lacan, Book XVII, 1969-70*, trans. R. Grigg. New York: Norton.

Latour, B. (2004) 'Why has critique run out of steam? From matters of fact to matters of concern', *Critical Inquiry*, 30(Winter): 225-248.

Marx, K. (1976) *Capital: Volume One*, trans. B. Fowkes. London: Pelican.

Meyerson, D. (2003) *Tempered Radicals: How Everyday Leaders Inspire Change at Work*. Boston: Harvard University Press.

Pascal, B. (1966) *Pensées*. Harmondswood, UK: Penguin.

Peters, T. (2003) *Re-Imagine! Business Excellence in a Disruptive Age*. London: Dorling Kindersley.

Roberts, J. (2005) 'The power of the Imaginary in disciplinary processes', *Organization*, 12(5): 621-645.

Ross, A. (2004) *No-Collar: The Humane Workplace and its Hidden Costs*. Philadelphia: Temple University Press.

Roy, D. (1952) 'Quota restriction and goldbricking in a machine shop', *American Journal of Sociology*, 57(5): 427-42.

Roy, D. (1958) 'Banana time: job satisfaction and informal interaction', *Human Organization*, 18: 158-168.

Sloterdijk, P. (1988) *The Critique of Cynical Reason*. Minneapolis: University of Minnesota Press.

Žižek, S. (1989) *The Sublime Object of Ideology*. London: Verso.

Žižek, S. (1991) *For They Know Not What They Do: Enjoyment as a Political Factor*. London: Verso.

Žižek, S. (1997) 'The supposed subjects of ideology', *Critical Quarterly*, 39(2): 39-59.

Žižek, S. (2006a) *The Parallax View*. London: Verso.

Žižek, S. (2006b) 'The interpassive subject', available at
    http://www.lacan.com/interpass.htm (accessed September 2010).

7

Danger! Neurotics at Work

Carol Owens

Within the study of (so-called) organizations, many have taken for granted the curious *pastiche* of human subjects – necessarily boundaried against other similar entities – with aim-oriented processes. We might wonder what sense at all can be made of speaking about an 'organization' as if it were anything other than the deployment of subjects in a particular manner? The recent contributions to this field by critical management theorists (variously informed by poststructuralist and Lacanian analytics) have allowed for a shift in focus; *from* the 'organization' itself as some kind of über-agency *to* the mode of 'organizing' within the organization. As such, a specifically Lacanian twist performs the much-needed singularizing of the research gaze so as to obtain on the one hand, a case-by-case examination of the organizing principles of any organization that may then be subjected to an analysis that yields the particularities of its effects on the subject within the organization, and on the other, mobilizes certain discourses within which the organization understood as a master signifier draws together a field of signification, notwithstanding its own vacuity.[1]

In this chapter I want to examine some of the modalities of the subject within the organization in order to consider if it is the case that a certain 'kind' of subject might be more or less commensurately locatable within specific hegemonic organizational practices of control and activity. If indeed it is the case that a certain kind of subject co-relates to, or co-exists with a certain kind of organizational practice, how might a specifically Lacanian psychoanalytic lens illuminate that subject? As such we need to consider *what* it is that a subject relates to when they relate to an organization. For Lacanians this kind of question usually requires some tracing of the fantasy in so far as it structures any relation with the Other. However, at the same time, we cannot ignore that this Lacanian *Big Other* is in somewhat of a decline and that we must therefore take into account contemporary symptoms in such a way as to consider the orientation of the subject – to what Miller has tagged 'transferable objects' as well as the more traditional investments the subject has in relation to *das Ding* as original lost object. These 'investments', variously understood, mobilise another key Lacanian trajectory, namely, the question of *how* the subject is so invested. As such, the terrain of *jouissance* (and its regulation) is implicated. In this chapter, the subject within-the-organization will be examined in the context of the workplace as the specific site of organizational activity according to these coordinates.

We will begin by making some general observations about the workplace as a particular location inhabited by neurotic subjects, which will allow us to make some initial comments about the transformation of the workplace in recent times and the effects this transformation has on subjects. We will then explore specific destinies emergent in the workplace according to Freud's assertions concerning the function of work *qua* sublimation and according to Lacan's assertions about the function of collective, socially accepted sublimations as colonizers of 'the field of *das Ding*'. We shall go on to consider recent work on neo-normative control as instancing a radical twist in the modalities of *jouissance* available to subjects in the workplace. Finally we will explore the notion of 'subjective disarray' as a feature of the contemporary workplace, and perhaps, of the contemporaneously unreliable Other.

Neurotics at work

> [A]s a path to happiness, work is not highly prized by men. They do not strive after it as they do after other possibilities of satisfaction. The great majority of people only work under the stress of necessity, and this natural human aversion to work raises the most difficult social problems. (Freud, 1991: 80, n. 1)

> Put the key of despair into the lock of apathy. Turn the knob of mediocrity slowly and open the gates of despondency. Welcome to a day in the average office. (David Brent, *The Office*)

Freud's statement above may seem at odds with the general thrust of his argument for the effective sublimation of the instincts (made functional in the yield of pleasure) that can be achieved through physical and intellectual work. Yet precisely, the world of work and the pleasures obtainable therein, the 'finer and higher' satisfactions, are in fact for Freud accessible to 'only a few people'. The rest of us labour 'under the stress of necessity' and our aversion to this forced labour foregrounds a neurotic subjectivity in ever more isolating conditions of existence. Late capitalism – with its devices of bureaucracy, mechanisms of 'operativity', such as appraisal schemes, systems of continuous professional 'development' and technological matrices – shore up a field of the subject; libidinalised with respect to the objects of his/her enjoyment through endless tasks and projects, and even through 'time' itself, in the case of computerized logged-hours. As such, we might wonder then, in the first instance, if in fact the 'difficult social problems' alluded to by Freud above are in fact the outcome of manifest pathologies created in the workplace as the conditions of an ever-more enjoying Other on the one hand, and on the other hand an ever-more inconsistent Other. This is to say that for some subjects, the ego ideal still functions in its place, i.e., in so far as symbolic identification with the organization's aims and objectives – *one's* organizational persona – entails a kind of neurotic solution in the form of a symptom, which continues to *work* for the subject (even if at times the subject needs a little help to maintain the symptom). However at this time, 'our time', (Lacanian) psychoanalytic practitioners are also speaking of a clinic of 'contemporary symptoms' where the decline of the paternal function, the dis*inclination* of the subject in relation to the name(s)-of-the-father, more than ever before, it seems, evidences a commensurate primacy of the *objet petit a* over that of the ideal. This primacy of the *objet a*, or rather *objets a* in the sense of all of those 'transferable objects' derived from the particular objects and advanced by Lacan in his tenth seminar as pertaining to the order of nature (Lacan, 1962-63) together with the objects of sublimation in their function of 'filling in' for the lost object, *das Ding*, are recognized in the subject's various over-consumptions, addictions, and derailing fugues.

In my practice in Dublin I am indeed struck by the apparent dovetailing of neurotic structure and symptom formation with certain job descriptions as if, incredibly, neurotic characteristics have become written into the requirements specific to certain positions of employment. Yet I also note the increased prevalence of *a kind* of subjective destitution, where the neurotic symptom fails to work in the Lacanian sense of holding the fantasy in place, and what Žižek (after Badiou) has called a 'passion for the real' comes to the fore (Žižek, 2002: 5-6). Of course the notion of subjective destitution is posited as one outcome of the end of analysis and, at least in that sense, is understood as a desirable end state of the work. We can recall here Lacan's comments in his seventh seminar regarding the end of the 'training analysis' where he proposes that the subject should reach and come to know the domain and experience of absolute disarray.[2] Commensurate with this theorizing of a subjective destitution in Lacan is a fall of the Other, where the Other ceases to exist, ceases to be guaranteed as it were. It is in this way that I think patients are encountering particular experiences of disarray in the workplace – where in fact the Other is more and more revealed to be lacking, inconsistent and not 'in its place' so to speak – that far from 'destitution' arising from any analytic work, in fact we begin the work of analysis with a condition of dis-identification where the old unfashionable signifiers of the workplace are absent. Clinical observation indicates that where the Other is not in its place, we find the desperate accumulation, consumption, stockpiling and storing of the *object*.

We can interpret the recent comments of various Lacanian psychoanalysts (Leader, 2008; Verhaeghe, 2004) who have drawn our attention to an increased incidence of depression, anxiety, and actual pathologies, as indexing a kind of subjective ahistoricity that appears to replace the traditional neurotic existential drama; where in the place of a story that once could be told in which the subject comes to inscribe themselves, there is instead an 'I don't know why I'm depressed/anxious/panicked… nothing happened'. This *'unbearable lightness of being'*, I believe, finds a natural homeland in so many of our contemporary workplaces where the 'call-centre' or 'the office' become less and less a recognizable instance of the symbolic (as in 'Darling I must go now or I'll be late for the symbolic order') and more and more an encounter with a 'staged fake' (Žižek, 2002: 14). In other words, where the workplace once functioned perhaps as the *place of work*, it has now become the location where selves can and indeed must be actualized. Moreover, the notion that self-actualisation is contingent upon the mobilization of the 'happy worker' conjures up the kind of 'terrorist civility' that Žižek speaks of in his *In Defense of Lost Causes* (Žižek, 2008: 18). It is not enough that we show up to do a day's work, but that we must be 'happy in our work'.

The compulsion to be 'happy in your work' is clearly another aspect of the super-egoic compulsion to enjoy; but as the obscene underbelly of the hegemonic practice of organizational control it is manifest in the idea that work is a route to self-fulfillment and happiness. As such, in this movement away from the idea of work as labour – the notion of labour as something dragged from the subject, often under conditions of torture – we have an instance of a 'Žižekian decaf' whereby 'we get the result without having to suffer unpleasant side effects' (Žižek, 2008: 47). The unpleasant side effects here are on the side of the organization that might be accused of unfair work practices, abusive employer/employee relations and so forth. Unsurprisingly, we can note here too the commensurate increase in the presence of the on-site organizational psychologist or counselor, usually schooled in cognitive behavioural therapy, whose methods of intervention of course foreclose any possibility of the analyses of unconscious complexes and drives. At the same time they mobilize and perpetuate the notion of the 'individual worker', who can be re-educated in order to 'gain the maximum' from his/her work experience. Indeed, many so-called traditional 'open systems' approaches to management foster the idea that a 'fit' between organization and employee can be brought about, allowing for inter-subjective as well as inter-organizational 'flux' – a notion that parodies somewhat the inherent characteristics of a narcissism of small differences!

As such, we could say that we are witnessing in the workplace a *virtualisation of reality*, where the 'work' in the 'workplace' has become emptied of any possible connotation of labour, where, as Žižek suggests, in keeping with late-capitalist consumerist society, 'real social life' itself acquires the features of a staged fake; with our neighbours – in this case 'workmates' – behaving like stage actors and extras (Žižek, 2002: 19). The old promotional tag for Mars bars, 'A Mars a day helps you work, rest, and play', neatly packaged a whole bundle of sublimatory gestures as both necessary on the one hand and achievable (with the help of a Mars bar of course) on the other. Are we not now seeing a kind of radical disruption of this tag, which announces 'All work and no play' as a kind of slogan for late capitalist subjects, where work is suddenly where you are really yourself, where you can be the self you dream of and yet al.so inevitably where for some, the dream ends. To play with another product slogan, where once it was proclaimed that 'Coke is Life' now it seems that we could cry out 'Work is life!' And I would argue, this latter dictum works very well for some neurotics but very badly for others, which readers who are familiar with Ricky Gervais's BAFTA winning BBC masterpiece *The Office* will no doubt have observed! Here, in what has been described as a 'mockumentary', we can gaze upon the habitat of the workplace in just the ways that I have outlined above: on the one hand we can see the *dangers* involved when neurotics are at work, how their various fantasies implicate them in their quest for *jouissance*, we get to enjoy (a little) ourselves, identifying with one or other character perhaps, at that safe distance, or indeed groan when a character makes a gesture that we find familiar from our own experience. On the other hand, are we not forced to consider the postmodern spectacle of the workplace as recorded by some unseen Other as the very staged fake it has become, a kind of made-up world where the Other has gone missing.

The Stress of Necessity (or What's Sublimation Got to Do with it?)

In *Civilisation and Its Discontents*, Freud poses the question: What does mankind demand of life and wish to achieve in it? He considers that the answer to this question can hardly be in doubt: happiness! Humans strive after happiness, wanting to become happy and to remain so (Freud, 1991: 76). The endeavour to be happy involves the reduction of the experience of pain and unpleasure, and at the same time, the experience of 'strong feelings of pleasure'. It is in this way that Freud will argue that what decides the purpose of life is none other than the programme of the 'pleasure principle'. A *strong* programme, Freud notes, that dominates the mental apparatus from the start. However, one which, he also remarks, has no possibility at all of being carried through since 'all the regulations of the universe run counter to it'. It is important to note here with Freud that happiness is defined as the (preferably sudden) *satisfaction of needs*. Unhappiness on the other hand, in the form of suffering, threatens us from three directions: from our own body, from the external world, and from our relations with others (this latter, according to Freud, is likely to cause us more pain than any other threat) (Freud, 1991: 77). The whole equation of maximizing pleasure and minimising pain affords a kind of mobilizing of what we can call (*pace* Lacan) a balancing of accounts in the economy of *jouissance*.

As an alternative to the 'strong' programme, we devote ourselves to the avoidance of unpleasure. Freud in his wisdom notes that some methods for avoiding unpleasure are extreme and some moderate. He introduces first what he calls the option of a total voluntary isolation: keeping oneself away from other people in order to ward off the threat of suffering through relating to others; this may remind us of Miller's recent interventions derived from Lacan's comments in his twenty-fourth seminar where he restates the cause of neurosis as social reality itself. Miller argues that in the contemporary clinic we are witnessing what he calls a 'disinsertion', a 'discontact' (Miller, 2008). In a time where the Other no longer exists, the radical nature of discontact or disinsertion indexes the subject's movement away from the pole of symbolic identification with the big Other *qua* ego ideal and towards a *jouissance* contingent upon the consumption of objects.

Another option for Freud involves, rather, a total immersion in (a total identification with) the community of 'men' and the utilization of science to ward off the threats posed by nature and/or the external world – let us say a more radically effective hysterical solution that cleaves to the existence of the Other (of science, of technology etc.) as the repository of knowledge.

Finally, the third option sketched out by Freud consists in solutions that are brought about at the level of the body, in other words, the real. For Freud, this latter option entails that non-satisfaction is not so painfully felt, but by the same token, neither is satisfaction so enjoyably experienced. Again, in Lacanian terms, we would see here the efforts of a self-administered *jouissance* unmediated by the Other.[3] At this point in his discussion, Freud will introduce the notion of 'sublimation' as part of this latter option for dealing with suffering. Sublimation effects a shifting of instinctual aims such that they cannot in the same way come up against frustration from the external world or the world of others, and it is as a by-product of his general discussion on the possibilities afforded by sublimation that Freud will comment for the first time on the function of 'work' as a sublimatory solution to the frustration of the instincts. Whereas the artist is capable of experiencing the joy of creating and the scientist the joy of discovery – these two terrains amounting to the obtainment of the higher and finer satisfactions for

Freud – the rest of us (non-artists and non-scientists) have to fall back on what Freud calls 'ordinary professional work'! Here, Freud makes some crucial remarks on the function of work as sublimation. He notes that 'no other technique for the conduct of life attaches the individual so firmly to reality as laying emphasis on work; for his work at least gives him a secure place in a portion of reality, in the human community' (Freud, 1991: 80, n. 1). He goes on to argue that 'work' offers the possibility of the displacement of a large amount of libidinal components (whether narcissistic, aggressive or even erotic) onto professional activity and onto the human relations connected with it. Even so, he notes that work is not highly prized by people who only really work because they 'need' to, not because it offers them a path to happiness.

Now, the whole trouble with the pursuit of happiness, psychoanalytically speaking, is that insofar as it involves pleasure, it also involves desire, and insofar as it involves desire, it also involves the unconscious drive in its circulation of what Freud has called *das Ding* and which in his 1959-60 seminar on ethics, Lacan will posit as 'beyond the pleasure principle'. What we find in the clinic of psychoanalysis is the neurotic's attempt to regulate his behaviour precisely so as to avoid what is often seen quite clearly as the goal of his desire; for, the pleasure principle is also involved in the order of avoiding excess, the 'too much' of pleasure. What regulates the function of the pleasure principle is the relation of the subject to *das Ding*.

Reference to 'the thing' in Lacan is based on Freud's term *das Ding*, which he had used in his *Project for a Scientific Psychology* to describe that which is perceived but cannot be recognised by the activity of thought, but that stays together as a thing. In Lacan's seminar on ethics, he sets up a structural opposition which poses the Freudian system of unconscious representations regulated by the pleasure principle against the unrepresentable *das Ding* situated beyond the pleasure principle. This thing will be inscribed by Lacan as something fundamentally lacking in a relationship to an individual but at the same time it is here in this primordial place of lack where Lacan locates the impetus of desire. This place of lack causes desire to be set in motion. Insofar as *das Ding* is in the place of the lost object, the pleasure principle governs the search for the lost object and imposes the detours which maintain the distance in relation to its obtainment.

The pleasure principle is the symbolic law, what we might regard as the 'safeguard of homeostasis', which tries to prevent as much as possible the occurrence of painful pleasure i.e. *jouissance* in Lacanian terminology. But it is precisely this *jouissance* which is attached to the satisfaction of the drive. Desire is that which is set in motion by lack. It is sustained by a fantasy that masks the *jouissance* of the drive, but as it is trapped within the confines of the pleasure principle, it remains unsatisfied in its quest to arrive at the object which would in some way respond to the lack.

Now, for Lacan, civilization in the form of collectivities deludes itself on the subject of *das Ding*; in fact it 'colonizes the field of *das Ding* with imaginary schemes' (Lacan, 1992: 99). He goes on to argue that this is how collective, socially acceptable sublimations operate. And it is evident that one of the terrains so colonized by the field of *das Ding* with imaginary schemes is the workplace itself. As such, imaginary schemes in the workplace can include a whole plethora of collective socially accepted sublimations: from the elevation of the 'team' – i.e. the object 'team' raised to the dignity of *das Ding*[4] where subjects are praised for their 'team-effort', 'team-achievements' and 'team-playership' – to the enforced acceptance of the ritualized practices of hierarchical mechanisms of bureaucracies. Even the 'social outlets' provided by some organizations requiring participation and involvement, in the form of 'team dinners' and 'team-bonding days', capitalize upon the subject's tendency to sublimate individual instincts in favour of the overall benefits for all group/team members. The law of the pleasure principle, as *jouissance*-regulating drive, becomes harnessed in the pursuit of a redistributed *jouissance* among the collective/team/organization.

I have noted this radical imposition of redistributed *jouissance* in some of the large multi-national organizations that have taken up residence in Ireland over the past ten years or so due to the highly skilled labour force and desirable financial incentives. In these organizations team dinners and outings are not at all optional since absenteeism is interpreted as disinterest in the firm. 'Friendly' competition is fostered between teams of different nationalities and each team's territory on the vast office floor is demarcated by national colours and relics of various kinds. Individual team 'agents' are encouraged to fight for their team in weekly and monthly sales target competitions. A surprising number of these 'agents' have come to see me over the years crippled by their 'inability' to give themselves up to the team. One woman working in an international call centre was regularly taken to task over the length of time she spent speaking to customers on the telephone. She was accused of 'letting the team down' since she took too long to deal with enquiries. What is of interest is that where once she might have been reprimanded for not adequately managing aspects of her job and perhaps re-skilled or re-trained, the accusation here is not that she is not doing 'her job' well, but rather that she is letting the team down, not fighting, not being a proper team-player. It is of course what happens when the imperative of the call for collective sublimation fails to operate in the singular, notwithstanding this particular subject's signifying history, which revolves around being truly helpful and patient in her dealings with others!

As forms of neurosis correspond for Freud and for Lacan to specific forms of sublimation, we find that the hysteric worker and the obsessional worker are drawn into these imaginary schemes for collective sublimations differently. The hysteric's style of sublimation is caught up with the organizing of an unconscious representation of *das ding* around an empty space.[5] In other words, she will attempt to posit a 'some-thing' there where there is a no-thing. Typically, then, the hysteric is most vulnerable to the tendency to install, even to initiate the 'office-drama';[6] to find 'satisfaction' in the 'storying' into existence of the 'petty gossips around the photocopier'; to find wonder in the circulation of 'the latest news', and at her best to be – if not the epi-centre of the office – then at least the one who is in support of the 'epi-centre'. I am thinking here of a female hysteric analysand, who was 'the life and soul of the office', the One who kept it all ticking along smoothly, organizing office parties, birthday cards, and cakes for fellow office workers. However she was also the one who, in the course of her analysis, attested to her absolute disarray outside of the office, on the weekend and in the evenings; laying awake at night when she did not know what to do with herself. She spoke of the enormous energy required in order to sustain the position she occupied at the office and the phenomenal anxiety she experienced when she was transferred to a different department and the sublimation offered to her in the workplace became jeopardized. When sublimation fails, either because it is no longer available to the subject, or when it is not operational at the level of the singular, the subject is brought back to the catastrophic unbearable (absent)presence of *das Ding*.

In contrast, the form of sublimation that corresponds to the obsessional neurotic structure is in avoiding the emptiness which characterizes the relation of the subject to *das Ding* via displacement and substitution.[7] There is a lost object, and there is a promise that it will be restored.[8] The sublimatory gestures of many obsessional neurotics revolve around the things they do for the Other, the ways in which they sacrifice themselves for the Other, and the ways in which they deprive themselves of pleasures so that the Other can profit from their sacrifices. It is in this way that the obsessional may in fact be the 'team-player' *par excellence*, since *he* appears to impassion himself with the dedication to detail, to procedure, to the organization itself, in the typical *oblative* gesture of 'everything for the Other!' It is in this way that obsessional symptoms and sublimatory gestures appear to dovetail with the recipe for the ideal employee at times. However although it may be true that the obsessional at work is often the ideal employee, it would surely be a mistake to overlook the obsessional's particular signifying history that brings about this purely happenstance fit between worker-subject and organization.

Here I am thinking of a young man in his late twenties who came to me to see how I could help him to stop worrying. He has been worrying about one thing or another since he was fourteen years old. What does he worry about? He worries that he has done so many bad things in his life that he will be punished either by God in the hereafter, or by his girlfriend in the here and now, since she would leave him if she was to find out everything he has been up to; or by the Law if it finds out about the many ways in which he has broken it; or even by himself by worrying so much that he might cause his heart to arrest, or the blood to clot in his brain or most probably by his body being unable to process such a high amount of stress that it will surely respond by growing a cancer in his cells. He worries that he is guilty of doing many wrongs or thinking about doing them, which is just as bad. He worries that because at the age of fourteen he wished that his father would die, and his father did in fact die of cancer shortly afterwards, that he is guilty of having caused his father to die. This is the 'real' crime that this young man suffers with. The unconscious source of the guilt that this boy suffers from has become displaced onto all the other crimes he believes he has committed. 'Guilty' of killing his father, he is desperately looking for a punishment, which would be commensurate with this ultimate crime. But just as soon as he thinks he has found one, he realizes that instead of being able to assume a sustaining guilt *vis-à-vis* one of his 'worries', he finds that he is innocent of these 'crimes' after all, since *they* can never be pinned unequivocally on him.[9]

He has spent his working life thus far in the frantic organization of grand-scale fundraising activities in his place of work, for children's hospitals, cancer research, and third-world community developments that aim specifically at the improvement of children's lives. His activity in the workplace, alongside of his actual work, has raised hundreds of thousands of euros. His symptom has been in the service of rehearsing a never-ending quest for the punishment that would be commensurate with his Oedipal crime. In the meantime his acts of sublimation, his endless good will and devotion in the service of others, allow him to obtain a pleasure that is without guilt – since it is (for now at least) a way of making up for his crimes. Along the way though, he has been marked as an employee with tremendous potential and (not surprisingly) secured a pathway to senior management based upon his ability to organize so many goodwill events. (These have generated accolades for the entire organization such that the organization itself has shot to fame, winning national and international awards for its fundraising activities!)

As such we can say that if 'work' *qua* sublimation *does* function in the service of a 'shifting of instinctual aims', it follows that the object(ive)s of the workplace become nothing other than libidinalised substitutes for *das Ding* itself. Straight away we can begin to grasp the pathological outcomes of what happens when sublimation fails to effectively function in this way, since in clinical work with hysterical and obsessional neurotics what is also evident is in fact this failure, or increasingly, the threat of its failure. We might playfully modify a section of Freud's opening commentary on sublimation in his *Civilisation and Its Discontents* thus:

> *Work*[10], as we find it, is too hard for us; it brings us too many pains, disappointments and impossible tasks. In order to bear it we cannot dispense with palliative measures… There are perhaps three such measures: *powerful deflections, which cause us to make light of our misery; substitutive satisfactions, which diminish it; and intoxicating substances, which makes us insensitive to it. Something of the kind is indispensable.* (Freud, 1991: 7, emphasis added)

Neo-normative Control

Curiously enough, these latter 'measures' indicated by Freud above as palliative in dealing with the disappointments of life – *and I believe*, absolutely the case with regard to work – can be seen as an emergent form of 'identity management' or what some researchers have termed 'neo-normative control' in (post)modern organizational practice (Cederström and Grassman, 2008). Fleming (Fleming and Sturdy, 2006; Fleming, 2009), for example, has noted how the limitations of normative approaches to controlling employees has led to the development of a new and distinct form of what he calls 'identity management'. Here, employees are encouraged to 'just be themselves', and this is supposed to deflect workers away from disgruntlement in the face of 'normal' organizational control. Their happiness remains contingent upon the freedom to be themselves, which in turn is supposed to make them more productive (Bains, 2007, cited in Fleming and Sturdy, 2006). Of course, and as Fleming notes, the apparent emancipatory initiative inherent in neo-normative organizational control is nothing other than a radical (new) form of identity regulation belied in the talk of 'freedom' that circulates in this discourse. This discourse emphasizes and privileges the 'self' over the organization, even to the extent that the subject is encouraged to be authentically self-centered, since the alternative is some kind of non-existence as suggested in the imperative 'Be distinct or extinct!' (Fleming and Sturdy, 2006: 19). Can we not see here the powerful deflection of which Freud speaks? Deflected away from the notion that the organization is controlling the employee in order to achieve optimum productivity towards the notion that in fact the organization just wants you to be yourself and in so being, the results will invariably benefit all.

Again, can we not also see the substitutive satisfactions that Freud speaks of revealed here in the attempt to mobilize a substitution of self over collective, of play over work, again with the end result of capitalizing upon the subject's inherent proclivity to minimize suffering? In their examination of the 'neo-normative' culture of Google, Cederström and Grassman (2008: 45) highlight the whole-life experience that work in the *Googleplex* entails. Google employees are invited to enjoy themselves at work as who they are. Again this norm of difference relies upon the (Googled) subject behaving as if they were at home, since it is presumed that when we are 'at home', we are truly ourselves. Indeed, according to Cederström and Grassman's research on the Googleplex, the idea of home and homeliness feature strongly in the founding of the whole imperative to 'just be yourself', where food, entertainment, gyms, playfulness in the corridors, and medical help for the ill, etc., etc., meet an employee's every possible need. If we are to regard such neo-normative organizational control practices as bringing about the necessary deflections from life/work misery, or putting into place substitutive satisfactions which diminish ordinary human unhappiness in the workplace, what are we to make of an organization that apparently cares less about the health and wellbeing of its employees?

In their research, Cederström and Grassman also draw our attention to a London based consultancy firm which they refer to as Leo-Ebing. Here, there are no perks, no happy hype, no gym, no snacks, no concern for employees' wellbeing! Instead, what appears to be on offer is 'reflexivity'. That is to say that employees are not required to be happy in their work, nor to be themselves, in the illusory sense displayed in the examples provided by Fleming and in that of Google. Rather, a 'healthy' dose of self-hatred and corporate cynicism prevails together with a masochistic bent in which you can in fact 'just hate yourself' instead of 'just be yourself' for what you do, and of course hate the organization that you do it in! It would, on the face of it, appear to be a more freeing environment for the subject insofar as authenticity hinges less on being distinctively happy than say indistinctively cynical were it not for the fact that (as Cederström and Grassman point out) this cynicism is itself also something that employees are compelled to express! Notwithstanding Cederström and Grassman's insightful commentary upon the ways that Leo-Ebing manages to exploit the subject's tendency to enjoy his/her symptom, we can also note here the way in which Leo-Ebing employees are encouraged to overeat, and binge-drink as compensation for working for the organization (Cederström and Grassman, 2008: 45). We can see here Freud's idea that a desensitizing of the subject via the use of intoxicating substances – what we now refer to as the overconsumption of the object in the toxicomanias and 'eating disorders' – is brought into service in some organizational practice as a kind of obscene payment.

What this recent research on neo-normative control in organizations highlights is the way in which ideals, fostered by the organization, are mobilized as palliative measures; compensations for the discontents experienced by individual subjects in the workplace. On the other hand are we not forced to recognize an either/or trajectory at work in the form of: *either* the mobilization of the acceptance of an ideal that fosters identity-formation in the workplace (as contingent upon the acceptance of the new norms at work, i.e. just be yourself, be distinct, be authentic, so long as acceptance of those imperatives co-respond to the ideals of the organization), *or* the mobilization of an ideal that encourages the radical refusal of an organizational paternalism – where to be a sick subject, intoxicated and addicted to a whole plethora of 'unhealthy' objects, is just as radically controlling. Are these organizations not extolling the virtues of a perverse *jouissance* instead of the valorising of collective sublimations?

We might recall here Lacan's earliest preoccupations with the 'decline of the paternal imago' and its consequences. In the formation of the ego ideal and super-ego functions, a bastardization of the paternal imago is formed as just a 'bigger fucker' rather than an (ideal) ego ideal, and commensurately 'being fucked over by the bigger fucker' indexes the tyrannical obscene version of the super-ego, rather than its original 'repressive' function. In *The Ticklish Subject*, Žižek points out how Lacan's take on the Oedipus complex,[11] reveals the 'truth' of the Oedipus complex. What is this 'truth'? None other than a condensing of the 'two functions of the father' (the pacifying ego ideal as the point of ideal identification, and the ferocious superego, the agent of cruel prohibition), united in one and the same person (Žižek, 1999: 313). It is in this way perhaps that we can interpret what appears to be a distinct difference in the ways that organizations 'manage', as contingent upon either the fostering of a pacifying ego ideal, or, on the contrary, the putting into place of the cruel aggressive bastard of the ferocious superego – in Žižek's words, the 'obscene jouisseur' (ibid.).

Disarray in the Workplace: To Enjoy (Your Work) or Not to Enjoy (Your Work) is Hardly Ever the Question!

Perhaps, after all, there are worse destinies in the workplace than being a 'typist locked in the toilets' (Lacan, 1991: 128). In the balancing of our accounts of *jouissance*, we humans are caught up with the avoidance of the terrorising proximity to *das Ding* which, as we have seen above, entails various sublimatory devices that, let us say, 'work' at least some of the time and are structurally commensurate with the symptom. On the other hand, our dedication to the strong programme of the pleasure principle, of aiming for an unrestricted satisfaction of every need, catapults us into a trajectory that places enjoyment before caution, and as such brings with it its own punishment. For the domain of the 'strong' programme of the pleasure principle is the domain of the drive, which always succeeds in being satisfied even insofar as it inevitably causes mayhem in and for the subject. The superego as the imperative, 'Enjoy!' – as the tyrannical completion of the ego following the Oedipus complex – demands that we throw caution to the wind in the service of *jouissance*. And as we have seen in the previous section, this requirement can be insidiously written into the employment contract itself!

Why should it be surprising that we find so much subjective disarray manifesting itself in the subject's relation to the workplace, since it is there that so many subjects live out the trajectory of the signifier most succinctly? I am thinking of a man who has spent much of his life not 'crossing the line'. Crossing the line has a rich signifying history for him. As a school boy at a religious institution, a line was drawn on the ground outside the school building indicating a prohibited area in which the boys were not allowed to walk or play. He would regularly find himself with one foot across this line and the fact of this transgression was called to his attention by one of the teachers, whereupon he would be punished. In his working life as a senior accounts executive he meticulously sought out ways to avoid crossing the line, i.e., in the devotion to bureaucratic mechanisms of procedure and protocol even as he laboured with the anxiety that some day he might be called into the office of a superior and called to task. The action that led him to my office was a fierce crossing of the line of moral standards: caught masturbating in a public place – he was detained for questioning by the police and required to seek psychotherapy. In this way we can see the superegoic compulsion to enjoy working in such a way as to guarantee *jouissance*, even as it guarantees a certain subjective disarray. What was avoided in the workplace was unavoidable outside of it. We can see, quite clearly, that what is repeated on this day where he steps 'over the line' of acceptable moral behaviour and is required to accompany the police officer to a room where his actions are admonished, is nothing other than a repetition of what he had been compelled to do as a child and later on suffered from in the form of anxiety. Here indeed we have an instance of the signifier suffering from 'the thing'.

We can see, I think, in this case that what is aimed at by the drive in terms of a satisfaction that might be achieved is also indeed what is prohibited, forbidden and catastrophic. The *jouissance* of the action is a horrific *jouissance* that is ineffable and yet we can see that it satisfies the drive big time. Perhaps one of the most wonderful aspects of Ricky Gervais' *The Office* is that we get repeated glimpses of David Brent's *jouissance* at work. Juxtaposed with the 'civilized desire' of the imported manager from the Maidenhead branch of the firm, Brent appears as hostage to his own drive where he habitually says the 'wrong' thing (in his crude sexist and racist comments), does the 'wrong' thing (in the hideous and deeply inappropriate gyrating and displaying of his body in his dance routines and management talks and addresses to his employees), and in the gradual debasement of his character over the term of the series, is revealed as just being the 'wrong' thing (where finally he is made redundant). And yet, we cannot help but feel huge sympathy for his character even as we squirm at the consequences of the David Brent drive.

We have seen earlier how the 'obscene and ferocious imperative of the superego' is, at the service of the law of the superego, translated into the compulsion to enjoy one's work! Not only must we submit ourselves to the stress of necessity, but in Freud's words, we must also enjoy it![12] We can surely agree then that the ideal that fosters a being 'happy in one's work' is a convenient artifice of late capitalism and a supplement extraordinaire in the resources available in the repertoire of global transnational mechanisms of production and of course pertinent in the recent research in neo-normative control. The 'happy' hype promoted in the localized language of the organization – organizational *llalangue*, why not? – is often supported by a dedicated team of what Miller has recently called 'techno-shrinks', counselors, behavioural and cognitive behavioural psychologists, and psychotherapists, who interrogate the worker/subject for signs of what has become a pathology of unhappiness. Lest we be too quick to dismiss this (however disingenuously) strategic use of the organizationally domesticated superego, i.e. the imperatives of the superego 'organ-ized' into the service of the organization's aims, I would argue that the appraisal system at work, almost universally in organizations, is a method for divining those worker/subjects who are less than happy in their work and thus suitable for in-house psycho-services. (And I remember one patient who was threatened with a visit to the in-house cognitive behavioural therapist if he didn't manage to 'pull his socks up and look happier'.)

We are but a few steps away from the mobilization of a 'Stepford Wives for the Workplace', where a smile and a happy face guarantee success within the organization and where there is zero-tolerance for the grumpy typist who would much rather be locked in the toilets! Indeed, the grumpy typist, far from her place in Lacan's sketch of the typist in Queneau's story (Lacan, 1991) who clearly enjoys at the expense of the Other, is in other scenes the one who repeatedly takes 'sick leave' or is required to, since her 'sick presence' reveals (what I have referred to at the beginning of this chapter as) the 'staged fake' of the workplace. In other words, she has become the symptom of the evolution of the workplace from the place of work – with all of the old-fashioned signifiers in place (the boss, the manager, the coffee break, the 'holiday', etc.) – to the workplace re-fashioned as a virtual location deprived of its reality and Otherness.

In this virtualisation of reality, a concept that Žižek elaborates in his *Welcome to the Desert of the Real*, the Other is systematically deprived of its Otherness, and products are deprived of their substances (e.g. coffee without caffeine, cream without fat, beer without alcohol, virtual sex without sex, etc.). And what about work deprived of labour? This is the final outcome of the staged fakery of the workplace as indeed the place where you go to experience an aspect of being, rather than to sell your labour in exchange for coin, even if that coin is caught up within the economy of your *jouissance*. This is at least one of the outcomes of twenty-first century neo-liberalist strategies of capitalism: where once there was the boss, now there are team-leaders; the One is multiplied in a device that redistributes Otherness. Where once there was the manager, now there are human relations operatives. Where once there was the employee, now there are agents. Where once there was a desk with your name on it, now there are 'hotdesks' belonging to everyone and no one. Where once there were discernible cuts in the time you sold to the workplace in the form of coffee breaks and holidays, now there is flexi-time and 'leave' of various kinds, such that the subject's very relationship with time itself is complicated, restructured, and de-signified.

An Unbearable Lightness of Being / Has the Other Gone Missing?

Let us recall that, for Lacan, anxiety is the outcome of what he calls the lack of lack. When the Other is on your back, when there is no possibility of the experience of lack itself, when the desire, demand, and *jouissance* of the Other is too present for the subject, that is when anxiety and the acts pertaining to the state of anxiety (i.e., for Lacan, acting-out and *passage-à-l'acte*) are staged.[13] In other words, it is in consequence of an all-present Other, that the subject becomes anguished. The clinic of psychoanalysis has long borne testimony to this experience of the subject in anxiety and indeed, a large part of the clinician's work up until now has been dedicated to a direction of the treatment in the terms of an analysis of the subject in relation to this Other. Increasingly however, it is as if the Other has gone missing and a new clinic of symptoms indexes the consequence of the Other's departure from the scene. In place of the *Che vuoi?* as the driving force behind the trajectory of desire, there is a *Chi vuoi?*, as nowadays it is not so clear that there is an Other who wants something of you. It is in this way that we can say that there is a kind of dis-insertion taking place, which we find most obviously emergent in the workplace. Contemporary subjects are not ignorant of the ways in which the big Other has been stripped of Otherness, but it seems that they are discombobulated with it all the same.

A woman in her forties came to see me following a 'breakdown' where she had increasingly felt 'invisible' at work, as if nobody would notice whether she was there or not. One way that she has tried to make herself noticed, that is, to (re-)insert herself into the field of the Other is to become sick. Curiously, through the course of her analysis, she has returned to the workplace as a 'sick' subject and has staged a type of radical protest there, by insisting upon her entitlements (i.e., working part-time, requesting formalized assistance, actively delegating tasks to various 'underlings', and demanding that senior employees and management respond to her 'sick' presence at team meetings by giving her appropriate notice and due respect in the myriad of projects assigned to her for completion).

But we might still want to ask: has the Other really gone missing or is it just so redistributed or de-instanced of its Otherness as to be emptied of its radical utility? Žižek suggests that it is a commonplace, globally acknowledged, that there is no 'big Other' any more in the sense of a substantial shared set of customs and values (Žižek, 2008: 34). On the other hand, he remarks that what *is* missing in today's social bond, is a small other, which 'would embody, stand in for, the big Other – a person who is not simply 'like the others', but who directly embodies authority'. Paradoxically, he seems to suggest that the 'human, all too human' character of the small other ('fallible', 'imperfect' and at times 'ridiculous', we can think here again of poor David Brent!), preserves the purity of the big Other 'unblemished by its failings' and renders it all the more pervasive (Žižek, 2008: 35). Here, Žižek seems to be suggesting that it is as if a series of small imperfect others, none of which functions as the stand-in for the big Other, creates the conditions for a claustrophobic anxiety where the subject, lacking any structuring point (a symbolic coordinate topographically contingent on the existence of the Other) is caught up in the *meconnaissance*(s) of imaginary captation. If this is the case, we may begin to see that what Žižek has elsewhere tagged as the 'virtualisation of reality' is also commensurate with what we might prefer to figure as a displacement of the big Other. Indeed as far as the workplace may be said to be made virtual, in this particular sense of deprived of its particular Otherness – where let's say, work was work in the Hegelian sense, but now work is something other – subjects seem to be experiencing an unbearable lightness of 'being'; where dis-insertion and dis-contact are commensurate with new forms of melancholia; where anxiety – once the neurotic symptom *par excellence* of the employee – has become replaced by subjective disarray or a destitution brought about by a de-identification with an ego ideal. This a consequence, then, of the big Other missing in action, indeed, though not necessarily, a consequence of the big Other on permanent leave!

Notes

1 A vital and invigorating aspect of the implementation of a Lacanian analytic brought to bear on critical research in general in recent times has afforded a re-examination of the whole question of 'agency' (and I thank Carl Cederström for bringing to my attention recent innovations in critical management research on this theme). Moreover, it is interesting to see how critical management theorists, in focussing upon the organization as master signifier, mobilise analyses of organizations so that, what is highlighted and brought out, is the *jouissance* that subjects derive from the master signifier (e.g. Cederström and Grassman, 2008: 41-57).

2 In his seminar on the ethics of psychoanalysis, Lacan makes explicit comments regarding the end of analysis. In particular, what he calls the 'true termination of an analysis', the kind of analysis that prepares someone to become an analyst is figured as the one which at its end 'confronts the one who undergoes it with the reality of the human condition'. He goes on to remark that at the end of the training analysis the subject should reach and

know the domain and the level of the experience of absolute disarray (Lacan, 1992: 303-304).

3   Rik Loose has developed this theme of the self-administration of *jouissance* in his book *The Subject of Addiction* (2002).

4   In fact Lacan's definition of sublimation reads as follows: 'the most general formula that I can give you of sublimation is the following: it raises an object… to the dignity of the Thing' (Lacan, 1992: 112).

5   Lacan will remark in this context how primitive forms of architecture were always organized around emptiness. He will say that artists use their techniques precisely to make something appear there where there was nothing. Art will always function as a something in the place of a nothing but it will do so insofar as it allows the unconscious representation of the Thing as something else. *Das Ding* cannot be represented by anything and therefore can only be represented as some-thing (cf. Lacan, 1992: 129-130). The object of art, of work of art can yield a pleasure both in its creation as well as in its viewing (or for that matter in its reading, or listening) in such a way as to afford a primitive satisfaction of the drives but also curiously, allows the circulation of such objects as 'goods'.

6   We recall here Lacan's comments on the Hysteric's appetite for drama from his seminar on transference. He argues that the devotion of the hysteric, her passion for identifying with every sentimental drama, to be there, to support in the wings anything thrilling that may be happening and which nevertheless is not her business, this is the mainspring, this is the principle around which waxes, proliferates all her behaviour (Lacan, 1960-61: April 19, 1961).

7   Religions of many forms produce the notion that that which was lost will be restored, a state of grace, life as we know it, the son of God who died as a man and is resurrected as a God, our mortal coils shucked off on the day of judgement when we will be restored to glory to sit alongside the holy Trinity in the garden of Heaven.

8   In 'The Future of an Illusion', Freud argues that religion is the universal obsessional neurosis of humanity (Freud, 1991: 43). He suggests that it arises in a similar way as the Oedipus complex in children, that is, out of the relation to the father. In Freud, 'thou shalt not kill' is less a religious imperative than it is a social imperative. Indeed we can say that the Oedipus complex lends itself to religion because it substitutes for the emptiness of the Thing (there is no God) the idea that there is an object there which one could have were it not prohibited, that is, an object that could be attained via some form of sacrifice (God is everywhere: I am the way, the truth and the life).

9   From a Lacanian psychoanalytic standpoint, when a subject speaks of
    his/her guilt, they generally have very good reasons for doing so. See E.
    Laurent's discussion of guilt and shame in his chapter entitled 'Symptom
    and Discourse' (2006). See also, J.-A. Miller's chapter, 'On Shame' (2006) in
    the same volume. Lacan speaks extensively about guilt in his seminar on the
    ethics. Notwithstanding his aphoristic comments regarding the subject's
    guilt as being correlated with the extent to which desire has been
    compromised, he also delimits guilt as staking out the bonds of a
    'permanent bookkeeping', insofar as guilt occupies the field of desire
    (Lacan, 1992: 318). Žižek of course has also discussed guilt (via Lacan)
    extensively throughout his work but see in particular his chapter 'Superego
    by Default' in Žižek (1994).

10 In fact the first word in the quotation proper is 'Life' (my emphasis added).

11 Žižek is referring here to Lacan's early writings on the subject, 'Family
    Complexes in the Formation of the Individual' (Lacan, 1938).

12 I find it interesting though that some work is supposed not to be enjoyable
    since any enjoyment that might be accumulated could only be seen as a
    sadistic enjoyment. For me this strikes a personal note since my children
    have long ceased to bid that I should 'enjoy' my working day as they have
    decided that my work could not possibly be appropriately enjoyed!

13 See in particular the session of December 5th, 1962, in Lacan (1962-63).

References

Bains, G. (2007) *Meaning Inc: The Blue Print for Business Success in the 21st
    Century*. London: Prolific Books.

Cederström, C. and R. Grassman (2008) 'The masochistic reflexive
    turn', *ephemera*, 8(1): 41-57.

Clemens, J, and R. Grigg (2006) *Reflections on Seminar XVII*. London:
    Duke University Press.

Fleming, P. (2009) *Authenticity and the Cultural Politics of Work*. Oxford:
    Oxford University Press.

Fleming, P. and A. Sturdy (2006) '"Just be yourself" Towards neo-
    normative control in organizations?' Working Paper, Cambridge
    University.

Freud, S. (1991) *The Standard Edition of the Complete Psychological Works of
    Sigmund Freud, Volume XXI: The Future of an Illusion, Civilisation and Its*

Discontents and Other Works, 1927-1931, trans. J. Strachey. London: Hogarth.

Lacan, J. (1938) *Family Complexes in the Formation of the Individual*, trans. C. Gallagher. Unpublished.

Lacan, J. (1960-1961) *Transference: The Seminar of Jacques Lacan, Book VIII, 1960-1961*, trans. C. Gallagher. Unpublished.

Lacan, J. (1962-1963) *Anxiety: The Seminar of Jacques Lacan, Book X, 1962-1963*, trans. C. Gallagher. Unpublished.

Lacan, J. (1991) *The Ego in Freud's Theory and in the Technique of Psychoanalysis: The Seminar of Jacques Lacan, Book II, 1954-1955*, trans. S. Tomaselli. New York: Norton.

Lacan, J. (1992) *The Ethics of Psychoanalysis: The Seminar of Jacques Lacan, Book VII, 1959-1960*, trans. D. Porter. London: Routledge.

Laurent, E. (2006) "Symptom and discourse', in J. Clemens and R. Grigg (eds) *Jacques Lacan and the Other Side of Psychoanalysis. Reflections on Seminar XVII*. Durham: Duke University Press.

Leader, D. (2008) *The New Black: Mourning, Melancholia and Depression*. London: Hamish Hamilton.

Loose, R. (2002) *The Subject of Addiction, Psychoanalysis and the Administration of Enjoyment*. London: Karnac.

Miller, J.-A. (2008) 'Psychoanalysis in close touch with the social', online at http://www.lacan.com/jamsocial/html (accessed September 2010).

Verhaeghe, P. (2004) *On Being Normal and Other Disorders: A Manual for Clinical Psychodiagnostics*. New York: Other Press.

Žižek, S. (1994) *The Metastases of Enjoyment: On Women and Causality*. London: Verso.

Žižek, S. (1999) *The Ticklish Subject*. London: Verso.

Žižek, S. (2002) *Welcome to the Desert of the Real!* London: Verso.

Žižek, S. (2008) *In Defence of Lost Causes*. London: Verso.

8

Lacan in Organization Studies

Campbell Jones

IGNORANCE

DISMISSAL   STYLE

VULGARISATION   HUMOURLESSNESS

INCORPORATION   RADICALISM

SURREPTION   BITS

SYCOPHANCY   LOVE

X

In this short text I seek to account for something of the reception of Jacques Lacan in organization studies. This is a task set for me by another, or by two others to be more precise, so I hope to satisfy these two young fools, at least a little, but also to satisfy you a little bit too.[1] I must however admit my frustration with the setup, and with the idea that organization studies might be a satisfactory address or addressee. Indeed, the problem with the task that I have been set is that, as I put it some years ago, in the strict Lacanian sense, 'organization studies does not exist'.[2]

This is not to say that organization studies does not continue to operate as a legitimising fiction. It remains an effective signifier, that is, at least in the sense that it stands in the place of many otherwise well-functioning subjects. But that functioning is far too often taken to close over the irreparability of the fractured life of organization, or, perhaps worse still, to reduce the study of organization to a matter of 'perspective'. But this distaste for organization studies is today perhaps more a matter of indifference, of not giving a damn, which is another way of saying that organization studies is not in command of my, or could I say 'our', desire.

This text is broken in two. First are seven responses that have been made to Lacan in organization studies to date. These seven styles of appropriation, which I place here on the left hand side of the page, are designated: ignorance, dismissal, vulgarisation, incorporation, surreption, sycophancy and crossing. As the names no doubt intimate, I will have some rather nasty things to say about at least six of the ways in which the name 'Lacan' has been signified in organization studies.[3]

I

Ignorance is of course a rather savage claim, at least to those who pretend to be lovers of knowledge. But here by ignorance I am not only thinking of the act of being uninformed, or of *ignoring*, but more so of an ignorance that speaks. It takes a certain pretence to know, without a shadow of a doubt, the contents and merits of a work in the absence of the labour of reading. In this way ignorance is both more active than ignoring, but also involves a duplicity which claims both to be informed and simultaneously, that the content in question is of so little import that it is just as well to not be informed. One might then be tempted to think that ignorance is the dominant relation to Lacan in organization studies.

But not only satisfied with 'walking on by', Lacan is also often treated in organization studies in much the same way that Freud is now treated in psychology; that is to say, with stupid and uninformed brutality. The alleged crimes will be familiar to those here: Lacan is a structuralist, which automatically implies an essentialism and an inferiority with respect to something called poststructuralism; the idea of Lack implies a vulgar metaphysics and an inability to see the positive nature of desire.[4] Others come with objections that perhaps cut closer to the bone: I am thinking here of the question of gender in Lacan, although again in organization studies this is often treated in such a one-sided way, so keen to put Lacan aside, or in his place, that it fails to account for the way that Lacan has *also* been a key point of reference in some of the most important developments in feminist theory in recent years.

This brings us to a third reception strategy, and perhaps you will already see the instability of my first typology exposing itself, but I will paper over this at least momentarily. Vulgarisation is perhaps least noticeable because of its near universality, and in this sense we shouldn't be surprised to see the overlap between this and strategies of ignorance and dismissal. Of course a certain vulgarisation is *required* in order to ignore or dismiss Lacan, but I am referring here to those who, with the best will in the world, squelch Lacan in order to make him more palatable, more fit for consumption, in short: more likeable. Here vulgarisation is almost indistinguishable from the pedagogical impulse, something which should not be disparaged and is perhaps unavoidable, particularly for those of us who are incarcerated in universities. But I will later come back to the question of the risks that come not with simplification, but with making Lacan likeable, and in particular with making his work comprehensible and above all *possible*.

I am not entirely sure whether incorporation is merely a variety of vulgarisation, but here I am thinking of the act of placing Lacan within a larger body or corpus, and on the basis of that incorporation concluding, one way or the other. This might operate negatively, as in the way that Lacan is often dismissed on the basis of his alleged membership in the psychoanalytic community, although it can also operate in exactly the opposite fashion. But the specific dynamic that I am referring to here is often marked by a process in which Lacan appears in a 'chain of equivalence' whereby his name appears in a list alongside other (usually French) thinkers, but where he possesses no distinctive character in his own right. Once duly incorporated, it is then possible to attribute specifically Lacanian theses to others and to attribute to Lacan the ideas of others. Such misattributions have certainly marked discussions of, for example, the decentrement of the subject, as this idea has been imagined in organization studies.

Maybe I am making a meaningful distinction or maybe I am merely elaborating on the previous two categories when I raise the matter of the surreptitious introduction of Lacan via the work of others. For some, or even many, in organization studies, the first encounter with Lacan has been through the ample pages of the writings of one particular Slovenian critic.[5] It would be unfair to bemoan this pathway, other than to note that a shortcut is a shortcut. And if we are not aware of the particular shortcuts of this particular student – as we must equally be aware of Lacan's own shortcuts with respect to his own Master, Freud – then we find one thing under the cover of another, and think that the mere appearance of the thing is the thing itself.

But that being said, there are those who have gone to the man himself, who have shaken off their little shoes and taken the plunge. But we face the risk here that has so marked the reception of other French theorists in organization studies. Yes, I am referring to the infatuation, idolatry, and projected self-love of those who have encountered intellectual work of such a daunting magnitude that the critical faculties are forgotten and global defence is required, *beyond all reason*.[6] And the risk is particularly alarming given that Lacan not only accepted cultic status and sycophantic students, but actively encouraged them. We then face the danger that Lacan might play the part of the new master theorist rather than one that we can love 'warts and all'.

Which brings me to the seventh category, which you can take as either a distant possibility or as a depiction of all of the work that has been published since this talk was first given. I invite here the image of the Greek letter *Chi*, by which we also symbolise the intercrossing or reversal of what in anatomy is called a *chiasma* or in grammar a *chiasmus*. This figure of a hinge also marks, in various practices of reading that we learn from Derrida, the admission of the aporetic, of a crossing of a text that inhabits but also passes through, a reading that gives to a text its 'hinge' and the possibility with this of its unhinging. Neither with nor without, which means learning to live with, or without, which is also to say learning the love of Lacan.[7]

II

This brings me to my second set of concerns, which I will deal with in the time that remains. Here I turn somewhat more to the future, to possible alternative receptions, both of Lacan and of others, both within and outside organization studies. To this end I will turn to our second list and speak on the questions of style, humour, radicalism, fracture and love.

As is well known, with Lacan 'The style is the man himself', and in a short piece that appeared recently I argued that something of the promise of Lacan, with respect to his possible reception in organization studies, relates to his style, and in particular to his unreadability.[8] In fact, of all the strategies outlined above, the fact that Lacan has not been publicly accused of unreadability by those working in organization studies perhaps says something about the lack of reading that has been going on there. As is also well known, much has been made of the matter of style in organization studies,[9] which – let us note in passing – has hardly been a matter of sartorial elegance but rather a call for a writing in conformity with a particular set of norms of literary elegance or stylisation. Which is not to contest this demand for style, but rather to ask for more, always more.

For the style of organization studies is, if nothing else, humourless. Which is not to say that it is not very funny, indeed, on the contrary. The issue is, however, that it does not realise its comedy-value and indeed quite insists 'No, we are not joking'. Thus, even in the reception of Lacan in organization studies – and perhaps this is due to the goal of seeking to make Lacan respectable as an important and legitimate theorist – Lacan is so often rendered *without the jokes*, without the play, with a conceit towards the proper 'good style', and in doing so, we might rightly ask how much of Lacan is lost in the process. Not that realism will cut it, but that those working in actually existing organizations have a sense of the improbability of the demands put on them daily; they see that improbability, and they laugh.[10]

This raises the question of what prospects Lacan might hold for radicalism, and in particular for a radical critique of organized modernity, something that I sense more than one person in this book's readership is aiming for. There are of course serious questions as to the adequacy of Lacan's own politics, in particular in light of the place of the political economy in Lacan and in Lacan's relation to the critique of political economy. Should we excuse Lacan by insisting, with Miller, that 'there is… but one ideology Lacan theorizes: that of the "modern ego", that is, the paranoic subject of scientific civilization, whose imaginary is theorized by a warped psychology in the service of free enterprise'?[11] If one senses in Lacan a general radicalism, we need both to account for the unspeakably great import of Lacan's critique of the subject of free enterprise, at the same time as we recognise how limited Lacan's own comments on the subject of free enterprise are.

This is not to cleave Lacan in two, so that the wheat can be sorted from the chaff. It is rather to leave him in bits, or for those starting out, to start with him in bits. This is the fracture that runs through us, not a resoluble fracture but a radically irreducible cut, an open wound. The pretence of a Lacan made whole, and available to us, or maybe progressively unfolding, is the stupefying fiction of a generation of commentators who, we must stress, should have known better.

So would the future Lacan that might be imagined be the one who would finally be able to nestle down in organization studies, as if it were possible to imagine not merely Lacan *for* organization studies or Lacan *with* organization studies but Lacan *in* organization studies? Lacan at home in organization studies might be somewhat more unhomely, as it perhaps does not surprise you to hear me say. Lacan will therefore find no place in a critical management studies that conceives of itself as a home or a church, no matter how broad. Such would then resist all domestication and maybe even institutionalisation. If there are spaces in which such thoughts might be considered even thinkable then these are spaces that we must live with, and must love. Which is not an unpainful or an unquestioning love but is perhaps best called the love of Lacan.[12]

Notes

1   The text that appears here is an almost completely unmodified version of a talk that was presented at the 'Lacan at Work' conference held at Copenhagen, 4-6 September 2008, although these explanatory notes have been added. I would like to thank the 'two young fools', Carl Cederström and Casper Hoedemaekers, for their encouragement and assistance throughout, and also Alessia Contu and Michaela Driver for their part in organizing that event, as well as for so much more. I might also introduce a little hesitation against the text by referring interested readers to Lacan's lecture in which he speaks of the fool/knave distinction, in *Seminar VII* (Lacan, 1992). This recourse has a long heritage: in Hegel we hear that 'Fools, according to Aristophanes, have great intentions for the state, but bring about the opposite' (2007: 123, n. 151). Such simplicity should alert us both to what should be the obvious dangers of a prejudicial binary and also to the simultaneous charm and risk when Lacan rubs up against the political.

2   See Jones and Böhm (2004), Böhm (2006). Such a framing of the impossibility of organization studies repeats Lacan's maxim that 'woman does not exist' – notions that have been put to productive use by, amongst others, Ernesto Laclau (1990), Joan Copjec (2002) and again and again by

Slavoj Žižek (for example 1990). Such ideas inform our claim that entrepreneurship does not exist (Jones and Spicer, 2005; 2009).

The consequences of the admission that organization studies does not exist nevertheless require considerably more clarification. Important steps in this direction can be found in an important text by Anna Wozniak, 'The dream that caused reality: The place of the Lacanian subject of science in the field of organization theory' (2010). Here Wozniak notes the moves of avoidance that theorists of organization have taken – whether relativistic or in seeking to construct a 'metaposition' – to avoid the traumatic real of organizational life. Organization theory is then an imaginary construction in the Lacanian sense, a massive investment of (disavowed) libidinal energy put into something that it is dreamed might, above all, exist.

3   The situation regarding the responses to Lacan in organization studies has of course changed and is in the course of change, as the existence of this book makes apparent. One might even imagine or hope that it changes with every page that is read.

4   The worst instances of this often appear under the guise of ideas attributed to Deleuze. Against this one might point to the work of for instance Daniel W. Smith (2004).

5   I refer of course to Slavoj Žižek, who has done so much to popularise Lacan over the past twenty years. Here I might only add that the fetishism of Žižek at the expense of Lacan should not be substituted for some presumed notion of a return to a purer Lacan who might have existed before Žižek. All I will say is that Žižek's work remains indispensible for us today.

6   The most shocking instance of this has been the case of Foucault, who in organization studies has far too often been subject to either uninformed outright dismissal or on the other hand to idolatry. The notion of defending Foucault 'against all reason' comes from the work of Steven Brown (2007: 202).

7   The 'love of Lacan' in the sense proposed here is taken from Derrida (1998). Chiasmus appears in this text (pp. 62ff), but also governs Derrida's writing much more broadly.

8   'The style is the man himself', Lacan opens his *Écrits*, before stressing 'the fact that man is no longer so sure a reference point'. Here, as so often, Lacan is already quoting, here from Buffon. On the promise of the unreadability of Lacan working to 'save him' as he entered/enters organization studies see Jones (2007).

9   See, for instance, a text whose title gives away perhaps too much of what will follow, both by this author and others: John van Maanen, 'Style as theory' (1995).

217

10 There are, however, many very different ways of laughing at organizations and at organization studies. The point here is to stress that the opposition should not be set between the high seriousness of organization studies, or the apparently humourless life inside organizations. Rather, the question is to learn from those who laugh at the insanities of the world, to learn how to laugh differently. If such is possible, then to laugh 'with more reason'. If one wishes then this might be a project, as Sloterdijk (1988) has it, 'in search of lost cheekiness'. I remark on the humourlessness of the reception of Foucault in Jones (2009).

11 See Miller's 'Classified index' to the *Écrits* (Lacan, 2006: 852).

12 Would this then also be one of the meanings of what Lacan (2000) calls 'hateloving' (*hainamoration*)? If with this term Lacan seeks to indicate the 'limits of love', then this must also apply to him. One is reminded here of the way that Zarathustra, at the end of part 1, tells his students to go away and to learn to hate him. With Lacan, at one level we never get this instruction, although of course at one and the same time, at the level of the rebarbative signifier, we hear this message ceaselessly.

References

Böhm, S. (2006) *Repositioning Organization Theory: Impossibilities and Strategies*. Basingstoke: Palgrave Macmillan.

Brown, S. D. (2007) 'After power: Artaud and the theatre of cruelty', in C. Jones and R. ten Bos (eds) *Philosophy and Organization*. Oxford: Routledge.

Copjec, J. (2002) *Imagine There's No Woman: Ethics and Sublimation*. Cambridge, MA: MIT Press.

Derrida, J. (1998) 'For the love of Lacan', in *Resistances of Psychoanalysis*, trans. P. Kamuf, P.-A Brault and M. Naas. Stanford, CA: Stanford University Press.

Hegel, G. W. F. (2007) *Lectures on the Philosophy of Spirit, 1827-8*, trans. R. R. Williams. Oxford: Oxford University Press.

Jones, C. (2007) 'Read', *ephemera*, 7(4): 615-621.

Jones, C. (2009) 'Poststructuralism in critical management studies' in M. Alvesson, T. Bridgman and H. Willmott (eds) *Handbook of Critical Management Studies*. Oxford: Oxford University Press.

Jones, C. and S. Böhm (2004) 'Handle with care', *ephemera*, 4(1): 1-6.

Jones, C. and A. Spicer (2005) 'The sublime object of entrepreneurship', *Organization*, 12(2): 223-246.

Jones, C. and A. Spicer (2009) *Unmasking the Entrepreneur*. Cheltenham: Edward Elgar.

Lacan, J. (1992) *The Ethics of Psychoanalysis: The Seminar of Jacques Lacan, Book VII, 1959-60*, trans. D. Porter. London: Routledge.

Lacan, J. (2000) *On Feminine Sexuality, the Limits of Love and Knowledge: The Seminar of Jacques Lacan, Book XX, 1972-73*, trans. B. Fink. New York: Norton.

Lacan, J. (2006) *Écrits*, trans. B. Fink. New York: Norton.

Laclau, E. (1990) 'The impossibility of society', in *New Reflections on the Revolution of Our Time*. London: Verso.

Miller, J.-A. (2006) 'Classified index of the major concepts', in J. Lacan *Écrits*, trans. B. Fink. New York: Norton.

Sloterdijk, P. (1988) *The Critique of Cynical Reason*, trans. M. Eldred. Minneapolis: Minnesota University Press.

Smith, D. W. (2004) 'The inverse side of the structure: Žižek on Deleuze and Lacan', *Criticism*, 46(4): 635-650.

van Maanen, J. (1995) 'Style as theory', *Organization Science*, 6(1): 133-143.

Wozniak, A. (2010) 'The dream that caused reality: the place of the Lacanian subject of science in the field of organization theory', *Organization*, 17(3): 395-411.

Žižek, S. (1990) 'Beyond discourse analysis', in E. Laclau *New Reflections on the Revolution of Our Time*. London: Verso.

www.ingramcontent.com/pod-product-compliance
Lightning Source LLC
Chambersburg PA
CBHW051418090426
42737CB00014B/2718